ANDRÉ GIDE
AND THE
GREEK MYTH

ANDRÉ GIDE
AND THE
GREEK MYTH

A Critical Study

BY

HELEN WATSON-WILLIAMS

OXFORD
AT THE CLARENDON PRESS
1967

Oxford University Press, Ely House, London W. 1

GLASGOW NEW YORK TORONTO MELBOURNE WELLINGTON
CAPE TOWN SALISBURY IBADAN NAIROBI LUSAKA ADDIS ABABA
BOMBAY CALCUTTA MADRAS KARACHI LAHORE DACCA
KUALA LUMPUR HONG KONG TOKYO

PRINTED IN GREAT BRITAIN

PREFACE

THE following study is a revision of a thesis presented for the doctorate of the University of Paris in 1958.

The subject was suggested to me by Professor Jean Fabre of the Sorbonne who directed my researches in 1956 and in 1958 and I take this opportunity of expressing my gratitude for his help.

Revision has entailed certain changes. To begin with, Gide's influence on later writers is too great for summary treatment and has been omitted. On the other hand, it is difficult to appreciate Gide's use of the Greek myth without some survey of hellenism in nineteenth-century France. The critical discussion of his works has been reshaped and expanded.

A part of chapters VIII and IX of the original French version was published in *The Modern Language Review* (vol. lviii, no. 2, April 1963) as 'Gide and Hellenism', and I have to thank the editors for permission to use the relevant section.

My thanks go finally to the University of Western Australia for the leave which enabled me to undertake the work of preparation, presentation, and revision.

H. W.-W.

Oxford, 1965

CONTENTS

ABBREVIATIONS

O.C.	André Gide. *Œuvres complètes*, édition augmentée de textes inédits établie par L. Martin-Chauffier. 15 tomes. Paris, Nouvelle Revue Française, 1932–9.
Narc.	*Le Traité du Narcisse* (*Théorie du symbole*).
PME	*Le Prométhée mal enchaîné.*
Phil.	*Philoctète ou le traité des trois morales.*
RC	*Le Roi Candaule.*
'Pros.'	'Proserpine.'
'Myth. grecque'	'Considérations sur la mythologie grecque: fragment du Traité des Dioscures.'
Grain	*Si le grain ne meurt.*
Œd.	*Œdipe. Théâtre*, Paris, Gallimard, 1942.
Pers.	*Perséphone. Théâtre.*
Journal	*Journal 1889–1939*. Paris, Bibliothèque de la Pléiade, 1948. *Journal 1939–1949*. Paris, Bibliothèque de la Pléiade, 1954.
André Gide	G. Brée. *André Gide l'insaisissable Protée*, étude critique de l'œuvre d'André Gide. Paris. Société d'Édition 'Les Belles-Lettres', 1953.
Gide	G. Brée. *Gide*, New Brunswick, Rutgers U.P. 1963.
L'Hellénisme	R. Canat. *L'Hellénisme en France pendant la période romantique. La renaissance de la Grèce antique (1820–1850)*. Paris, Hachette, 1911.
Paganisme	C. Clerc. *Le Génie du paganisme*: essais sur l'inspiration antique dans la littérature française contemporaine. Paris, Payot, 1926.
La Jeunesse d'A.G.	J. Delay. *La Jeunesse d'André Gide*. T. 1. Paris, Gallimard, 1956.
Le Rêve hellénique	F. Desonay. *Le Rêve hellénique chez les poètes parnassiens*. Paris, H. Champion, 1928.
Notes sur A.G.	R. Martin du Gard. *Notes sur André Gide (1913–1951)*. Paris, Gallimard, 1951.
Message poétique	G. Michaud. *Message poétique du symbolisme*. 3 tomes et *La Doctrine symboliste: Documents*. Paris, Nizet, 1947.
De l'humanité	J. Michelet. *Bible de l'humanité*. Paris, Chamerot, 1864.

Bibliographie critique H. Peyre. *Bibliographie critique de l'hellénisme en France de 1843 à 1870.* New Haven, Yale U.P. 1932.

Des religions Edgar Quinet. *Le Génie des religions. Œuvres complètes,* T. 1. Paris, Pagnerre, 1857.

Prométhée R. Trousson. *Le Thème de Prométhée dans la littérature européenne.* 2 tomes. Genève, Librairie Droz, 1964.

BAGB *Bulletin de l'Association Guillaume Budé.*

MLN *Modern Language Notes.*

N.R.F. Nouvelle Revue Française.

INTRODUCTION

La fable grecque est pareille à la cruche de Philémon, qu'aucune soif
ne vide, si l'on trinque avec Jupiter. (Oh! j'invite à ma table le Dieu!)
Et le lait que ma soif y puise n'est point le même assurément que celui
qu'y buvait Montaigne, je sais — et que la soif de Keats ou de Goethe
n'était pas celle même de Racine ou de Chénier.[1]

IN 1919 André Gide in a characteristically mythological trope
drew our attention to the inexhaustible imaginative potentiality
of the Greek myth, as he himself, following so many great predecessors, had discovered it. The use he had made of mythological
subject-matter in the first decade of his literary life lay behind him
as he wrote and his two most considerable works, *Œdipe* and
Thésée, which were to close his creative life, still lay far ahead.
He was not to know at this time that in France, as elsewhere, 1919
formed the threshold of a renaissance of Greek mythological
matter, transformed by the imagination of the twentieth century.
Gide's own early works played their part in the coming renaissance
of the myth, as Trousson particularly notes of his influential
method of *désacralisation* in treating Prometheus,[2] and this has
also been observed of his experimental drama, *Le Roi Candaule*
and *Saül*.[3] He very properly admitted the strong attraction the
myth exercised for him as for others and the way in which the
Greek fable answers the need of different ages and of different
men. As, indeed, it may answer different needs in the same man.

The intention of this study is to trace the origin and development of Gide's lifelong interest in hellenism, chiefly, of course,
as it is embodied in works of imagination, both narrative and
dramatic. But it is also apparent in Gide's critical writing, for
mythology leads him to formulate his own interpretation of its
inner meaning and to frame a theory of aesthetics. The same

[1] 'Myth. grecque', O.C. ix. 147.
[2] R. Trousson, *Le Thème de Prométhée dans la littérature européenne*, Genève,
Lib. Droz, 1964, ii. 435.
[3] G. Brée, *Gide*, New Brunswick, Rutgers U.P. 1963, p. 99.

interest incites him to re-examine, in his own highly personal way, the familiar term of 'classicism'. This has many facets in Gide's interpretation. It may concern the *matter* of art, that is, the given fable; or the *manner* of its artistic presentation; and it is extended to include the *morality* of the artist, and by easy transfer of man himself. The 'idéal d'équilibre, de plénitude et de santé' that Gide, in recalling his youth,[1] later describes as his first impulse towards 'classicism' becomes a personal code of ethics and of conduct: the hero of *Thésée* is its imaginative incarnation. In 1858 Renan had said: 'On ne comprend bien que le culte qui a provoqué en nous le premier élan vers l'idéal.'[2] Gide's autobiography records how deeply Greek literature influenced his adolescence and early manhood, at first in harmonious collaboration with his Protestant upbringing, later in definite opposition.

Such an enduring concern with hellenism therefore seems to demand a basically chronological approach which must first be adopted. However, the myths employed in the imaginative works raise other and more general aspects that must also be considered. There is, for instance, the essentially revelatory aspect of personal choice. At twenty-one Gide defines the heroic role as one of manifestation of truth at whatever personal cost. It is an interpretation that is astonishingly close to the later opinion of R. Caillois who, in 1938, writes: '*Le héros est par définition celui qui trouve* [aux situations mythiques] *une solution, une issue heureuse ou malheureuse. C'est que l'individu souffre avant tout de ne jamais sortir du conflit auquel il est en proie. Toute solution, même violente, même dangereuse, lui apparaît désirable: mais les prohibitions sociales* [la] *lui rendent impossible psychologiquement plus encore que matériellement. Il délègue donc le héros à sa place: . . . Le héros est donc celui qui résout le conflit où l'individu se débat: . . .*'[3] When the hero is allotted such a heavy task by the young Gide we are naturally drawn into an examination of the particular heroes he chooses to manifest truth as he understands

[1] *Grain*, O.C. x. 350.
[2] E. Renan, 'Les religions de l'antiquité', *Études d'histoire religieuse*, Paris, Lévy, 1858, p. 7.
[3] R. Caillois, *Le Mythe et l'homme*, Paris, Gallimard, 1938, pp. 27–28.

it and the situations which they are called on to resolve. Nevertheless we shall most fruitfully confine our own discussion to what we may learn of the attributes of the heroic character and the aspects of his predicament which combine to form the Gidian vision of human experience. His choice of a few myths among many, as well as his manner of presenting them, throws light on the problems and experiences that most nearly concern him. By means of the myth, used in ways that range from the handling of allegorical abstractions to the expression of imaginative truth about human life, and thus to the creation of his own myth, Gide explores the central problem of man's relationship with his surrounding world. But although in Gide's opinion France was the natural heir of Greek antiquity, we shall be forced to ask how fully Gide himself understood the Greek spirit and how successful his re-creations of Greek myth may be thought. In 1926 a critic specially concerned with contemporary French literature inspired by antiquity totally ignored Gide's contribution to the body of imaginative or critical work.[1] Admittedly, Gide's two most ambitious works, *Œdipe* and *Thésée*, were still to come, but in 1926 his early works and his critical essays were all available. Was such neglect justifiable?

Finally, André Gide, in exposing his theory of the two types of artistic nature, placed himself in the same category as Goethe and Racine, as belonging to the *extrême milieu*. The last task here will therefore be, not the almost impossible question of an absolute evaluation, but the more modest one of an attempted estimation of Gide's creative works founded on the Greek mythology he so long and so profoundly admired.

[1] C. Clerc, *Le Génie du paganisme*: essais sur l'inspiration antique dans la littérature française contemporaine, Paris, Payot, 1926.

I

FIRST IMPRESSIONS

ANDRÉ GIDE's first real meeting with Greek literature came about in the winter of 1887–8 when, at the age of eighteen, he returned to his first school, l'École Alsacienne, to prepare his *baccalauréat*. After a childhood and early adolescence disturbed in many ways after the death of his father in 1880, a period filled with travels, changes of school, and illness, he came back to Paris with his mother to settle down for the first time to formal education.

This is the phase of his life so supremely re-created in his auto-biography,[1] the phase dominated by the growing influence of his 'Emmanuèle' (his cousin, Madeleine Rondeaux, later to become his wife); by his friendship with his rival in the class for French composition, Pierre Louis (later Louÿs), when they took first place turn and turn about; and by the explorations in European literature which the two young men undertook together. The days come to life in Pierre Louÿs's vigorous diary: 'Je cause souvent avec Gide', he writes in May 1888, 'bien qu'il soit pour presque tout d'un avis contraire au mien; mais c'est le seul de la classe qui ait des goûts littéraires, le seul qui s'enthousiasme comme moi, le seul à qui on puisse parler d'autre chose que des p'tites femmes, avec qui on puisse causer sérieusement sans qu'on vous réponde: "Tu m'fais mal!"'[2] He is equally exuberant when he records his discovery of the Greeks, a discovery which Gide shared with him, doubtlessly with equal enthusiasm: 'Je suis fou des Grecs depuis huit jours. Je ne sais comment, lundi dernier, il me vint tout à coup une envie folle de posséder les traductions de Leconte de Lisle. Je me les suis commandées aussitôt et le

---

[1] *Si le grain ne meurt*, vol. i, 1920; vol. ii, 1921; Paris, N.R.F. 1926; O.C. x.

[2] *Journal inédit* (Impressions de jeunesse: 1887–8), Paris, Éditions Excelsior, 1926, pp. 256–7.

lendemain j'avais Homère, Eschyle et Sophocle. J'ai commencé par *Prométhée*, qui m'a tout à fait emballé. Et c'est une traduction! Oh! Si je pouvais lire cela dans le texte!... Celle de Leconte de Lisle est idéale. Quelle pureté! quelle limpidité! comme ces mots sonnent clairement! On se croirait sous le ciel de la Grèce'[1]. Pierre Louÿs's admiration for the translations of Leconte de Lisle was one shared by his time. Indeed, for another quarter of a century, they remained the general reader's classical Bible.[2] If Gide's account of the same discovery seems flat in comparison with his enthusiastic companion's it is, regrettably and inevitably, the result of age. A lifetime has passed and time has imposed its own distance on the event: 'C'est en ce temps', he writes in his autobiography, 'que je commençai de découvrir les Grecs, qui eurent sur mon esprit une si décisive influence. Les traductions de Leconte de Lisle achevaient alors de paraître, dont on parlait beaucoup et que ma tante Lucile (je crois) m'avait données.'[3] There is a curious tone here that suggests the fortuitous element in the influential accident. Had it not been for an aunt, Gide allows us to think, would he ever have made the same encounter? But this interpretation, with its diminishing detail, comes from a man of nearly fifty, not from a young man of eighteen. We are perhaps entitled to read Pierre Louÿs's ardent account of discovery, with its sense of immediacy and wonder, as an experience that, for all the two young men's customary debates, his literary friend, André Gide, shared with him. So, too, another young man very little older than these two made a similar discovery in the 'realms of gold', knew the same sense of wonder at the world opening before him, and celebrated it splendidly in poetry: Keats's sonnet, 'On first looking into Chapman's Homer', could speak for others besides himself.[4]

Like Keats, both Louÿs and Gide came to the Greeks through translations. This reliance on an intermediary for the works that were of capital importance to him was a weakness that Gide was

[1] *Journal inédit*, pp. 155–6, 7 février 1888.
[2] See M. Delcourt, *Étude sur les traductions des tragiques grecs et latins en France depuis la Renaissance*, Bruxelles, Lamertin, 1925, pp. 248–9.
[3] *Grain*, O.C. x. 262.
[4] Written in 1815, when Keats was twenty.

never forgiven. The fact that his Greek studies were elementary and never pursued beyond the Greek translation required for the first part of the *baccalauréat* in 1888, that he drew on Mallarmé's collection of mythological tales, *Les Dieux antiques*, itself derivative,[1] and on other accounts, laid Gide open to the charge of superficial hellenistic studies and a failure to understand the Greek spirit. He has been described by one critic as a humanist, not a hellenist, acquainted only with university humanism where 'l'antiquité y est comme digérée par le dix-huitième siècle français'. J. Prévost regretting that Gide who had made such admirable efforts in other literatures had remained satisfied with his inadequate studies in Greek and hellenism as a whole, writes: 'Homère, Eschyle, Pindare, il n'a pu boire directement à ces grandes sources naturelles. Il les respecte, il les admire, on ne l'en a pas nourri.... La conséquence importante de cette espèce d'éducation, c'est qu'il croira posséder assez ses classiques.'[2] Just how well Gide understood the Greek spirit is a question we will have to consider later when we attempt to evaluate his works based on Greek mythology. What concerns us here are the concepts the young Gide formed of hellenism and the attitudes he adopted towards it as he emerged from adolescence. If these ideas and attitudes were formed from works in translation rather than in their original form they were nevertheless capable of exercising an equally powerful influence. W. B. Yeats, although he regretted that he had met Greek and Latin authors only 'through the poor mechanism of translation', still thought them the 'builders of [his] soul'.[3] And so they may be seen in the sporadic, spontaneous, and varied reading of the young Gide as it is suggested in *Les Cahiers d'André Walter* and the early entries of the *Journal*. *Les Cahiers* have been described as 'cette "somme" littéraire d'un adolescent',[4] but so, too, is the *Journal*.

[1] S. Mallarmé, *Les Dieux antiques: nouvelle mythologie*, d'après G. W. Cox, Paris, Gallimard, 1925 (1e éd., 1880).
[2] J. Prévost, 'André Gide critique', *Hommage à André Gide*, Paris, Éditions du Capitole [1928], pp. 163–4.
[3] 'Reveries over Childhood and Youth', *Autobiographies*, London, Macmillan, 1926, p. 72.
[4] J. Delay, *La Jeunesse d'André Gide*, T. I, Paris, Gallimard, 1956, p. 555.

Alongside the Greeks came Goethe's 'Prometheus', that poem explosive in its own content and capable of arousing explosive feelings in others, as Goethe recalls in his autobiography.[1] It had lost nothing of its force by the time Gide, as a young man, read it for the first time. Forty years later he could remember its impact on him and recognize the profound effect it had on his development: 'Il me semble qu'aucun coup de ciseau, pour dégager ma figure intérieure, n'a enfoncé plus avant (même ceux de Nietzsche par la suite) que ne firent, lorsque je les lus pour la première fois à vingt ans, ces vers admirables du *Prométhée*. Rien de ce que je lus de Goethe, ensuite, ne put modifier cette première intaille, mais bien seulement la parachever et je dirais plutôt: l'adoucir.'[2] But the effect of this formative—because self-revelatory—influence could only be fully understood and acknowledged later. At the moment of immediate impact what did Gide find so personally disturbing in the ode? 'Prometheus' is, of course, whatever Goethe may have written later of his preference for 'that peaceful, plastic, and always patient opposition which, recognising the superior power, still presumes to claim equality',[3] a shouting, rebellious voice. It is essentially a challenge to divine authority, a rejection of worshippers as 'hope-besotted fools', a declaration of total independence, an affirmation of the self:

> Thou!—thou, my soul, burning with hallow'd fire,
> Hast not thyself alone accomplished all?[4]

Most of these themes became central to Gide's most characteristic work and he heard them, perhaps for the first time, certainly at the most propitious time, in the words of the 'Titanic, gigantic, heaven-storming character' that Goethe was to think unsuitable material for his 'poetic art'.[5] They are the expression of Goethe's own youth when he discovered personal independence in the

---

[1] In Book xv; see *The Auto-biography of Goethe: Truth and Poetry*, translated from the German by John Oxenford, London, Henry G. Bohn, 1848–9, ii. 39.

[2] André Gide, *Journal 1889–1939*, Paris, Bibliothèque de la Pléiade, 1948, p. 906, 15 [janvier] 1929.

[3] *Truth and Poetry*, p. 39.

[4] 'Prometheus', *Poems and Ballads of Goethe*, translated by Aytoun and Martin, London, Blackwood, 1907, p. 118.

[5] *Truth and Poetry*, p. 39.

exercise of his creative talent, an experience which Prometheus, as creator of men and his own world, so splendidly embodies. They struck fire in Gide's mind and helped him in his turn to self-knowledge and, ultimately, to independence. And they were stamped with the authority of Germany's great poet. Small wonder then that Gide should remember his first reading of this poem all his life.

But Goethe had many other riches to offer him which Gide never failed to acknowledge. In the *Second Faust* which, as he writes in 1940, had long nourished him, he found admiration for the world of antiquity, enjoyment of the natural world and, above all, belief in the supremacy of artistic power. For instance, when Chiron describes the mythological heroine to Faust he claims complete imaginative freedom for the poet:

> The learned dons, I see,
> In this have hoodwinked both themselves and you.
> In myth the heroine is fetter-free,
> And as the poet needs she comes to view.
> She never comes of age, grows never old,
> But still is appetizing to behold,
> Abducted young, and loved when past her prime:
> Enough, the poet knows no bonds of time.[1]

This is a concept that touches Gide closely, whether it concerns the poet's use of the figures of myth or of historical personages. In a lecture delivered in Brussels in 1904 he quotes Goethe's opinion of history as presented by the poet: ' "Il n'y a point, à proprement parler, de personnages historiques en poésie; seulement, quand le poète veut représenter le monde qu'il a conçu, il fait à certains individus qu'il rencontre dans l'histoire, l'honneur de leur emprunter leurs noms pour les appliquer aux êtres de sa création." '[2] And Gide goes on to defend this order of priority where poet takes precedence over historian against Victor Hugo's earlier disapproval. The present age, Gide considers, accepts the idea of the poet's freedom from demands of accuracy.

[1] Goethe, *Faust Part Two*, translated by Philip Wayne, London, Penguin Books, 1959, p. 120.
[2] 'L'évolution du théâtre', O.C. iv. 208.

Certainly, in 1904, Gide himself had already demonstrated such poetic licence in his handling of mythological figures and he was to continue to do so. His imagination plays freely over the traditional matter of mythology. Goethe's authority is called on to support a creative method which Gide had already adopted.

Yet it was Goethe's love and admiration for the spirit of Greek antiquity and his opinion of the 'Grecian mythology [as] an inexhaustible mine of divine and human symbols'[1] that exercised the greatest influence on Gide. He became indeed so identified with the Greek ideal in Gide's mind that Gide could later use 'l'idéal grec ou gœthien' as interchangeable terms in opposition to the Christian ideal.[2]

As he became more familiar with the Greeks, whether directly, as it were, by his own reading of their poets, or indirectly, through the idealizing imagination of Goethe, Gide's attitude changed in nature though not in intensity. The more meaningful an idea may be to us the more it is capable of transformation, of integrating itself with developing thought. So Gide's attitude to hellenism, initially emotional, moved through aesthetic interest to a philosophic basis which was, admittedly, a personal interpretation but which was nevertheless focussed on the Greeks.

The emotional nature of his first appreciation of Greek poetry may well have been affected by the love he had for his father. For Paul Gide, Professor of Law at the University of Paris, held unusual ideas about educating his only son and he read him passages from the *Odyssey* among a varied literary fare of Molière, Italian comedy, adventures of Sindbad or of Ali-baba.[3] Forty years later Gide could re-create the awe-inspiring effect of his father's study where these readings took place: 'Je ressentais pour mon père une vénération un peu craintive', he writes, 'qu'aggravait la solennité de ce lieu. J'y entrais comme dans un temple; dans la pénombre se dressait le tabernacle de la bibliothèque; un épais tapis aux tons riches et sombres étouffait le bruit de mes pas.'[4] It is not hard to imagine the impact such readings made on

[1] *Truth and Poetry*, p. 39.
[2] 'Réponse à Mauriac', *Hommage à André Gide*, p. 137.
[3] *Grain*, O.C. x. 40.   [4] Ibid., p. 38.

the six-year-old child nor the persistent emotional aura that was to surround the chosen passages in the future. A biographer records 'les enchantements qu'il trouvait dans la compagnie de son père, leurs promenades du soir dont il revenait "ivre d'ombre, de sommeil et d'étrangeté", les lectures fabuleuses dans le cabinet de la rue de Tournon . . .'.[1] And when that study was locked up by Madame Gide after her husband's death, when the son had to wait some years to be allowed in, when he then found his father's favourite works of Greek and Latin poetry in their place of honour in this hallowed place, the writers of antiquity must have been endowed with the powerful associations of affection, authority, and inaccessibility.

Just how disturbing the first direct meeting with the Greeks could be for a sensitive young reader we learn in the thinly disguised autobiography which appeared in 1891 as the experience of André Walter. The fictional account, written so close to the experience and protected by the *persona* of the romantic young hero, restores the emotional nature of the encounter in a way that the distanced view of middle age cannot or, rather, does not do in Gide's memoirs. As André Gide shared his discoveries with his cousin Madeleine, André Walter and his Emmanuèle know the increased excitement of a common enthusiasm:

Le grand frisson, à la fois moral et physique, qui vous secoue au spectacle des choses sublimes, et que chacun de nous croyait seul avoir, de sorte qu'il n'en parlait pas à l'autre, — quelle joie quand nous le découvrîmes l'un chez l'autre pareil: ce fut une grande émotion. Quelle source de joies, après, en lisant, de l'éprouver ensemble; il nous semblait nous unir dans un même enthousiasme. Et ce frisson, bientôt, nous le sentîmes l'un par l'autre, l'un dans l'autre; la main dans la main et très proches, nous nous y confondions éperdument.

Et, quand nous lisions, par ma voix, tantôt déclamante ou grisée, je savais les accents, aux passages aimés, qui nous feraient frissonner ensemble.

· · · · ·

Skamandros, Simoïs, aimés des Priamides.

— Les noms seuls, ces noms grecs aux terminaisons larges, éveillaient

[1] Delay, *La Jeunesse d'A. G.*, p. 146.

en nous des souvenirs si splendides, que d'avance ils soulevaient les enthousiasmes latents, aux éclats de leurs sonorités.[1]

The great names kept their evocative and emotional power for some time: fifteen years later Gide could be moved to tears in a theatre by the single name of Agamemnon.[2] But gradually the miraculous aura seemed to dwindle as rational man replaced the mythological being in his estimation. As a young man he wrote: 'L'admirable, sur cette terre, c'est qu'on est forcé de sentir plus que de penser.'[3] As an older man would he still place feeling above thought? We must return to this question later.[4] Certainly, at this stage of his life, his whole conception of mythology was shot through with emotion. If his own experience had endowed things Greek with this intensity of feeling, he was also sharing, in a more personal way, the generally accepted idea of Greece as the source of poetic imagination.

But it could be seen, too, as the origin of beauty, an ideal Beauty made manifest in the works of the poets. And the schoolboy, debating literature with his friend Louÿs, found a new interest in aesthetics emerging from his reading. As he writes of Leconte de Lisle's translations: 'A travers elles, je contemplais l'Olympe, et la douleur de l'homme et la sévérité souriante des dieux; j'apprenais la mythologie; j'embrassais, je pressais sur mon cœur ardent la Beauté.'[5] Later he looked back on this period of peaceful coexistence of Christian and pagan worlds with some surprise, since these two concepts so soon clashed. Their unusual compatibility seemed to the mature mind looking back on his adolescence to be due to their common quality of beauty. But the period of tranquillity at which all manifestations of beauty were welcome and held in harmonious equilibrium was brief. If for a moment Gide's adolescence possessed the harmony and unity proper to this stage of his development, so that Charles du Bos can describe it as 'investie d'un certain caractère d'adolescence idéale',[6] the moment quickly passed. As soon as philosophic interests came

---

[1] *Les Cahiers d'André Walter*, O.C. i. 36–37.
[2] *Journal*, p. 216, [13] mai 1906. [3] Ibid., 'Feuillets', p. 99.
[4] See ch. VIII and IX. [5] *Grain*, O.C. x. 262.
[6] Charles du Bos, *Le Dialogue avec André Gide*, Paris, Corrêa, 1947, pp. 43–44.

to dominate aesthetic pleasures the two worlds of Christianity and of antiquity were thrown into opposition. Hellenism became paganism and thus the antagonist of Gide's 'première formation (ou déformation) chrétienne'.[1] This conflict became one of the main elements of his character and provided him with one of his major literary themes. It appeared as André Gide left adolescence behind him and as his emotional response to hellenism was replaced by his personal philosophic interpretation.

Even the most rapid glance at this first Christian formation (or deformation) of his development must acknowledge the influence of his mother. Protestant like her husband, Madame Gide seems to represent one side of her son's divided nature. Indeed, she personified dogma for him and a whole code of morality which at once attracted and repelled him. Psychological analysis reveals that: 'Chez Gide, l'image maternelle s'identifia à une religion, une morale, une classe sociale, une province, et dans ses sentiments vis-à-vis du protestantisme, des mœurs puritaines, de la bourgeoisie traditionnelle et de la Normandie, se retrouvera toujours une secrète attirance sous une évidente hostilité.'[2] Yet, both parents shared the same faith and belonged to the same class, although their individual influences on their only child differed so greatly. The father aroused poetic emotion in his son, the mother the moral conscience: 'Et c'est peut-être là une des origines de l'étrange partage que fit assez longtemps son imagination entre le monde de l'art qui lui paraissait masculin et le monde de la morale qui lui paraissait féminin', Delay observes.[3] The explanation for such diverse influence may well be found in the characters of Gide's parents. When the father shared his literary pleasures with his son he was offering him what he personally delighted in; when the mother, in her turn, dominated his doctrinal and moral development she, too, was offering him what was closest to her own nature. Gide's account suggests indeed that her behaviour, inflexible and over-conscientious, as it may seem to us, was the natural expression of her own perfectionist disposition: 'Elle allait toujours s'efforçant vers quelque bien, vers quelque mieux,

---

[1] *Journal*, p. 1051, 16 juin 1931. [2] Delay, *La Jeunesse d'A. G.*, p. 271.
[3] Ibid., p. 77.

et ne se reposait jamais dans la satisfaction de soi-même. Il ne lui suffisait point d'être modeste; sans cesse elle travaillait à diminuer ses imperfections, ou celles qu'elle surprenait en autrui, à corriger elle ou autrui, à s'instruire.'[1] But he was not to understand the intimate connexion between his mother's belief, behaviour, and nature until much later. As he reached manhood she represented for him the code of morality and restraint that he was so long and so painfully to oppose.[2]

His growing ideas of the value of individual human beings were enough to set him against his mother. She was governed by the Calvinist or Jansenist doctrine of 'le moi haïssable', as Jean Delay writes: 'Pour elle le devoir était de contrarier la nature au prix d'un "constant effort" et c'est dans cet esprit qu'elle éleva son fils. L'accent fut mis, comme dans toute éducation hugue-note, sur la pureté sexuelle.'[3] While Pascal's 'moi haïssable' may never have been formulated to André Gide as doctrine, the attitude it produced offered a challenge which he was ready to accept eagerly. As for the emphasis on sexual purity, on restraint or abstinence, this posed the most burdensome problem of all to the young man just emerging from adolescence. It forms the principal subject of his first book, *Les Cahiers d'André Walter* (1891), translated into the spiritual agony of the young hero driven towards madness and death. Gide could analyse it more coolly later when he wrote, in a characteristic metaphor: 'Mon éducation puritaine avait fait un monstre des revendications de la chair.'[4] It is this over-disciplined process of growing up, with its inevitable sense of constraint in physical maturity, that we should remember when we try to distinguish some of the many attractions hellenism held for Gide.

It had the full weight of public approval. Not only were the works of classical antiquity praised and esteemed by unanimous general opinion but they were also, as it were, perpetuated by great and honourable figures of the nineteenth century. When such writers as Goethe and Leconte de Lisle followed the literary tradition of paganism that opposes the Christian view their per-

[1] *Grain*, O.C. x. 210. [2] *Journal*, p. 934, 27 septembre 1929.
[3] Delay, *La Jeunesse d'A. G.*, p. 88. [4] *Grain*, O.C. x. 301.

sonal authority brought respect, and respectability, to the confrontation. Leconte de Lisle's adoration of beauty led him to
praise paganism and condemn the austerity of Christianity for its
neglect of beauty.[1] Goethe's essential nature associated him even
more closely with the spirit of antiquity: 'Il est . . . naturellement
et spontanément païen', Gide writes. Acquaintance with Greece
and Rome merely taught him to know himself.[2]

And Gide himself was to undergo something of the same
experience of self-revelation as a result of what he considered to be
'le classicisme'. With his hereditary traits, however, paganism did
not come naturally or spontaneously; it had to be assiduously
cultivated. Nevertheless, we find more or less what we seek and at
this point the apparent opposition of antiquity and Christianity
seemed to offer freedom from restraints and conventions that had
produced nothing but unhappiness.

No doubt Gide was also aware of the interpretation of paganism
that flourished in the shadow of the asceticism and the aesthetics
of a Leconte de Lisle. There is the frankness of Théophile Gautier:
'Ce qui me plaît dans le paganisme, c'est qu'il n'a pas de morale.'[3]
And there is the lyrical celebration of a classical trinity, stemming
rather from Anacreon than the tragic poets, that expresses the
familiar opposition in other and more concrete terms:

> Coupe! Sein! Lyre!
> Triple délire
> Où ne peut lire
> L'œil d'Israël!
> Sous ton déisme
> Se brise au prisme
> Le synthétisme
> Originel![4]

Certainly Gide, in the year of his first entry into literary circles
in 1891, welcomed the authors who treated the life of physical

---

[1] F. Desonay, *Le Rêve hellénique chez les poètes parnassiens*, Paris, H. Champion,
1928, p. 300.
[2] *Préfaces*, Neuchâtel and Paris, Ides et Calendes [1948], p. 112.
[3] Quoted by Clerc, *Paganisme*, p. 131.
[4] Théodore de Banville, *Les Cariatides*, Paris, Pilout, 1842, p. 193.

pleasure. Taine's account of Renaissance life (*Littérature anglaise*) encouraged him to think: 'Peut-être était-ce là la vraie beauté; toute physique. Il y a quelque temps, tout ce déploiement de richesses m'eût laissé froid. Je le lis au bon moment: celui où cela peut m'intoxiquer le plus. Ma pensée devient voluptueusement impie et païenne. Il faut exagérer cela.'[1] And he set himself a reading list of the authors (Stendhal, the *Encyclopédie*, Swift, Condillac, . . . 'puis les nerveux et surtout les mâles: Aristophane, Shakespeare, Rabelais') who could most strengthen him in the way he wanted to develop. As he self-mockingly describes his motive: 'pour dessécher le cœur (assécher est mieux; on y moisit, dans mon cœur). . . . J'ai assez de larmoiements dans mon âme pour irriguer trente livres.'[1]

But his reading had an even more direct influence on his developing ideas. When he came to Euripides' *The Bacchae* he discovered his own personal problem set out in the experience of Pentheus and explored in all its destructive aspects. He later described this tragedy as 'inquiétante, révélatrice entre toutes',[2] encountered at a phase of his life when its impact could be most intimate and immediate. This, too, was one of the works that he read 'au bon moment', when the mind is open and ready for new experience. Fifty years later he wrote: 'Sans doute le bouleversement profond, lors de ma première lecture, dut-il beaucoup à l'opportunité de celle-ci. Je rencontrai *Les Bacchantes* au temps où je me débattais encore contre l'enserrement d'une morale puritaine. La résistance de Penthée, c'était la mienne, à ce qu'un Dionysos secret proposait. Sur la route que j'entrevoyais, je craignais de ne trouver que désordre et disharmonie.'[3] Here are the elements of his own disturbed state: the fascination of what should be thought temptation, resistance due as much to timidity as to conviction, and a fearfulness of the unknown future. When he understood that the Dionysiac spirit only proves dangerous to those who resist it, how quietly the possessed Bacchantes could

---

[1] *Journal*, p. 21, 10 juin 1891.
[2] André Gide, *Journal 1939–1949*, Paris, Bibliothèque de la Pléiade, 1954, p. 48, 21 août 1940.
[3] Ibid., p. 49.

sleep under the trees, how profoundly the denouement must have touched him. Pentheus' intransigence and death thus served to emphasize the message that seemed so reassuring to the young reader. Submission to temptation need not necessarily lead to debauch and disgrace; indeed, obstinate repression of instinctive behaviour may bring its own dangers. Euripides, across the centuries, seemed to speak to him as directly as Goethe's Prometheus had; and the voices reinforced each other.

Besides the thematic content of *The Bacchae* that touched Gide so personally, the figure of Pentheus provides yet another illustration of one of his most cherished concepts, that of the heroic destiny and its relationship to human behaviour. At twenty-one he formulates his theory of heroic duty: 'Le héros ne doit même pas songer à son salut. Il s'est *volontairement* et *fatalement* dévoué, jusqu'à la damnation, pour les autres; pour manifester.'[1] Shortly afterwards when asked by a friend to define his future work in a single sentence he expresses himself in much the same way: 'Nous devons tous représenter.'[2] The hero as representation, as manifestation, as allegory or symbol; this is an idea that is to run through the work of a lifetime, from Narcissus to Icarus in *Thésée*. Gide was, of course, by no means unique in holding such a concept in the 1890's. It was much discussed among those who held esoteric views of art and the poet. Guy Michaud traces the development of their ideas from Carlyle and from a statement of Novalis: 'Tout être créé est "une révélation de la chair".'[3] A contemporary poet such as Saint-Georges de Bouhélier used the terms of mysticism to describe the lives of heroes: 'Ils incarnent le Destin d'un Dieu. Mais les divinités habitent en paradis. Or les Héros les reflètent sur la terre. Et ils reçoivent, hommes des Ciboires, le Sang sacré.'[4]

In Gide's case the influence of Schopenhauer may well have played a decisive part in shaping his ideas. First introduced to his *Le Monde comme volonté et comme représentation* during his year of

[1] *Journal*, p. 18, novembre 1890.

[2] *Grain*, O.C. x. 332.

[3] Guy Michaud, *Message poétique du symbolisme*, Paris, Librairie Nizet, 1947, iii. 468–9.

[4] Saint-Georges de Bouhélier, *La Résurrection des dieux*, Paris, Vanier, 1895, p. 66.

philosophy (1888–9), a work which gave him inexpressible delight, he returned to it with equal interest and pleasure in June 1891, as his letters to Valéry show. In the following year a short work dedicated to André Gide by a friend echoes the philosophic ideas in a way that closely resembles the contemporaneous Gidian *dicta*: 'Nous ne connaissons qu'une partie de l'Univers: le mouvement', writes Maurice Quillot in *Le Traité de la Méduse*. 'La vie est la manifestation d'une lutte et c'est en l'homme que la vie arrive au plus haut degré d'intensité consciente. L'homme est nécessairement imparfait, puisqu'il est la représentation d'une fraction de l'Univers. Sa loi est donc l'action. Joies ou souffrances, qu'importe, s'il se passionne.'[1]

Such ideas of the heroic, or the simply human duty to express the multiplicity of the world in representative action were bound to appeal to a young man fretted by his conventional surroundings, constricted by his upbringing, and longing for a legitimate means of escape. The concept of man's life as 'manifestation' authorizes, even commands, diversity of nature and its expression in characteristic behaviour. Gide adopted it eagerly, developing it in his own terms as a philosophy of eccentricity based on the unique quality and destiny of each human being. Social conformity thus appears as self-betrayal rather than as a trap; a crime against one's irreplaceable gift of individuality. As Gide describes these ideas much later he stresses the representative aspect of human life, with its implications of dramatic action: 'Je me persuadais que chaque être', he writes, 'ou tout au moins: que chaque élu, avait à jouer un rôle sur la terre, le sien précisément et qui ne ressemblait à nul autre; de sorte que tout effort pour se soumettre à une règle commune devenait à mes yeux trahison . . . et que j'assimilais à ce grand péché contre l'Esprit "qui ne serait point pardonné", par quoi l'être particulier perdait sa signification précise, irremplaçable, sa "saveur" qui ne pouvait lui être rendue.'[2] When Gide qualifies the general rule to distinguish the elect from the multitude he recognizes and admits the differences in human endowment

---

[1] M. Quillot, *Le Traité de la Méduse*, Essai de mystique transcendante, Dijon, Imprimerie Darentière, 1892, p. 26.

[2] *Grain*, O.C. x. 333.

which are to affect Theseus' administration of his newly founded city. And when Gide, characteristically enough, opposes the influence of Christianity it is in biblical phraseology. For it was precisely the Christian ideal, as he thought, that by attempting to discipline human nature prevented the encouragement of natural diversity and inhibited potential individuality. When Gide turned towards the cult of classical antiquity he was, therefore, deliberately adopting one that seemed to offer freedom for self-fulfilment.

His first departure for Africa in 1893 marks the entry on a new phase of life, as such departures so often seem to do. When Gide and his friend, Paul Laurens, young writer and young artist, set off for Algeria they were fully conscious of the importance of this first journey overseas. It seemed as if an unknown continent offered a new attitude to life. For the first time in his life Gide travelled without his constant companion, the Bible, and he was well aware of the significance of this apparently minor event. Later he was to interpret his state of mind on leaving France as his first movement towards 'classicism'. As he writes: 'Ce fut, je crois bien, ma première aspiration vers ce qu'on appelle aujourd'hui le "classicisme"; à quel point il s'opposait à mon premier idéal chrétien, c'est ce que je ne saurais jamais assez dire; et je le compris aussitôt si bien, que je me refusai d'emporter avec moi ma Bible.'[1] But it is one thing to know what one is leaving, even to glimpse the reasons for leaving; it is quite another to know where one is going. When Gide defined his goal at that time as 'un idéal d'équilibre, de plénitude et de santé' he was framing in his own way the rather nebulous concept of the hellenic spirit which was current in his youth. If the historians stressed the moderation of the Greek mind and nature or the healthy mind and body produced by education,[2] the artist imagined their lives

[1] Ibid., x. 350.

[2] See A. and M. Croiset, *Histoire de la littérature grecque*, Paris, Thorin, T. 1 (Maurice Croiset), 1887, p. 4: 'les Grecs . . . alliaient l'énergie du caractère à l'intelligence. . . . L'Hellène a toujours eu de la raison dans l'imagination, de l'esprit dans le sentiment, de la réflexion dans la passion. Jamais on ne le voit entraîné totalement d'un seul côté.' See also J. Michelet, *Bible de l'humanité*, Paris, Chamerot, 1864, p. 194: '[L'être sain] marche la tête haute, il va dans sa sérénité.'

as dedicated to plastic beauty,[1] while the poet celebrated Greece as the origin of all beauty. As Pierre Louÿs expresses this splendid if vague ideal: 'Grec. C'est un mot que la lumière environne. Il suffit que la voix le prononce pour que l'esprit imagine l'eau bleue, le ciel bleu, le marbre blanc, le soleil de feu pur, l'atmosphère toujours limpide où le sentiment de la beauté pour la première fois devait prendre forme, la rive où sa déesse naquit des amours du ciel et de la mer. . . . En Grèce, tout est beau par soi-même, de sorte qu'il n'y a pas de contrée où la soif de l'idéal nous entraîne moins loin de la réalité, puisque dans cet horizon calme la matière est l'égale du rêve.'[2]

Some such ideas may well have been implicit in Gide's impulse towards classicism and his rejection of romanticism, as he later described his change of orientation. But it originated in unhappiness and the description is clearly a rationalization of the very natural if unconscious movement towards self-fulfilment of a tormented young man. What both men set out to find in Africa was freedom, offering and encouraging self-realization. And once Gide left his mother and his familiar surroundings this is what he found. Nevertheless it is his way of describing this movement towards freedom that is of particular interest. It suggests what the spirit of Greece later meant to him: the opportunity to live freely and fully and to shed the constraints and conventions of his over-protected Protestant family background. The departure from Marseille in 1893 closed a phase of life as it opened the way to liberty. Gide's later explanation of his motives reinforces an already strong interest in hellenism which persisted and was demonstrated in many ways. When he came to choose the subjects that could express his own experience and the figures that could embody it, his attraction to the Greek spirit and his concept of the hero's representative duty guided him naturally to the great mythological figures of Greece.

[1] Desonay, *Le Rêve hellénique*, p. 51.
[2] Pierre Louÿs, *Pages choisies* [Paris], Éd. Montaigne, 1927, pp. 30–31.

2

THE SITUATION OF THE FIRST HERO

ANDRÉ GIDE's developing ideas about hellenism in the years immediately preceding his Algerian journeys were, as we have seen, personal and imprecise. They can be assembled only from the *Journal* entries of 1889–1893, the disguised autobiographical experience of *Les Cahiers d'André Walter*, and the interpretations of the much older man when he analysed his own youth. While in some ways they reflect the general floating impressions of the 1890's they are too vague, too personally selective to represent informed opinion of current Greek studies. Whereas Gide's first work to make use of the Greek figure of Narcissus belongs strictly to his literary age, with its new poetic and its approach to mythology, his general ideas of hellenism had been absorbed from the thought of a century concerned with hellenistic studies of many kinds.

If his *Le Traité du Narcisse*, planned in 1890,[1] written and published in the following year,[2] is to be properly understood there must be some recognition of the prevailing and immediately preceding literary ideals and aspirations. It will be, therefore, necessary to examine the creative writers' concepts of hellenism in some detail from their appearance in the middle of the century in order to appreciate Gide's contribution to his literary world some forty years later.

Similarly, the newly awakened critical spirit which Renan distinguishes as characteristic of the beginning of the century[3] cannot be disregarded as an indirect influence on Gide's thought. Its various manifestations include such events as the publication

---

[1] *Journal*, p. 16, 8 mai 1890.

[2] 'Le Traité du Narcisse', *Les Entretiens politiques et littéraires*, janvier 1891; Paris, Librairie de l'art indépendant, 1891.

[3] E. Renan, *Études d'histoire religieuse*, pp. 1–2.

of Creuzer's *Symbolik und Mythologie der alter Völken* (1810–12) which reached France ten years later in its original version and through many derivative works or adaptations;[1] the initiation of courses in archaeology at the Bibliothèque nationale in 1818, followed by the foundation of the *Revue archéologique* (1844) and l'École française d'Athènes (1846); the increasing flow of travellers to Greece from 1820 onwards, who may well have been disappointed by the absence of glades and nymphs in the astonishing land they found;[2] or the studies in philology, anthropology, and comparative religion which turned back to the East as the cradle of civilization (Quinet's 'L'Olympe recule jusqu'à l'Himalaya'[3] comes to mind).

All such works were expressions of the new scientific spirit of the century. All may be seen as governed by the belief in human reason which Renan, discussing popular astonishment at the disparity between the reputation of classical Greece and its drunken and adulterous gods, constantly involved in scandalous adventures,[4] claims as the fundamental principle of scholarship: 'Il faudrait cependant partir de ce principe', he writes, 'que l'esprit humain n'est jamais absurde à plaisir, et que toutes les fois que les œuvres spontanées de la conscience nous apparaissent comme dénuées de raison, c'est qu'on ne sait pas les comprendre. . . . N'est-il pas bien probable que, si nous nous placions réellement au point de vue où étaient les anciens, cette prétendue extravagance disparaîtrait, et que nous reconnaîtrions que les fables, comme tous les produits de la nature humaine, ont eu raison en quelque chose?'[5] In other words, humility and open-mindedness are the essential prerequisites of the scholar. Instead of starting with certain accepted dogmas or ideas and attempting to impose them on the confused pattern of the past there should be an honest attempt to return

[1] See J.-D. Guigniaut, *Religions de l'Antiquité*, 4 tomes, Paris, Treuttel et Würtz, 1825–51; B. Constant, *De la Religion*, Paris, Bossanqe père, 1824–31. René Canat, *L'Hellénisme en France pendant la période romantique. La Renaissance de la Grèce antique (1820–50)*, Paris, Hachette, 1911, discusses the importance of Creuzer's work in France (pp. 88–89).

[2] Canat, *L'Hellénisme*, ch. IX.

[3] Edgar Quinet, *Le Génie des religions. Œuvres complètes*, T. I, Paris, Pagnerre, 1857, p. 53.

[4] Renan, *Études d'histoire religieuse*, p. 7.   [5] Ibid., pp. 7–8.

to the point of departure, to reconstruct the conditions of an unfamiliar age. As Quinet defines his intention in the 'Notice' to the first edition of his *Le Génie des religions* (1841), he can only succeed by shedding all his contemporary concepts: 'j'ai cherché plutôt à dépouiller l'homme de nos jours, pour revêtir l'homme antique', he claims, '. . . Si dans ce livre quelque chose subsiste de l'âme religieuse de l'antiquité, j'ai atteint mon but; si, au contraire, on n'y reconnaît que les pensées laborieuses d'un commentateur du dix-neuvième siècle, cet ouvrage est à refaire jusqu'à la dernière page.'[1] Such an approach needs no exposition today but it was, at the time, a new development in humanist studies.

The critical spirit is all the more remarkable in the field of comparative religion, a subject particularly vulnerable to pre-conceptions and prejudice. Profoundly stirred by the discovery of the East, the recovery of the classical past, scholars sought the key to the understanding of ancient civilizations in their religious beliefs, in their mythologies. The eighteenth-century encyclopaedists in their attempt to understand the past endowed primitive man with their own deductive powers and social preoccupations; the nineteenth-century interpreter deliberately explored the depths of earlier consciousness and traced all political and artistic achievements back to their common source in religious belief: 'Ne croyez pas, en effet, connaître un peuple si vous n'êtes remonté jusqu'à ses dieux.'[2]

And how many gods there were to know, how many civilizations to understand through their mythologies! Besides India, Persia, and Greece, those 'trois foyers de la lumière' in Michelet's phrase,[3] there were the gods of Egypt and of Babylon, the prophets of the desert and the diviners of Etruria, the gods and heroes of the North. But however bewildering the multiplicity of mythologies may have seemed, however misguided some of their civilizations may have been, however monstrous their temples and rites, there was a way of reconciling them in the ever-lengthening, increasingly complex history of the human race. All contained some evidence of man's striving towards the good

---

[1] Quinet, *Des religions*, p. 8. [2] Ibid., p. 12.
[3] Michelet, *De l'humanité*, p. 131.

and the beautiful, all contained some revelations of universal truth, all demonstrated the fundamental brotherhood of men in all ages and in all societies. Each in turn had shown 'un rayon de l'éternelle vérité' through which they had endured.[1] Increasing knowledge of past faiths became in itself an act of faith in mankind.

In what particularly concerns us here, the understanding of mythology, the essential elements of the nineteenth-century experience may be summarized as the attribution of reason to the hitherto incomprehensible; the attempt to return to an earlier state of consciousness free of prejudice; the recognition of religious aspiration as fundamentally formative; and the reconciliation of the multiplicity of mythologies within the governing concept of changing ideas of God.[2]

These general ideas, as we shall see later in detail, were not without their influence on Gide's thought but his interpretation of them was personal. When he, in his turn, examines Greek mythology he, too, stresses the underlying rationality of the fable, but he extends his understanding of human reason to include the subconscious springs of action and desire; and his approach is governed by his own time, not by the attitudes of antiquity. The formative effect of religious training was a force which he acknowledged all his life, chiefly as it concerned himself in his childhood although, again, he later generalizes this argument to explain the glory of the City-State by the harmonious diversity of Olympus. As for the contemporary manner of reconciling alien mythologies, it may well be paralleled if not reflected in the ecstatic but transient phase of his adolescence when, as we have seen, the intensity of his Christian feeling was exalted by his fervour for Greek paganism. Both were expressions of Beauty and were thus congenial. As he later describes this enthusiastic experience shared with his cousin Madeleine, his imaginative simile recalls the spirit of the age into which he was born: 'Au vrai,' he remembers, 'le temple de nos cœurs était pareil à ces mosquées qui, du côté de l'orient, restent béantes et se laissent divinement envahir par les rayons, les musiques et les parfums.

---

[1] Quinet, *Des religions*, p. 81.
[2] Ibid., p. v, Avertissement de la deuxième édition, 1850.

L'exclusion nous semblait impie; en nous quoi que ce fût de beau trouvait accueil.'[1]

Nevertheless, among all the newly recovered mythologies a divine light still shone on Olympus. Greek civilization had produced 'la plus lumineuse histoire que le génie humain ait laissée de lui-même',[2] however chronologically and geographically extended learned interests may have become. Every aspect of the great Greek period was endlessly fascinating to the nineteenth century: its genetic origin;[3] its heroism of body, will, and mind;[4] its City-States;[5] its triumphant arts of architecture,[6] sculpture,[7] and of letters, whether the work of tragic poet, philosopher, or historian.

Indeed scholarly concern with every branch of Greek literary achievement in the first half of the century was so marked that it has been called a second *renaissance* comparable to the great Renaissance, although manifesting itself principally at first in investigation, interpretation, and adaptation.[8] But however specialized the field of individual scientific studies, however mediocre the interpretations or literary adaptations may have been, they were governed by an ideal of Greek antiquity which had captured the imagination of the century and held scholar, critic, theorist, and later, poet alike.

It was an ideal formed from the Greek pursuit of beauty in all things, from their identification of gods with men, of gods in men, from their society which unified diversity in gods and in men and taught its children to act splendidly, in harmony, health, and joy.[9] It may be summarized in the unspoken counsels offered

[1] *Grain*, O.C. x. 263.

[2] Michelet, *De l'humanité*, p. 135.

[3] See C. O. Müller, *The History and Antiquities of the Doric Race*, translated by Henry Tufneil and G. Cornewall Lewis, 2 vols., Oxford, J. Murray, 1830.

[4] Quinet, *Des religions*, pp. 342, 354. See also idem, *Vie et Mort du génie grec*, Paris, Dentu, 1878.

[5] See Michelet, *De l'humanité*, pp. 175–93.

[6] Quinet, *Des religions*, p. 321.

[7] Ibid., p. 101. See also Canat, *L'Hellénisme*, chs. xii–xv, for an account of the debates that arose about the nature of Greek art.

[8] Canat, *L'Hellénisme*, p. 276.

[9] See Michelet, *De l'humanité*, pp. 193–214.

by the statues of gods and heroes to the child on his first pil-
grimage to Delphi: 'Approche et ne crains rien', the mute statues
seem to say. 'Vois ce que nous étions, d'où nous partîmes et où
nous sommes… Fais comme nous. Sois grand d'actes et de
volonté. Sois beau, embellis-toi de formes héroïques et d'œuvres
généreuses qui remplissent le monde de joie… Travailel, ose,
entreprends! Par la lutte ou la lyre, chantre, athlète ou guerrier,
commence! Des jeux aux combats, monte, enfant!'[1]

Could Michelet's imaginary 'enfant' have been called Theseus?
As Gide in his old age creates the childhood and youth of his
greatest hero, listening to the advice of Egeus and Daedalus, he
comes close to the child initiated into the mysteries of Greek
civilization.

For a man like Quinet, living in the 'désert moral' of a disabused
and disturbed world,[2] the rediscovered religions of the East were
refreshment for the mind. But he nourished his heart when he
evoked Greece at its greatest:

si l'on recherche en quel temps l'homme a vécu le plus satisfait de
la terre [he writes], il est aisé de voir que ce fut pendant le règne de
cette religion de poëtes. Il avait renoncé à creuser les anciennes questions;
où il trouvait un abîme, il plaçait une divinité qui en cachait les pro-
fondeurs sous la pourpre. Ces divinités indulgentes, toujours près de
lui, jeunes, imprévoyantes comme lui, nées de l'hymne, le rassuraient
constamment sur sa propre destinée: il s'endormit sous leurs regards. …
Il y eut un moment de trêve pour lui. Nourri de nectar, sa sérénité fut
même si profonde, qu'à peine elle fut troublée par la chute de la société
grecque. Les villes tombaient en ruine, qu'il refusait encore de s'inquiéter.
Pour le réveiller sur les roses, il fallut que le Christianisme vînt dé-
chaîner en lui une ambition sans limites. Depuis cette heure, il a regardé
la terre avec dédain. … Que sont le nectar et l'ambroisie pour celui
qui a soif de la vie de l'esprit? La vallée de Tempé est devenue une
vallée de larmes; par un contrat héroïque, l'homme a conquis l'infini
au prix de l'infinie douleur.[3]

Admittedly this is the personal view of one man whose nostalgia
for Paradise lost overpowers the compensations he may find in
more complex spiritual thought. It is, nevertheless, sufficiently

[1] Michelet, De l'humanité, p. 207.
[2] Des religions, pp. 135, 71.   [3] Ibid., pp. 324–5.

representative of its age in its suggestions of the anxieties of the present, its consequent adoration of the past, and its opposition between Christianity and the age of Greek paganism.

The impact of hellenism on the world of letters during the first half of the nineteenth century was more gradual. In 1852, however, with the publication of Leconte de Lisle's *Poèmes antiques*, a new era opened, of creative writers fired by that imaginative appeal of Greece which has perhaps always transcended men's factual knowledge of her civilization. The divergency in them, is clear, between the given matter and the created. Mind works in quite other ways than memory. The creative mind finds its own food which may have little to do with facts. Leconte de Lisle, for all his advocacy of contemporary theories, worked imaginatively with subjects drawn from East and West. The case of Mallarmé is even more striking. While he espoused the current dominant scientific theory of mythological meaning as representations of physical phenomena in his adaptation of G. W. L. Cox's *Les Dieux antiques* (1880), and justified his preference for Greek mythology on those grounds, he himself did not use its figures in the same way. Even as he announces the priority he gives to Greece before Rome with all the authority of accepted scientific opinion, he characteristically enlarges his justification: 'A qui demanderait pourquoi, dans cette double mythologie, grecque et latine, les mythes grecs prennent une valeur que n'ont pas les mythes latins, je répondrais: parce que l'on peut dire des seuls mythes grecs, plus anciens, que ce sont des *personnifications vivantes de phénomènes naturels*. En même temps que l'imagination humaine leur communiquait ses formes heureuses, ils ont reçu d'elle une vie véritable.'[1] It is the imagination which brings the physical laws to life; the poet must play his essential part. Mallarmé thus adopts the scientific explanation but goes beyond it to claim the supremacy of the poetic imagination. His own use of mythology as a Symbolist poet and his inclusion of mythological poems by Banville, Victor Hugo, and Leconte de Lisle in the Appendix to his *Dieux antiques* demonstrate the liberty of the poetic imagination and establish its freedom from theory.

[1] *Les Dieux antiques*, p. 43.

The Preface of the *Poèmes antiques* sets out the fundamental tenets of the 'École du Parnasse'.[1] It is always dangerous to speak of a 'school', perhaps more particularly so in the case of the Parnassians, because to do so imposes arbitrary limitations of content and time. The three volumes of *Le Parnasse contemporain*[2] are made up of the work of three generations of poets, and among a wide range of subjects barely a score out of a 160 poems are concerned with Rome and Greece.[3] Again, if the Parnassian movement may be said to have lasted some twenty years (1850–70), similar attitudes are to be seen in Théodore de Banville's *Les Cariatides* (1842), and they are present in Heredia's *Les Trophées* published as late as 1893.[4] They were certainly still strong enough to influence the young Pierre Louÿs in 1891 when he founded a new periodical, *La Conque*, on the Parnassian ideal, although admittedly he was exceptional in his admiration. As he writes to André Gide in January 1890: 'C'est inepte de faire un mouvement littéraire sur notre pitié mystique. Au fond c'est la sensiblerie vague du xviiie siècle qu irevient sur l'eau. . . . Assez! Assez! . . . Ce qui reste, c'est la forme avec un grand F, et ma Forme ne veut de votre idée que domptée et asservie. . . . Vois-tu, ce qu'il faut c'est la Beauté impassible . . . et cela n'empêche pas d'avoir un cœur quand même et de le laisser crier quand la tête a fini de produire et qu'on a posé la plume.'[5]

With all reservations made, however, there are common motives in the poets of the Parisian Parnassus. They may be understood as: 'Vieille habitude littéraire qui persiste; mépris de la morale chrétienne, nostalgie d'un temps où ne sévissait point dans l'âme un conflit paralysant; ou désir au contraire de revivre ce conflit plus près de ses origines; haines des laideurs présentes, évasion vers une vie plus belle; ou refuge dans la mort silencieuse . . . telles sont quelques-unes des causes de ces modernes retours

[1] See Desonay, *Le Rêve hellénique*; H. Peyre, *Bibliographie critique de l'hellénisme en France de 1843 à 1870*, New Haven, Yale U.P. 1932; Clerc, *Paganisme*.

[2] Paris, Lemerre, 1866, 1869, 1876.

[3] Clerc, *Paganisme*, p. 83.

[4] Desonay, *Le Rêve hellénique*, p. 44.

[5] P. Iseler, *Les Débuts d'André Gide vus par Pierre Louÿs*, Paris, Éd. du Sagittaire, 1937, pp. 87–88.

à l'Antiquité.'[1] There are also common technical ambitions, for instance experimentation in poetic rhythms, as Banville declares:

> Car il faut assouplir nos rythmes étrangers
> Aux cothurnes étroits de la Grèce natale,
> Pour attacher aux pas de l'Ode aux pieds légers
> Le nombre harmonieux d'une lyre idéale.[2]

There is the emphasis on the picturesque that follows naturally from the doctrine of impersonality; and the desire for accuracy in the re-creations of the past. Leconte de Lisle describes his poems as studies, without personal emotion or topical allusion, and he consciously draws on contemporary discoveries to give them greater realism and conviction. Poet and scientist alike should return to antiquity in order to understand its thought, its beliefs, and its actions, he declares, and greater knowledge of the past can only confirm the essential similiarity of human nature throughout the ages: 'Il est du reste un fonds commun à l'homme et au poëte', he writes, 'une somme de vérités morales et d'idées dont nul ne peut s'abstraire; l'expression seule en est multiple et diverse.'[3] If there are great truths that hold good for men of every age then the poet's chief duty is to express them cogently and well. The desperate pursuit of originality in poetic thought can lead only to idiosyncrasy and artificiality (as Samuel Johnson had thought of the Metaphysical poets). Given the essential similarity of human nature, the poet who can most convincingly present the spirit of Greece is re-creating human experience at the time of its finest flowering.

But the link between present and past may not simply lie in a participation in a common humanity. It may also be formed by intellectual tradition. Théodore de Banville describes the Greeks as 'nos véritables aïeux spirituels', and the originators of the 'culte de la beauté et de l'héroïsme'.[4] Hellas, for Louis Ménard, represents

---

[1] Clerc, *Paganisme*, p. 27.
[2] Théodore de Banville, 'Les Stalactites', *Poésies complètes*, éd. définitive, Paris, Charpentier, 1879, p. 220.
[3] C.-M. Leconte de Lisle, *Poèmes antiques*, Paris, Marc Ducloux, 1852, Préface, p. vi.
[4] 'Le Sang de la coupe', Préface, *Poésies complètes*, p. 280.

L'art sacré, la sainte Poésie,
Et la Beauté divine, enfant des immortels.[1]

And when concepts of triumphant paganism, basically opposed to Christianity, as in Banville's formula: 'Coupe! Sein! Lyre!', are added to the adoration of nobility, heroism, and beauty, we have some idea of the Parnassian poets' ideal of hellenism.

Whether it was authentically Greek or not does not matter. It could kindle their poetic imagination and direct their interest and efforts. Their willingness to amalgamate recent discoveries made in all fields of hellenist research produced poetry of rare fervour and conviction while providing a highly original vision of ancient Greece.[2] They can be seen as consolidating the experimental approaches of the first half of the century and, as Mallarmé thought, in successful poetry: 'De très grands poètes ont su . . . vivifier à force d'inspiration et comme rajeunir par une vision moderne les types de la Fable.'[3] Not every reader would agree with Mallarmé since, for some of us, the desired impersonality impoverishes rather than improves the total effect. However, in the history of French hellenism in the nineteenth century they were the first creative writers to approach antiquity conscientiously and with great sincerity—with the exception of the lone genius of Maurice de Guérin, whose influence on his work Gide later so strongly denied.

Their general influence did not last long. Well before his death Leconte de Lisle's glory as creative writer had passed away and by 1890 he had little to offer most of the rising young writers. Paul Valéry recalled the opinion of the majority (to whom Louÿs forms an exception) when he wrote: 'En ce temps-là, Leconte de Lisle, tout vivant et vénérable qu'il était, était déjà pour un grand nombre une ombre vaine. . . . Les très jeunes orgueils se cherchaient des poétiques nouvelles, que les uns désiraient plus complexes, et les autres tout autres que la sienne.'[4] The 'new poetics' are, of course, those of the Symbolist movement whose theory André

---

[1] [L. Ménard] L. de Senneville, *Prométhée délivré*, Paris, au Comptoir des Imprimeurs Unis, 1844, p. 92.
[2] Peyre, *Bibliographie critique*, p. 60.   [3] *Les Dieux antiques*, p. 281.
[4] Paul Valéry, *Variété II*, Paris, Gallimard, 1930, p. 162.

Gide had expressed in his *Le Traité du Narcisse* (*Théorie du symbole*). Indeed its publication in 1891 had coincided with the official establishment of Symbolism, as Michaud interprets the events of that year: '1891 est bien l'heure du symbolisme. . . . En 1886, la révolution de la sensibilité était faite; en 1891, la révolution intellectuelle est consommée.'[1]

But the young revolutionaries, like their Parnassian predecessors, also turned back to antiquity and the Greek myth for inspiration. So constant was their interest in Greece, so changed their way of seeing and of re-creating it that they illustrate Louis Ménard's claims for the inexhaustibility of mythological truth and his perspicacious and prophetic analysis of changes in interpretation, made as early as 1855: 'Les mythes sont vrais dans quelque sens qu'on les prenne,' he writes; '. . . Mais, selon le caractère des peuples, des époques, des individus, tel aspect des types divins prend plus de relief que tel autre. Le sens des mythes paraît tantôt plus matériel, tantôt plus moral, car l'idéal ne varie pas seulement d'une race à l'autre, il se transforme selon la nature des intelligences individuelles.'[2]

Symbolist sensibility transformed the eternal myths in a manner which was totally opposed to the Parnassian aspiration. Where the earlier poets sought clarity and definition of outline, with the plastic and picturesque qualities thrown into relief and the whole conception solidly supported by the new information provided by scholarship, the later poets turned inwards towards the shaded vision of the dream. Evocation replaces declaration, suggestion precision, and scholarship, seen as pure pedanticism, must be completely banished. Even Henri de Régnier and J. Moréas, the most erudite of the group, made no attempt to re-create an authentic Greek world but contented themselves with a decorative Greece, in Renaissance style, 'très raffinée et un peu mièvre'.[3] Indeed each poet had his own vision of Greece, a dream formed by mood and temperament and by a common desire to escape from

[1] See Michaud, *Message poétique*, ii. 399; H. Peyre, *L'Influence des littératures antiques sur la littérature française moderne*, *État des Travaux*, New Haven, Yale U.P. 1941, pp. 72 sqq.

[2] L. Ménard, *Poëmes*, Paris, E. Dentu, 1855, Préface, p. xxii.

[3] Desonay, *Le Rêve hellénique*, p. 59.

the immediate and mediocre present.[1] Not all of them were as frank as Samain in acknowledging how slight was his real concern with Greece itself when he wrote to a friend: 'Ce qu'il y a de grec dans ces vers n'est qu'apparent; les noms de mes petits bergers, quelques appellations usuelles, et puis c'est tout. Au fond, ce ne sont que des visions où mon âme s'est plue.'[2]

The true matter of poetry, as Samain suggests, is the vision created by the individual soul. It is not the exhibition of concrete objects or physical conditions however beautiful they may be. This subjective criterion was shared by the whole group of poets, whether they used the world of antiquity as setting, as décor, or whether they drew on its myths. For just as the physical world came to represent or embody the poet's feelings instead of reflecting or contradicting them, once Verlaine had altered the relationship between observer and observed, so the myth lost its independent life and became absorbed in the subjective experience of the poet who used it. Only the poet's inner experience could endow myth and physical matter alike with meaning.

Henri de Régnier's early poetry is characteristic of the Symbolist attitude to hellenism. He finds his inspiration in the classical world where 'l'éternelle verdeur de l'antique laurier'[3] endlessly glows; he symbolizes it in Pegasus, 'le vieux Cheval divin';[3] he uses the figure of Ariadne to express his own mood:

> Les ailes d'un oiseau de mer qui vole et plane
>   Font choir une ombre double aux plages de soleil
> Où mon ennui s'accoude en poses d'Ariane.[4]

But when the Symbolist poets go beyond the experience of the individual man to seek a wider meaning in antiquity they look not for the underlying unity of human nature as the Parnassians did but for a means of reaching universal, absolute truth. As Mallarmé declares: 'La matière éternelle du poème, c'est le mythe.'[5]

[1] Clerc, *Paganisme*, p. 198.
[2] Quoted by Michaud, *Message poétique*, iii. 499.
[3] H. de Régnier, *Les Jeux rustiques et divins*, Paris, Mercure de France, 1897, p. 112.
[4] Idem, *Épisodes, Sites et Sonnets*, Paris, Vanier, 1891, p. 40.
[5] Quoted by Clerc, *Paganisme*, p. 258.

More analytically, Charles Morice in *La Littérature de tout à l'heure* (a work that in 1889 seemed to represent a whole generation of poets) recognizes a common motive among his contemporaries in their approach to classicism: 'le besoin de vérité qui est en nous . . . nous qui faisons . . . le grand effort de renouer les bonnes, les belles traditions que [le monde] a rompues.'[1] The return to antiquity, with its creed and its philosophic beliefs, its legends and its traditions, can be seen as doubly desirable: both as contact with men's first communications with the Absolute and hence as a return to the original source of all art;[2] and as a means of re-establishing traditions of poetic thought.

The myths and legends of antiquity had to be understood in a new way. Henri de Régnier's definition of Symbolism, which Michaud considers the most admirable, discusses the contemporary approach: 'Les poètes récents ont considéré autrement les Mythes et les Légendes. Ils en cherchèrent la signification permanente et le sens idéal: où les uns virent des contes et des fables, les autres virent des symboles. Un Mythe est sur la grève du temps comme une de ces coquilles où l'on entend le bruit de la mer humaine. Un Mythe est la conque sonore d'une Idée.'[3]

The metaphor of the shell is important in Henri de Régnier's poetry. It also influenced other writers. In his early poem, 'Ariane', the poet on the seashore picks up the shell that he may blow to recall the divine past and to summon a passing god:

> je ramasse
> Une conque en spirales torses d'émail dur
>
> Où je souffle un appel à quelque dieu qui passe.[4]

Here the shell is a concrete object with its own form and texture; it is used by the poet's active will. It is he who appeals to the gods. When it is employed metaphorically in the address of some years later to symbolize the myth the emphasis has changed. The past

---

[1] Quoted by Michaud, *Message poétique*, ii. 379.

[2] Michaud, op. cit. ii. 379.

[3] 'Poètes d'aujourd'hui et poésie de demain', Conférence faite le 6 février 1900 à la Société des Conférences; quoted by Michaud, *Message poétique*, iii. 515.

[4] *Épisodes, Sites et Sonnets*, p. 41. See also Henri de Régnier, 'Églogue marine', *Les Jeux rustiques et divins*, p. 151.

may communicate only with the passive and attentive mind; the myth may express eternal Ideas only to the mind prepared to receive them, the shell murmur only to the waiting ear.

It is in the first sense that Pierre Louÿs, in collaboration with André Gide, named his 'anthology of the youngest poets', *La Conque*, in March 1891, using the last verse quoted above as epigraph. Poetry may be the means of summoning the passing gods. What Gide later described as 'la part de Dieu' in his creative writing may well have sprung, although unconsciously, from this Symbolist 'appel à quelque dieu qui passe'.

For this is the Symbolist world of letters which André Gide entered both socially and intellectually with the publication of *Le Traité du Narcisse* in 1891. As an adolescent he had been filled with admiration for Leconte de Lisle as interpreter of the classics; as a young man he became a disciple of Mallarmé for whom his admiration touched on adoration: 'il nous enseignait la vertu', he wrote in 1947. 'Oui vraiment c'est comme un saint qu'il m'apparaît et que je le considère. . . .'[1] From 1890 he enthusiastically frequented the rue de Rome on Tuesdays where he was made welcome. Mallarmé called him 'le Rare Intellectuel', and specially invited him to his home. He was among the ninety-four guests at the 'banquet des Symbolistes', as Paul Valéry named the banquet that celebrated the publication of Moréas's *Le Pèlerin passionné* on the 2nd of February 1891.[2] Gide was so closely involved in the Symbolist group that he naturally avoided the less congenial atmosphere of Heredia's rival receptions, while circulating freely, with Pierre Louÿs and sometimes Paul Valéry, among those men of letters who shared his aesthetic tastes. As he writes to Valéry in August 1892: 'As-tu lu que Bernard Lazare, parlant des revues et de *La Conque*, nous trinitise: "Trois jeunes écrivains du plus grand talent"?'[3] His two publications, *Les Cahiers d'André Walter*, despite its lack of popular success, and *Le Traité du Narcisse* entitled him to a certain respect among the

[1] André Gide, 'La leçon de Mallarmé', *Érasme*, T. II, no. 16, avril 1947, p. 146.
[2] *Correspondance d'André Gide et de Paul Valéry 1890–1942*, Préface et notes par Robert Mallet, Paris, Gallimard, 1955, p. 51.
[3] Ibid., p. 170.

young writers, his comfortable financial circumstances made life materially easy for him, and the friendship of Mallarmé gave him a position of some distinction.

Much later in his autobiography he describes this period as the most confused of his life, as one of 'dissipation, d'inquiétude',[1] which he was relieved to bring to a close when he left for Africa. It may well have seemed such when considered in retrospect; his personal state of mind was, as we have seen, disturbed enough; but the letters he wrote to Valéry at the time suggest that he was pleased enough to participate in the Parisian world of letters. Certainly he never recovered the same stimulating and agreeable world again when he came back to it after his Algerian experiences. *Paludes* (1895) provides witty and ironical proof of his later attitude. But *Paludes* could not have been written in 1890-1. There is no place for irony in *Les Cahiers* and no satire in *Le Narcisse*.

There is instead a predominantly serious interpretation of the current theory of poetics as his sub-title, *Théorie du symbole*, announces. Yet conventional as the principal ideas may appear there is a sense of urgency not only in the much-quoted note: 'Nous vivons pour manifester . . .',[2] but within the text itself, that individualizes the familiar conception. 'Ce curieux petit livre dogmatique', as an early critic described it,[3] has little that is curious in its aesthetic doctrine but much when the arguments, details, and tone of certain passages are closely considered.

The central line of thought is orthodox enough; a search for the Absolute strongly influenced by Plato's concept of reminiscence experienced in the world of flux and time.[3] The physical phenomena of this imperfect world are symbols that are capable of interpretation by those prepared to understand. Everything that appears in this world of ours is symbol, Gide declares.[4] And everything, properly understood, may recall the original condition of perfect Being, source of Truth, source of Ideas: 'Chaste Eden!

[1] *Grain*, O.C. x. 312.   [2] *Narcisse*, O.C. i. 215 n.
[3] Tancrède de Visan, *L'Attitude du lyrisme contemporain*, Paris, Mercure de France, 1911, pp. 374-5.
[4] *Narcisse*, O.C. i. 217 n.

Jardin des Idées! où les formes, rythmiques et sûres, révélaient sans effort leur nombre; où chaque chose était ce qu'elle paraissait; où prouver était inutile.'[1] Paradise, once lost by Adam's destructive act, can still be regained by contemplation and by comprehension. And these are the particular capacities of the poet: 'Le Poète est celui qui regarde. Et que voit-il? — Le Paradis.

Car le Paradis est partout; n'en croyons pas les apparences. Les apparences sont imparfaites: elles ballutient les vérités qu'elles recèlent; le Poète, à demi-mot, doit comprendre. . . .'[2] His duty takes him further since he must re-tell the truths he understands. In his turn he must re-create the Idea in its eternal form: 'Le Poète pieux contemple; il se penche sur les symboles, et silencieux descend profondément au cœur des choses, — et quand il a perçu, visionnaire, l'Idée, l'intime Nombre harmonieux de son Être, qui soutient la forme imparfaite, il la saisit, puis, insoucieux de cette forme transitoire qui la revêtait dans le temps, il sait lui redonner une forme éternelle, *sa* Forme véritable enfin, et fatale, — paradisiaque et cristalline.'[3] The work of art is therefore the product of the whole cyclical process of Idea, its embodiment (so to speak) in the symbol, its contemplation and recognition by the poet, and its re-creation. It epitomizes man's spiritual history, regaining Eden by its inner harmony, re-presenting Paradise, as part for the whole, and, by its own purity, allowing the Idea to bloom again: 'Car l'œuvre d'art est un cristal — paradis partiel où l'Idée refleurit en sa pureté supérieure; où, comme dans l'Eden disparu, l'ordre normal et nécessaire a disposé toutes les formes dans une réciproque et symétrique dépendance, où l'orgueil du mot ne supplante pas la pensée, — où les phrases rythmiques et sûres, symboles encore, mais symboles purs, où les paroles se font transparentes et révélatrices.'[3] Despite its Platonic overtones Gide's exposition of aesthetic theory is thoroughly traditional. The inner reality symbolized by the world of appearances is the doctrine to be understood in the poetry of

---

[1] *Narcisse*, O.C. i. 210.
[2] Ibid., p. 216.
[3] Ibid., p. 217.

Baudelaire, Rimbaud, Mallarmé,[1] as well as in the thought of such a contemporary as Valéry to whom the *Traité* is dedicated.[2]

So, too, is Gide's choice of the Narcissus myth: it embodies the spirit of the poetic age: 'Narcisse, on le sait', writes a critic, 'est le dieu favori de la mythologie symboliste, dieu du solipsisme, de l'onanisme esthétique.'[3] The solitude of Narcissus, the turning inwards on himself to discover truth and beauty, the mistrust of the physical world that reinforces his isolation: the myth readily carries the Symbolist message: 'nos sens nous trompent', Villiers de l'Isle-Adam states, '... *nous ne pouvons pas* voir les choses telles qu'elles sont ... Je ne sors pas de moi-même. C'est l'histoire de Narcisse.'[4]

Many poets drew on it. Henri de Régnier, again, found it deeply influential;[5] as did also Saint-Georges de Bouhélier[6] among others. But Valéry's contemporary poem, 'Narcisse parle', published in the first number of *La Conque*, is of the greatest interest not only for its absolute value but for its association with Gide's use of the myth. Two young men with immortal longings sat one day in the Montpellier cemetery under the cypresses by the tomb linked by tradition with the poet Young's daughter, the young girl whom he celebrated poetically as Narcissa. (Valéry recalls the origin of his 'Narcisse parle' in *Les Cahiers du Sud*, 1946.) Gide recognized the importance of his friend's poem, wrote him an intelligent appreciation of it, and had every intention of following his poetic example by a poem of his own. In March 1892 he sent Valéry part of a poem, intended for *La Conque*, which he called 'Narcisse secret'. But the poem was never finished and Gide's use of the myth remains his poetically expressed *conte* of 1891.

The *conte*, or *récit*, or *traité*, the brief story carrying a deeper

---

[1] R. Derche, *Quatre Mythes poétiques*, Paris, Société d'Éd. d'Enseignement supérieur, 1962, pp. 95–6.

[2] Michaud, *Message poétique*, ii. 389–90.

[3] R. Fernandez, *André Gide*, Paris, Corrêa, 1931, p. 60.

[4] Quoted by Michaud, op. cit. i. 87.

[5] See 'L'allusion à Narcisse', *Les Jeux rustiques et divins*, p. 16; *Le Bosquet de Psyché*, Bruxelles, P. Lacomblez, 1894.

[6] Saint-Georges de Bouhélier, *Discours sur la mort de Narcisse*, ou l'impérieuse métamorphose — théorie de l'amour, Paris, Vanier, 1895.

meaning, so popular in the eighteenth century, came back into favour in the 1890's, partly on account, as Jean Hytier thinks,[1] of André Gide's use of a fictional form that was so congenial to him; his preference for it is well demonstrated in the collection of *Le Retour de l'Enfant prodigue*. Gide's immediate influence is apparent in Quillot's *Le Traité de la Méduse* (1892), where the dedication to Gide seems almost redundant so closely do form, ideas, and style follow Gide's *Le Traité du Narcisse*.

But within the short tale with its implicit moral message Gide has already adopted the characteristic Chinese-box narrative he was so often to use. For three different narrative stances are taken up in this short tale.[2] There is the voice of the author's *persona* which introduces and concludes the retelling of the Narcissus myth. If the tone of this voice is not yet overtly ironical it has a casualness that is meant to disarm criticism. The book opens by saying: 'Les livres ne sont peut-être pas une chose bien nécessaire'; it draws to a close on an equally nonchalant note: 'Ce traité n'est peut-être pas quelque chose de bien nécessaire.' The effect of this tone is essentially protective, just as the Gidian irony is later to be, and its use in a framing narrative device established a perspective of the Narcissus myth that, however unconsciously used, may well have opened the way to the attitude of mind which produced *Paludes*. It is not, however, over-emphasized here. The stylistic device of repeated phrases, 'Quelques mythes d'abord suffisaient . . .', gives an incantatory effect that works in its own way and diminishes the influence of the distanced perspective. Then comes the story of Narcissus alone in his melancholy Netherlands: 'Un morne, un léthargique canal, un presque horizontal miroir; et rien ne distinguerait de l'ambiance incolorée cette eau terne, si l'on ne sentait qu'elle coule.'[3] Small wonder that he is bored, for it is simple boredom that drives him to the river of passing time. The third dimension is brought about by his dream of Paradise, the original Ideal from which everything is to fall away. This is

[1] J. Hytier, *André Gide*, Algiers, Charlot, 1938, p. 15.

[2] Germaine Brée, *André Gide l'insaisissable Protée*, Paris, 'Les Belles Lettres', 1953, p. 43: 'Le traité gidien se développe en triptyque.' The three contemplative figures thus form independent but related scenes.

[3] *Narcisse*, O.C. i. 208.

presumably the central focus of the *Traité* for Gide goes out of his way to number—I, II, III,—the sections describing the Fall, the description of human aspiration, and of the poet's special duty. The return to Narcissus and his eternal contemplation seems almost perfunctory. Are we to identify him with the poet? By his contemplative pose and by his concern with the inner life it would appear so. Yet he does not fulfil the poet's duty of re-creation and remains at the end passive and attentive, picturesque and idle: the layman's imperfect idea of the artist.

The most personal part of the *Traité* is certainly found in the narrative set at a third remove from the reader. André Gide adopts a 'Presenter' who tells the story of Narcissus who dreams of Paradise and Adam's original existence. And only Adam acts. Where Narcissus is bored in the imperfect world of Time, Adam, surrounded by perfect Being, is equally bored. As the Ideal Spectator whose role is merely to observe, how is he ever to know himself? However perfect the environment may be, how-ever powerful his capacity to create that world in his own mind, how can he define his own limits, his individuality, without an act of will? 'A force de les contempler', he thinks, 'il ne se distin-gue plus de ces choses: ne pas savoir où l'on s'arrête — ne pas savoir jusqu'où l'on va! Car c'est un esclavage enfin, si l'on n'ose risquer un geste, sans crever toute l'harmonie.'[1] Adam's predica-ment is one of perfect adjustment that becomes intolerable to the seeker of Self. At this point Gide changes his narrative stance to identify himself with the hitherto distanced Adam: the first person takes over from the third, the colloquial tone from the meditative; 'Et puis, tant pis! cette harmonie m'agace,' Adam says, 'et son accord toujours parfait. Un geste! un petit geste, pour savoir, — une dissonance, que diable! — Eh! va donc! un peu d'imprévu.'[1] And Adam performs the first of man's unforeseen acts, predecessor of 'l'acte gratuit', breaks the branch of Ygdrasil, scatters the leaves of the sacred book of knowledge, destroys Eden, and creates the world of Time.

The presentation of Eden is Gide's own, partly because of the transformation of the Tree of Knowledge into the Scandinavian

[1] Ibid., p. 211.

tree that supports the sky,[1] partly because the mixture of Hebraic and Norse mythology could be artistically justified by the universal search for the Absolute under the 'single Night', although it reveals his current interests,[2] but chiefly because the narrative springs to life, to the present tense, to the first person expressing himself in active prose as Adam expresses himself in self-defining action: 'Et puis, tant pis!'

There is much in the detailed working out of the whole *Traité* that was to become characteristic of Gide's amalgamation of experience, much that reveals his personal preoccupations, but, as he wrote to Valéry, the actual process of writing it was in itself a self-revelatory experience, even if he was doubtful of its final success: 'Toujours l'effort pour l'écrire n'est-il pas perdu, car il m'a débrouillé toute mon esthétique, ma morale et ma philosophie. Et l'on ne m'empêchera pas de croire qu'il *faut* que tout *auteur* ait une philosophie, une morale, une esthétique *particulières*. On ne crée rien sans cela. L'œuvre n'est qu'une manifestation de cela.'[3] If the process of writing may clarify an author's thoughts it may also influence the author himself and so develop both the man and his thought. Gide's use of the term 'manifestation' for the expression of a man in his writing shows how intimate he considers the relationship to be between creator and creation. It is indeed an influence exercised in two directions: the writer may express himself as he writes but he is also being formed by *what* he writes. This double influence was to become the subject of Gide's next *Traité du vain désir*: as he describes it: 'J'ai voulu indiquer, dans cette *Tentative amoureuse*, l'influence du livre sur celui qui l'écrit, et pendant cette écriture même. Car en sortant de nous, il nous change, il modifie la marche de notre vie; comme l'on voit en physique ces vases mobiles suspendus, pleins de liquide, recevoir une impulsion, lorsqu'ils se vident, dans le sens opposé à celui de l'écoulement du liquide qu'ils contiennent. Nos actes ont sur nous une rétroaction.'[4] This relationship concerned him as early as 1891

[1] See A. H. Krappe, *La Genèse des mythes*, Paris, Payot, 1938, p. 266.

[2] *Correspondance*, p. 88 [2 juin 1891], Gide writes to Valéry of his fascination by the 'brutales et vénérables visions' of the *Eddas*.

[3] *Ibid.*, p. 134 [3 novembre 1891].

[4] *Journal*, p. 40, 1893.

in *Les Cahiers d'André Walter* and as late as the experience of Édouard in *Les Faux-Monnayeurs* (1926). The unhappy André Walter whose personal history parallels the headlong progress towards madness of his fictional character, Alain, furnishes the most sensational illustration of the intimate link between writer and work. But of course André Gide who creates both characters escapes unscathed from their common plight.

When his writing of *Le Traité du Narcisse* took him far beyond his original intention of presenting a theory of aesthetics he followed the developing thought wherever it might lead him. And it led him to the formulation of a code of morality and to a philosophy. For if it is the poet's duty to make manifest the Truth he glimpses in the world of transience it is also the human being's duty to embody and enact particular facets of human experience among the multiple physical phenomena. The duty is identical, for artist as for man: 'Tout homme qui ne manifeste pas est inutile et mauvais.' The difficulties in performing that duty which arise when the self intrudes in the relationship between vessel and Idea are similar: 'Tout représentant de l'Idée tend à se préférer à l'Idée qu'il manifeste. Se préférer — voilà la faute.' When the duty is common, the task and the obstacles to be overcome common, then artist and man must acknowledge the same demands and commands: 'Nous vivons pour manifester. Les règles de la morale et de l'esthétique sont les mêmes: toute œuvre qui ne manifeste pas est inutile et par cela même, mauvaise. Tout homme qui ne manifeste pas est inutile et mauvais.'[1] When the human duty to manifest some part of Truth is acknowledged judgement can only be passed on the performance, not on the nature of the act performed. And such an evaluation and such judgement have little to do with conventional codes of morality. They stem from an extended aesthetic appreciation and cover all manifestations of life: 'La question morale pour l'artiste', Gide writes, 'n'est pas que l'Idée qu'il manifeste soit plus ou moins morale et utile au grand nombre; la question est qu'il la manifeste bien. — Car tout doit être manifesté, même les plus funestes choses: "Malheur à celui par qui le scandale arrive", mais "Il faut que le scandale arrive." —

[1] *Narcisse*, O.C. i. 215 n.

L'artiste et l'homme vraiment homme, qui vit pour quelque chose, doit avoir d'avance fait le sacrifice de soi-même. Toute sa vie n'est qu'un acheminement vers cela.'[1]

The importance of this didactic and revealing note written, as Gide takes care to point out, at the same time as the *Traité* has always been recognized.[2] What has not, I think, been noticed is that the *Traité* itself embodies, in embryo form certainly, both the artist and 'l'homme vraiment homme' with their common self-transcending, self-sacrificing task. When Narcissus turns back from the river and the impossible act of embracing illusion he voluntarily assumes the contemplative role that symbolizes the artist's preparatory task at least: 'Grave et religieux il reprend sa calme attitude: il demeure — symbole qui grandit — et, penché sur l'apparence du Monde, sent vaguement en lui, résorbées, les générations humaines qui passent.'[3] But Adam, too, has his role to play, equally self-sacrificing, but taking a different form. Contemplation is not for him: 'A force de les contempler, il ne se distingue plus de ces choses.'[4] At whatever cost to himself, he must act to break his harmonious state of enslavement even if this act is to bring anguish and horror to him and introduce desire, dissatisfaction, and time into the world. If ever 'l'homme vraiment homme' finds suitable incarnation it is in the figure of Adam.

Le *Traité du Narcisse* is in more ways than one the preparatory work of a young writer. So Gide himself considered it and so, by its reliance on fashionable aesthetic theory which soon became distasteful to him, it may well appear. It earned him the approval of a group of writers who withdrew that approbation after his return from Algeria, who condemned, as did Henri de Régnier, *Les Nourritures terrestres* (1897) and everything that followed it.[5] It did in fact *represent* the age of Symbolism.

---

[1] *Narcisse*, O.C. i. 215–16 n.

[2] See R. Derche, *Quatre Mythes poétiques*, p. 96, who thinks the note is the only personal contribution to a conventional treatment of a banal doctrine.

[3] *Narcisse*, O.C. i. 218.   [4] Ibid., p. 211.

[5] Henri de Régnier writes in *Le Figaro*, 12 mars 1924: 'J'ai honte d'avouer que j'ai peine à m'intéresser à l'œuvre et à la personnalité de M. André Gide. Quelques livres de jeunesse annonçaient en lui un certain talent . . .'. Quoted by G. Gabory, *André Gide, son Œuvre*, Paris, Éd. de la Nouvelle Revue critique, 1924,

But in a deeper sense it is also preparatory since it contains personified sketches of the dichotomy between the active and the contemplative attitudes to life that runs through Gide's whole work. When his note ends on a question: 'Et maintenant que manifester? — On apprend cela dans le silence',[1] it suggests a delayed reply that has been referred to Gide's own life. But the *Traité* already offers two responses. 'Que faire?' Narcissus asks himself, and then replies, 'Contempler.'[2] 'Mais que sait-il de sa puissance', Adam demands, 'tant qu'elle reste inaffirmée?'[3] and he responds to his need for individual affirmation by action however destructive it may prove.

Contemplation and action; self-subordination and self-affirmation: these are the antithetic concepts that are found in Oedipus and Theseus at the end of Gide's long literary career. They are also explored in the first extended presentation of Greek heroes, in *Philoctète* and *Le Prométhée mal enchaîné*.

p. 15 n., who adds: 'Ces livres, c'étaient *Le Traité du Narcisse, La Tentative amoureuse,* et surtout *Le Voyage d'Urien.* Depuis, André Gide cessa d'exister pour M. Henri de Régnier et pour tous ceux de son groupe — alors que sans doute il commençait d'exister vraiment.'

[1] *Narcisse*, O.C. i. 216.   [2] Ibid., p. 218.
[3] Ibid., p. 211.

3

SUPERHUMAN REBELS

FROM 1890 to 1898—from Narcissus to Philoctetes and Prometheus, from Symbolist theory and fantasies to non-theatrical drama and to satiric *récit*, even burlesque as *Le Prométhée* has been called[1] —there are many changes of approach. But the years were filled with events and influences, and the discrepancies between genres and attitudes will surprise no reader of Gide. These were the years of journeys to Algeria in 1893 and 1895 besides travels in Europe; Gide's return to Paris and his brilliant externalization of personal discontent in *Paludes* (1895); the death of his mother and his marriage to his cousin, Madeleine Rondeaux (1895); his illness and recovery, and its exuberant celebration in *Les Nourritures terrestres* (1897).

Only those who follow Gide's interest in Greek myth will notice that an interval of some seven years separates the orthodox Narcissus from his eccentric successors of the resounding names. Allusions scattered through *Les Nourritures* throw up the interests that were developed later, like so many seeds that, to use Gide's life-long metaphor, germinate in another season. Meanwhile, the winter of 1898-9 produced Gide's first completely free choice of Greek heroes when *Philoctète* and *Le Prométhée mal enchaîné*, like a pair of wounded and suffering Dioscuri, appeared within a month of each other.[2]

There may seem little to surprise us in the choice of Prometheus, although the Sophoclean Philoctetes, despite Leconte de Lisle's translation (1877), seemed less predictable. For the Aeschy-

---

[1] E. Ludovicy, 'Le mythe grec dans le théâtre français contemporain', *Revue des Langues vivantes*, xxii, 1956, p. 390.

[2] 'Philoctète', *La Revue blanche*, 1ᵉʳ décembre 1898; Paris, Mercure de France, 1899; 'Le Prométhée mal enchaîné', *L'Ermitage*, janvier-mars 1899; Paris, Mercure de France, 1899.

lean Prometheus (Hesiod's less awe-inspiring figure could never have aroused the same response) dominated the nineteenth-century imagination, as indeed did Aeschylus himself.[1] Admiration for Aeschylus touched idolatry; as Victor Hugo, speaking for his age, expresses it: 'Une sorte d'épouvante emplit Eschyle d'un bout à l'autre; une méduse profonde s'y dessine vaguement derrière les figures qui se meuvent dans la lumière. Eschyle est magnifique et formidable; . . . Eschyle est le mystère antique fait homme; quelque chose comme un prophète païen. . . .'[2]

If Aeschylus himself exercised such power over the literary imagination his Prometheus seemed inexhaustibly rich to poets and scholars alike. Goethe's double use of the myth in 1773-4 and Shelley's *Prometheus Unbound* (1820) were outstanding precursors of the multitudinous versions, translations, and adaptations of the nineteenth century.[3] Michelet goes so far as to identify Titan, tragic poet, and humanity itself. In Prometheus 'l'humanité se plaint, — s'abaisse? non. Du fond de la douleur, elle est forte, se dresse. . . . l'héroïsme en l'homme est la nature.'[4]

Where the poets found personal self-expression in the Promethean myth the scholars discovered the relationships between the perennial story and the cultural patterns and beliefs of succeeding ages. A hellenist like Louis Ménard shows some of the ways in which the myth may be analysed and interpreted. Within the particular story of Prometheus, he sees an illustration of the continually developing process of mythological matter; as he writes in 1863: 'Comme le sens des mythes est toujours multiple, celui de Prométhée et de Pandore, dont Hésiode ne montre que le côté social, contenait d'autres idées qui se développèrent à mesure que l'élément mystique prévalut dans les symboles religieux.' He goes on to describe its central symbolic meaning as spiritual: 'Prométhée devint l'expression de l'âme humaine, cette flamme tombée du ciel et attachée au Caucase de la vie sous les

---

[1] Canat, *L'Hellénisme*, p. 240.
[2] Victor Hugo, 'Les génies', *William Shakespeare*, Paris, A. Lacroix, Verboeckhoven et Cie, 1864, p. 65.
[3] See Trousson, *Prométhée*, for a full examination of the Promethean myth from its origin to today and bibliography.
[4] Michelet, *De l'humanité*, p. 264.

dures chaînes de la matière, dévorée d'angoisses toujours renais-
santes, et ramenée dans sa patrie céleste par le bras rédempteur des
vertus héroïques.'[1] Again, the myth may personify the physical
mystery of fire.[2] It may even seem a prefiguration of the Christian
Passion.[3]

But to these concepts of the evolutionary process of mythological interpretation, the religious meaning myth may embody
or prefigure, the physical phenomenon or the universal human
spirit it may symbolize, all of which seem valid suggestions to us
today, the close of the nineteenth century in France added many
and various Promethean avatars. Prometheus may represent the
French nation liberated by the Revolution;[4] universal human
freedom born in France;[5] the racial history of all antiquity.[6] He
may be sacrificed for the cause of justice,[7] self-sacrificed for the
eternal progress of mankind.[8] He may be mankind's traditional
benefactor, cluttered up by Pandora;[9] or he may, as artist and
free-thinker, stand totally alone.[10] The possibilities seem infinite,
the adaptations of very variable quality. Nevertheless these predecessors and contemporaries of Gide's Prometheus show certain
common traits. They are uniformly solemn, they attempt the
noblest of themes, they present the loftiest of heroes; and they
are all in verse. Even Meyer's scientific study of the movement of
peoples lumbers along in rhymed couplets.[11]

This is the group into which Gide's Prometheus insinuates
himself, his story, 'cette gerbe de folle ivraie', as Gide describes his
work, flourishing in the cafés and pavements of Paris in May

[1] L. Ménard, *Du polythéisme hellénique*, Paris, Charpentier, 1863, pp. 58–59.

[2] Id., *Rêveries d'un païen mystique*, Paris, Lemerre, 1876, pp. 34–35.

[3] Ibid., p. 38. See Trousson, *Prométhée*, ch. II, 'Prometheus Christus'.

[4] É. Duneau, *Prométhée*: le peuple délivré, cantate pour le Centenaire de 1789,
Paris, juin 1889.

[5] H. Muratel, *Le Triomphe de Prométhée*, Paris, Vanier, 1893.

[6] A. Meyer, *Prométhée enchaîné*, étude lue le 5 février 1885 à l'Académie de
Marseille.

[7] Sâr Péladan, *La Prométhéiade*, Paris, Chamuel, 1895.

[8] S. Millet, *Prométhée libérateur*, drame antique, Paris, Ollendorf, 1897.

[9] J. Lorrain et A.-F. Hérold, *Prométhée*, tragédie lyrique, Paris, Mercure de
France, 1900.

[10] I. Gilkin, *Prométhée, poème dramatique*, Paris, Fischbacher, 1899.

[11] A. Meyer, op. cit.

189 . . ., while the prevailing wind blew from the Caucasian crags. It seems an audacious book on all counts, this *Prométhée mal enchaîné*. Its plot is complicated, gods and men are indistinguishable; its structure is complex; its hero's voice changes from tenor to bass without warning; its speech is prose; and, above all, heroism and nobility when they appear are as unstable as shadows in a river. Its immediate provocative impact is produced, of course, by the free, even carefree, presentation of the suffering and sacrosanct Titan whose size, speech despite its overtones, and desires are wholly human. Nonetheless this familiar human figure may well still play his traditional role of benefactor to men whatever the vagaries of his fortune or the eccentricities of his attitudes.

It is well to remember, before judging *Le Prométhée mal enchaîné* by his contemporaries, that the tradition of comic or satiric drama is at least as old as tragedy. The Euripidean *Cyclops* shows us what the concluding play of festival tetralogies must have been. And it would seem that even Prometheus made his first appearance with the satyrs.[1] No one was sacred to the Greeks. Even the suffering and prophetic Titan could be presented by Aristophanes as sheltering under hood and umbrella from the wrath of Zeus.[2] But the Greeks were capable of holding two simultaneous views of the hero. The Aeschylean Prometheus was not diminished by the satiric treatment. The shuddering comic figure could not diminish the Titan, indomitable of mind, confident in his destiny, who could challenge Zeus to 'hurl [his] body utterly to black Tartarus with the savage eddies of Necessity' without fear of pain or death.[3] All that we know of the Greek spirit suggests that the double view of human behaviour could be simultaneously valid. All depends on situation and mood.

There is also the fact that the passing of time brings its own modifications. Prometheus, as Lucian of Samosate presented him in the second century, is a shifty and garrulous character who is

[1] L. Séchan, *Le Mythe de Prométhée*, Paris, Presses Universitaires de France, 1951, p. 85.
[2] Ibid., pp. 47–48.
[3] Aeschylus, *Prometheus Vinctus*, translated by F. G. Plaistowe and T. R. Mills, London, University Tutorial Press, n.d., pp. 27–28.

lucky to escape with one devouring vulture instead of the sixteen that Hermes thinks he deserves for his argument against Zeus.[1] If the 'sophist of Samosate' seems irretrievably to belittle the splendid heroic figure with his religious aura, his lively and disrespectful treatment is as potentially creative as it is destructive: 'il est aussi le premier alchimiste de la grande transmutation', Trousson writes, 'qui fera, au cours des siècles futurs, d'un dieu un homme, de Prométhée l'humanité. L'histoire du mythe dans l'antiquité s'achève donc comme se ferme une boucle: le monde du paganisme ne pouvait plus rien lui donner. Grâce à Lucien, la voie restait ouverte à une autre forme de la révolte, qui est encore la nôtre; avec lui, Prométhée s'engage insensiblement dans un autre combat, il se charge d'un autre symbole.'[2] And it was certainly the way opened by Lucien that was followed by Gide so many centuries later, although that path took him far from his contemporaries.

However, more interesting than the fact of divergence from the conventional view is the reason why the young Gide should adopt such an unorthodox attitude. When his great predecessors, Goethe whom he so admired and Shelley whose figure of Asia as Prometheus' beloved appears briefly in *Le Prométhée mal enchaîné*, both maintain the elevated tone and attitude of the tragedy, why should Gide adopt such a deliberately provocative tone? Are we justified in interpreting his handling of the subject-matter as a means of freeing himself from his own particular chains? The modification of Greek attitudes to their gods when mythology develops into comedy has been understood as the expression of a revenge taken by men against their former rulers. Disrespect readily replaces fear once divine authority is open to question. As the historical process has been described: 'A mesure que la crainte des dieux cesse d'être le premier mot de la sagesse, l'homme, devenu irréverencieux, se venge, par de cruelles railleries, du joug longtemps subi: la mythologie se tourne en sujet comique. Déjà Euripide et Aristophane bafouent les dieux sans merci; mais leurs plaisanteries semblent bien anodines auprès de celles que se

---

[1] Lucian, translated by A. M. Harmon, Loeb Classical Library, 1915, vol. ii, pp. 263-5.   [2] Trousson, *Prométhée*, i. 55.

permirent les auteurs de la moyenne comédie, qui firent des dieux et des héros des fantoches héroï-comiques du genre burlesque.'[1]

It is tempting therefore to see Gide's attitude in *Le Prométhée* as analogous on a personal level with that of the secularizing Greeks, for this early work, with the exception of the opera *Perséphone*, is the only one to include a divine figure. But the Eleusinian goddesses are treated with a respect that the character of Zeus, 'le Miglionnaire', does not receive. In the *récit* the omnipotent ruler controls money and therefore men; the Titan controls himself and therefore his fate.

This short work of Gide's has very properly received much attention. No one tracing the evolution of his thought can neglect it, no one studying the literature of later writers in France, particularly those who make use of the Greek myth, can fail to recognize its influence; it is, as Trousson writes, 'un sacrilège qui renouvelait singulièrement la portée du mythe'.[2] It has been examined in isolation, as a moral fable, as the exploration of key symbols, and as an artefact. Indeed Gide invites such examination when he draws attention in the dedication to his friend, Paul-Albert Laurens, to the 'bon grain' which may well be found in 'cette gerbe de folle ivraie'.

That seed, as we may interpret the tale from our own reading, lies in the ground of the Greek myth and its intervening interpreters. Just how much the myth contributed to the whole work has been questioned. It has been denied that he took more from the myth than the vaguest of starting-points: 'En dehors d'une vague donnée originelle, tout est de Gide', one critic writes.[3] Nevertheless, while no one would assert that the originality and individuality of *Le Prométhée mal enchaîné* arose from elsewhere than Gide's creative imagination, he did draw on the Promethean mythologem[4] for his general matter. Indeed the mythological

---

[1] G. Fougères, 'La mythologie classique chez les poètes modernes', *Revue Universitaire*, 15 juillet 1903, p. 129.

[2] Trousson, *Prométhée*, ii. 435. [3] Ludovicy, op. cit., p. 390.

[4] Kerényi's term for the traditional body of material from which mythology springs as a form of art. See C. G. Jung and C. Kerényi, *Essays on a Science of Mythology* (Revised edition), translated by R. F. C. Hull, New York and Evanston, Harper and Row, 1963, p. 2 (written in 1941).

pattern may be understood within the main development, over which play the provocative fantasies of a stimulating mind.

The essential elements of the myth are rebellion brought about by the Titan's generosity to men; punishment and physical suffering; and his knowledge of ultimate freedom that Hercules is to bring him. Thus rebellion, suffering, and liberation shape the history of Gide's Prometheus. There are, of course, no women in the main course of action. Io and the Ocean Nymphs follow Echo into the void; there is no place for Pandora. But the principal phases of the heroic story succeed each other in their customary order.

Gide takes many liberties within the general outline. That seems natural enough in a story essentially concerned with rebellion and with liberty. His modifications to the inherited story alter the original *schema*, audaciously transforming it almost to the point of unrecognizability, and complicate the plot both by additions to the main line of intrigue and by an extended inset narrative that comes very close to overwhelming the main plot development. The most obvious alteration is in the denouement when Prometheus frees himself from Zeus' domination without the aid of a superhuman saviour. It is he, not Hercules, who slaughters the retributory eagle, the 'winged hound of Zeus', whose daily onslaughts on his liver make up part of his traditional punishment and suffering. Indeed, it is roasted eagle that regales Prometheus and his friends after they have buried Damocles, and it provides the most delicious of dishes for the gayest of wakes. There is nothing to surprise us in the suppression of Hercules as saviour when Zeus the omnipotent receives such nonchalant attention. Yet it is possible to discern within the complexities of Gide's principal plot, a shadow of the Herculean role in the story of Damocles. If we remember that the main plot arises from the arbitrary actions of 'le Miglionnaire' (Zeus), who distributes with equal equanimity a blow to one stranger, Cocles, the gift of 500 francs to another, Damocles; who allows those two actions to ferment like yeast in the spirits of two very different men until one of them comes to terms with his lot, both the unmerited blow and subsequent loss of an eye, while the other, Damocles, dies of anxiety, a tormenting sense of debt, and ultimately despair, we may perhaps see in the death of Damocles a version of the self-sacrificing saviour whose descent into Hades will bring about the release of Prometheus. The Aeschylean Hermes prophesies that Prometheus will not be free until 'some one of the gods comes forth to bear thy sufferings instead of thee, and is ready go to unto the sunless realm of Hades and nigh about the gloomy depths of Tartarus'.[1] Damocles' death proves to be the turning point of the Gidian Prometheus' experience. When Prometheus fails in his attempt to bring comfort from Zeus to the moribund Damocles, he disposes of his own torturing eagle and presents himself at the graveside full of gratitude to the dead man for his present state of well-being. As he says: 'C'est à cause de lui pourtant, ou plutôt c'est grâce à sa mort qu'à présent j'ai tué mon aigle...'[2] Because of Damocles, thanks to Damocles therefore, Prometheus enters on his final phase of freedom and contentment. No one could seem less superhuman than Damocles, tormented by the sense of undischarged obligation and duty, delirious in his over-medicated bedroom, but nevertheless it is his death, voluntary or otherwise, that liberates Prometheus from conscientiousness, from guilt, and from Zeus. Whether Damocles descends into Hades is left uncertain; whether he wanted to do so is even less clear; but it is his unfortunate demise that allows Prometheus to tell his long parable of lost freedom in the tale of Tityrus, Angela, and the overpowering oak-tree which authorizes Prometheus' personal sense of freedom. The heroic figure of Hercules is hard to recognize in the only-too-human person of Damocles but the liberating function is similar.

Damocles' death and the funeral ceremony which allows Prometheus to tell his long tale of liberty lost and found as oblique explanation of his own state of mind mark the final stage of his liberation. But he is already partially free when his story opens. When Prometheus discovers that he is uncomfortable on the Caucasian heights, stretches himself, and presents himself on a

---

[1] Aeschylus, *Prometheus Vinctus*, p. 27.
[2] *PME*, O.C. iii. 150.

Paris boulevard one late May afternoon he has already experienced freedom without realization. The action of Gide's story covers the interval between the practice of partial freedom and the recognition of a totally free state. Prometheus acts almost unconsciously when he extricates himself from a physically disagreeable position; he is fully aware of his action when he eats his eagle and cuts his last connexion with Zeus. Gide's action thus takes place between the two phases of the mythological action. Eagle follows chains in the Aeschylean story, both successive parts of the same punitive action, chronologically ordered but simultaneous in intention. Prometheus has offended Zeus and must be doubly punished. What Gide has done, from the point of view of narration, is to separate these two connected phases, to show the Caucasian penance as preliminary action, and to pick up the story of his Prometheus as he leaves the mountain only to find himself still subject to the ubiquitous eagle even in Paris, where such suffering is out of place: 'A Paris c'est très mal porté. L'aigle gêne.'[1]

Gide's account thus opens in *medias res*. When Prometheus recalls his past benefactions to men, as in the Aeschylean matter and method, it is only to explain his eagle and its origin in human character. He passes lightly over the other aspect of his punishment, the confinement to the Caucasus, since it had not detained him once he felt inclined to move. The originality of Gide's narrative, therefore, lies partly in his separation of the two aspects of suffering and partly in the emphasis he places on the mobile eagle. Both innovatory aspects are to be understood in the light of Gide's fundamental concern with the evolution of conscious and voluntary behaviour from the instinctive expression of freedom in action. This is his solution to the Promethean predicament (whereas the full Aeschylean experience can only be surmised), and it is Gide's contribution to the mythological matter. It is also a theme of considerable importance and of constant urgency. The passage from instinctive to conscious, voluntary action is one that each of us must undertake not once but many times. Gide works it out in a plot of interlocking human destinies where supernatural

[1] *PME*, O.C. iii. 119.

assistance is withheld, and where men must make their own decisions.

When we examine the action between its tentative opening and its decisive close, we must encounter the Gidian eagle with its many ramifications of meaning. While it may seem to include too many meanings for complete clarity its main function is, I think, suggested in the first phase of Prometheus' punishment from which he, prematurely, considers himself to be free: 'Quand, du haut du Caucase, Prométhée eut bien éprouvé que les chaînes, tenons, camisoles, parapets et autres scrupules, somme toute, l'ankylosaient, pour changer de pose il se souleva du côté gauche, étira son bras droit et, entre quatre et cinq heures d'automne, descendit le boulevard qui mène de la Madeleine à l'Opéra.'[1] Here the single abstraction among so many concrete objects and practical actions points to the central meaning of the ambiguous eagle. It is the 'autres scrupules' that Prometheus finds as morally cramping as the chains are physically confining; it is the sensitivity of a scrupulous conscience that is embodied in the eagle. As Prometheus recounts his past history his own particular eagle sprang from its egg once he helped men with the gift of fire, once he felt responsible for their welfare: 'Ils étaient très peu éclairés; j'inventai pour eux quelques feux; et dès lors commença mon aigle. C'est depuis ce jour que je m'aperçois que je suis nu.'[2] In the history of men eagles came into being once their original consciousness of simple existence was transformed by Prometheus' anxiety for them into conscientiousness, into the desire to explain their existence and to justify it by improving it: 'non satisfait de leur donner la conscience de leur être', Prometheus says, 'je voulus leur donner aussi raison d'être. . . . Échauffant leurs esprits, en eux je fis éclore la dévorante croyance au progrès. . . . Non plus croyance au bien, mais malade espérance du mieux. La croyance au progrès, Messieurs, c'était leur aigle. Notre aigle est notre raison d'être, Messieurs.'[3] From consciousness to conscience, the evolution of human nature can be summarized by the linguistic pun, playing on the double meaning of 'conscience'.

This primary meaning of the eagle, the scruples of man's moral

[1] Ibid., p. 103.   [2] Ibid., p. 132.   [3] Ibid., p. 134.

conscience, thus develops directly from the opening paragraph of Prometheus' experience, unifying the process of suffering after a fashion, much as the Greek myth demanded. But the allegorical layer of meaning Gide imposes on his eagle extends its application to include the history of mankind as well as the story of one suffering hero. There can be personal eagles which distinguish individual men one from the other; there can also be, so to say, party-eagles which distinguish historical periods. Gide points to the second application above when he reiterates the importance of a 'raison d'être'.

However, each man starts with his own personal eagle. It is his claim to distinction. Not only must Prometheus so nourish his eagle at his own expense that his experience can be summed up in the prophetic: 'Il faut qu'il croisse et que je diminue',[1] but everyone must submit to a similar relationship. His advice to all his listeners is to cherish and appreciate the individual eagle that provides each man with his particular 'raison d'être', his unique distinction. He draws public attention to Damocles' indebtedness for his unsought money and uses it as a particular instance of a general principle: 'Voilà votre aigle à vous; il en est d'autres; il en est de plus glorieux. Mais je vous dis ceci: l'aigle de toute façon, nous dévore, vice ou vertu, devoir ou passion; cessez d'être quelconque, et vous n'y échapperez pas.'[2] The personal eagle then that every man of any quality must possess is here rather a ruling passion than a sensitive moral conscience. Whatever its form, it distinguishes man from his neighbour. But it will always be voracious, its function always to devour, its future always to flourish at the expense of happiness and health. Damocles provides the extreme example of the destructiveness of eagles. He dies from the sense of debt and obligation that he feels towards the unknown donor of the 500 francs, that same sense of debt that Prometheus describes as his personal eagle; as the waiter says of him: 'L'inquiétude le dévore. Il est maigri, maigri, maigri.'[3]

The eagle that distinguishes mankind in general, the common shared ideals of man in society, can be equally destructive. Prometheus rejoices to see the results of his gifts to men which

[1] *PME*, O.C. iii. 124. See John, iii. 30.   [2] Ibid., p. 138.   [3] Ibid., p. 143.

produce 'la dévorante croyance au progrès', a belief controlling a whole society. Prometheus at this point is nothing if not consistent. Just as he adores the beauty of his own eagle, nourished by his blood, soul, and love, so he praises the general process of history that had set ambitious ideals above the common joys of living: 'Le bonheur de l'homme décrut, décrut', he says, 'et ce me fut égal: l'aigle était né. Je n'aimais plus les hommes, c'était ce qui vivait d'eux que j'aimais. C'en était fait pour moi d'une humanité sans histoire... L'histoire de l'homme, c'est l'histoire des aigles, Messieurs.'[1] Naturally enough Prometheus is quite properly advocate of eagles for everyone: 'Messieurs, il faut avoir un aigle',[2] at whatever cost.

The eagle symbol thus holds many meanings which, while they are related to the central meaning of the scrupulous human conscience, spread out to encompass social man among his fellows and the general society of mankind. The relationship is invariable, however, always the diminution of the owner, and the domination of the parasitic visitor. It is this relationship that re-presents, in Gide's particular fashion, the element of suffering required by the Promethean myth. Indeed, so curious is the love–hate relationship that exists between Prometheus and his eagle, so amorous their play together when Prometheus sighs with pleasure: 'Doux aigle! qui l'eût cru? . . . Que nos amours seraient charmantes',[3] that it is only intelligible at the level of allegory. The direct physical torment endured by the Aeschylean hero is modified to suggest the delicate equilibrium of man's moral nature where the scrupulous conscience both dominates and delights.

When we come to the tale of Tityrus, which is Prometheus' indirect way of extricating himself from all obligations, he brings together the same cluster of moral implications engendered by the eagle. The rise and fall of Tityrus, from idleness to activity, from exhaustion back to idleness again, follows the same pattern as Prometheus' history up to date. But here the curve of experience is symbolized by the acorn planted in the swamp which becomes a giant tree whose care in turn requires a community of workers whose well-being demands provision of commodities, administration,

[1] Ibid. p. 134. [2] Ibid., p. 135. [3] Ibid., p. 126.

and jurisdiction. As the community grows in complexity and so in exigencies, like the House-that-Jack-built, the unfortunate Tityrus meets each new situation with pragmatic *savoir-faire* until one day he reaches the end of his tether. He laments to Angela: 'Tant d'occupations me tueront; je n'en puis plus; je sens l'usure; ces solidarités activent mes scrupules; s'ils augmentent, je diminue. Que faire?'[1] His story is Prometheus' experience of helping men; his plight the same as Prometheus' although he is obsessed by an oak-tree not an eagle; his sufferings and their cause are Prometheus' and when, having decided that 'somme toute, les occupations, responsabilités et divers scrupules' are no more binding than a rooted tree, his escape from his city, like Prometheus' escape from the Caucasus, brings him to the Paris boulevard at the same time of day as Prometheus. The tale told by Prometheus reflects in a more condensed and slightly altered form the problems and pattern of his own predicament.

This short tale that so faithfully reflects the principal experience is one example of Gide's favourite narrative device which he calls 'en abyme', a device adopted for his first work, *Les Cahiers d'André Walter*, and for many another work later. Gide at once recognized its usefulness: 'J'aime assez', he writes in 1893, 'qu'en une œuvre d'art, on retrouve ainsi transposé, à l'échelle des personnages, le sujet même de cette œuvre. Rien ne l'éclaire mieux et n'établit plus sûrement toutes les proportions de l'ensemble.'[2] If we may expect to find the subject of the whole *récit* reflected in the inset parable of Tityrus, properly transposed as Gide says, it deserves close attention. As an element in the tripartite structure of *Le Prométhée* it adds to the overall intricacy that one critic describes as an 'irritating complexity of composition and content'.[3] The effect of Gide's transposition is so to reduce the dispersed and apparently digressive story of Prometheus to its main outline that it tends to stand out from the whole and by its very economy and condensation satisfy the reader's need to an extent that endangers the total effect of the *récit*. The inset

[1] *PME*, O.C. iii. 154.   [2] *Journal*, p. 41.
[3] W. W. Holdheim, 'The Dual Structure of the *Prométhée mal enchaîné*', *MLN*, lxxiv, 1959, p. 714. See also Brée, *André Gide*, p. 118.

tale makes the points of the hazards of the over-scrupulous conscience on the personal level, and the consuming monster that a
progressive society can become, so effectively that it tends to
distract attention from the main narrative concern which is, after
all, the experience of Prometheus. Perhaps it is only when
Tityrus, in words that echo Prometheus' situation, repeats the
flight to Paris that we are reminded of the secondary function
of the parable and its place in the central story.

It comes at the pivotal point of that story in every sense. At the
narrative level it announces Prometheus' change of direction.
He tells it at Damocles' funeral, 'Let the dead bury their dead',
he has just killed his eagle and is about to sweep his friends off
to feast on it. Prometheus thus resumes his past in allegorical terms
and indirectly, though not explicitly, indicates his future. Gide,
as creator, reiterates his main moral comments and drives them
home to his reader by repetition and concentration. Within the
experience of Prometheus the allegorical tale expresses the growth
of self-understanding that forms the primary theme of the récit.
If we see his first flight from the Caucasus as the instinctive action
it appears to be then the self-knowledge demonstrated in the
parable authorizes the second and final stage of his liberation as
an act of the conscious will. The tale interprets his whole past in
fresh terms: the origin of his eagle with his sense of responsibility
for his protégés, men, is shown as the germination of a thought,
for the seed scattered by Menalcas is identified with thought:
'cette idée était la graine, et cette graine était l'Idée',[1] and the
seed requires care and develops the sense of responsibility. The
extension of social conscience and the corresponding proliferation
of eagles are expressed by the overwhelming tree and the community that develops in its shade; and the possibility of flight, as
suggested to Tityrus by Angela, is that phase of partial liberation
that Prometheus undertakes himself. The fact that he can thus
interpret his own past proves that he has reached full self-consciousness. If we were to summarize his past as the passage from
consciousness to conscientiousness then the final stage is that of
self-consciousness and hence independence.

[1] *PME*, O.C. iii. 150.

The story of Tityrus plays its influential part in the development of Prometheus, the great rebel. Gide's treatment of rebellion, that third element in the inherited myth, is as personal as are his versions of benefaction and of physical suffering. Gide's Prometheus undertakes the same preliminary intervention in men's lives as he tells us but his real rebellion takes place when he kills the eagle. This destructive and voluntary act manifests primarily a rejection of Zeus and so of divine authority. Prometheus is stupefied to learn that in this eagle-ridden world he encounters only Zeus is free from them and that he is indeed their origin: 'Les aigles (et Zeus riait), les aigles, c'est moi qui les donne.'[1] The final feast therefore symbolizes Prometheus' freedom from divine power. But the Zeus from whom he frees himself is not the Aeschylean god. In the power and cruelty shown in 'le Miglionnaire's' arbitrary acts there may be a suggestion of the Aeschylean god who so readily forgets the Titan's earlier aid when he punishes a new insubordination. But the main characteristic of the Gidian Zeus is his total detachment from the world of men. His refusal to show himself to the tormented Damocles, for reasons of prestige, exemplifies his total unconcern with the consequences of his arbitrary and gratuitous acts. His indifference and his irresponsibility mark him off sharply from the Aeschylean god whose fear links him to Prometheus. Because the Titan alone knows the secret of Zeus' destiny he is inextricably bound to the god in a pattern of terror and affliction. Their very interdependence opens the way to reconciliation in the future. No such relationship is possible under the icy reign of Gide's 'Miglionnaire'. His only contact with the world of men is made through the irresponsible play of his intelligence and the practice of so many laboratory experiments. Once Prometheus has understood this he is free.

So, too, once he recognizes the dangerous nature of an increasingly complex social system with its burdens of conformism, responsibility, and anxiety imposed on the individual man while the community as a whole suffers by its participation in 'la dévorante croyance au progrès', he can free himself from the

[1] *PME*, O.C. iii. 142.

code of society. Here, of course, the Gidian Prometheus is the product of his age. He is rebelling against the general belief in progress accepted by the nineteenth century, whose expression by Victor Hugo was ecstatically praised by Pierre Louÿs at the time of his close friendship with Gide: 'Cette marche parallèle vers le Bien, vers le vrai', the young man writes, 'n'est chantée nulle part avec plus de ferveur que dans le surhumain *Satyre*, résumé suprême et point culminant du livre, dernier terme du génie humain. *La Légende des siècles*, c'est donc avant tout un acte de foi en l'humanité, un acte d'espérance en son progrès illimité, un acte d'amour pour ses efforts actuels vers un but encore lointain.'[1]

In another sense, Gide's *Prométhée* is also an act of faith in humanity, but only in so far as human beings are capable of voluntary action based on their understanding of self and of their situation. To illustrate this belief in the progress of the individual man, if not in society's progress, the Gidian Prometheus shows a most unheroic inconsistency. The fervent advocate of eagles eats his own bird. Constancy of purpose is an outstanding characteristic of the Aeschylean Titan; contradiction of intentions is central in the Gidian experience. For in Gide's conception the denial of the past is the act of a hero. Prometheus, in rebelling against the confining and crippling situation he had contrived for himself, is suggesting the way to know personal liberty. Only the hero is strong enough to admit inconsistency. As Gide writes elsewhere at this time: 'J'ai la terreur des partis pris. Songez donc: c'est de vingt à trente ans qu'une carrière se décide; est-ce de quinze à vingt que l'on aura pu réfléchir! Qu'y faire? car c'est une fatalité. L'action seule vous éduque: on ne l'apprend qu'en agissant; un premier acte vous engage; il éduque, mais compromet; dût-on l'avoir trouvé mauvais, c'est le même qu'on va refaire . . . d'autres comptent déjà sur vous; changer ce serait les trahir. A trente-cinq ans vous n'avez fait que des écoles; mais vous apportez un passé qui dictera votre avenir.'[2] So the apparent betrayal of the past in the *récit* is the act of the heroic man (although not of the martyr

---

[1] Pierre Louÿs, *Journal intime 1882–1891*, Paris, Éditions Montaigne, 1929, p. 333, 28 août 1890.
[2] 'Lettres à Angèle', O.C. iii. 180. (*L'Ermitage*, 1898–1900.)

to a humanist cause as has been thought).[1] Nor should Prometheus be seen as the tragic hero as has also been suggested. One critic asks: 'Is the final scene a tragedy . . ., a triumph or, simply, a fact?'[2] Prometheus' practical acceptance of his own *volte-face* and his casual presentation of the parable that explains it suggest rather the simple fact.[3]

If his arguments and actions change direction their motivation has its own inner consistency. Prometheus' experience, like the earlier Adam's, is the search for consciousness of his own individuality. The eagle seems at first to express his unique quality, he introduces it to the waiter as his 'trait distinctif' and consequently urges others to welcome their own. When he learns that the eagle overpowers personality he continues his search for his individuality by destroying it. If he has mistaken the proper way, let him redress his errors without regret or remorse and reorientate his life.

But the new direction leads to an unknown goal. The ritual feast of emancipation ends this phase of Prometheus' experience. Where will the future take him? What will he do with his new-found liberty? What is the outcome of rebellion? One suggestion comes from the concluding lines of the *récit* when the double function of the dead eagle's feathers, almost another linguistic pun, closes one experience and opens another. Prometheus preserves his eagle's feathers; the unidentified narrator of the story whose first-person comments start and finish the action, as in *Le Narcisse*, makes use of one of them to record the history of Prometheus. Does the experience of suffering once past furnish Prometheus, too, with the subject-matter of an artist? When he re-creates his own problems in the parable of Tityrus he resolves them in literary creation as has been noted, yet in his personal experience he 'does not "integrate" the tragic fact of death: he simply turns his back on it'.[4] Is his future to be that of the artist, the artificer who can transform chaotic experience into artistic order? The

[1] G. I. Brachfeld, 'The Myth Maker', *L'Esprit créateur*, no. 1, Spring 1961, p. 33.

[2] J. R. Loy, 'Prometheus, Theseus, The Uncommon Man and an Eagle', *Yale French Studies*, vii, 1951, p. 36.

[3] See Brée, *André Gide*, p. 104, for a discussion of the 'style factuel' of the *PME*.

[4] Holdheim, 'The Dual Structure of the *PME*', loc. cit., p. 720.

mythological tradition would allow such a concept of Prometheus as maker, as creator. Yet the literary artist at work here is the anonymous *je* who introduces the tale and uses the eagle feather to recount it. The triple narrative method Gide adopts here does not confuse the general meaning of the *récit*; the first speaker amalgamates as readily with Prometheus as the hero does with his own created character, Tityrus. All three fictional *personae* merge smoothly enough to suggest that problems may indeed be resolved by artistic creation. Such a thought hints at one possible future for Prometheus.

There is another alternative future suggested in this story that has been so concerned with *how* people lead their lives as well as *why* they live as they do: 'Garçon,' asks Prometheus about the passing Parisians, 'où vont-ils?' Cocles and his compromise, Damocles and his defeat, Prometheus and his victory over circumstances have all suggested alternative attitudes. There is yet another in the inset tale of the careworn Tityrus, when Angela abandons him without a thought, to follow the charming, flute-playing, naked Meliboeus to Rome. She chooses in fact the instinctive, pagan, simple life of the senses, drawn irresistibly by the primitive melody of pipes, the life which Prometheus had led before the growth of conscience. Is this what the future holds for him? A return to primitive innocence and joy? It is another hint only, protected by its context, by its appearance in a tale at a double remove from the reader, but it is nevertheless a possible indication of the way Prometheus may profit by his renewed liberty.

The means of attaining freedom, the understanding of the nature of freedom as individuality, as self-consciousness, as self-chosen action, the use to which such freedom can be put in the future: these are the themes presented in *Le Prométhée mal enchaîné*, that 'Chronique de la moralité privée', as the narrator defines his subject of the experiences of Prometheus, Damocles, and Cocles attended by the Waiter and the 'Miglionnaire': 'Je ne parlerai pas de la moralité publique, parce qu'il n'y en a pas.'[1]

Philoctète ou le Traité des trois morales is no less explicitly didactic, no less concerned with a personal code of behaviour. Its form of

[1] *PME*, O.C. iii. 103.

traité and its inclusion in a volume of such works makes Gide's intention clear.[1] The common proselytizing attitude is natural enough in two works that are practically simultaneous expressions of Gide's thought at the end of the century. If we have discussed *Le Prométhée* first despite its month's delay in publication it is because of its more immediately attractive approach to its subject and because for all its *saugrenu* and occasional obscurity it establishes its own world as a valid artistic creation. For all its apparent lightheartedness it is the more ambitious of the two contemporaneous works.

The form adopted for the companion pieces, of *récit* and dramatic dialogue, marks more than a superficial difference of approach. The dialogue form is new to Gide at this stage although, as he makes clear in his later *Avant-propos*, it is not intended for the stage.[1] It is useful nevertheless, both thematically and technically. Since the action is concerned entirely with the confrontation of opposing concepts the movement of intellectual ideas manifests itself most effectively in direct speech: 'Les idées se dénudent plus loyalement, entièrement, sous les mains adverses du dialogue', one critic writes, 'et l'action, tout intellectuelle qu'elle soit, la garde sensuelle et vivante.'[2] Speech alone is enough for such a conflict. We do not need to visualize the speakers. Names categorize Ulysses and Philoctetes, youthfulness characterizes Neoptolemus. Technically, the dramatic form controls the evolution of the ideas. Rather as music controls its content by manipulation of pace, so the act and scene divisions here seem to control the *tempi* of the developing ideas. They emphasize the key points of argument and eliminate unnecessary passage of time; they can, as in Act I, Scene 1, indicate a significant silence (Philoctetes' silence is indeed the only action), as a musical pause makes its effect; and they can dictate the *rallentando* of the slow close when Philoctetes' murmured acceptance of abandonment: 'Ils ne reviendront plus; ils n'ont plus d'arc à prendre ... — Je suis heureux'[3], completes his experience as the whole action of the fifth and final act.

[1] *Le Retour de l'Enfant prodigue*, Paris, N.R.F. 29e éd., p. 112 (1912).
[2] R. de Souza, *Mercure de France*, février 1900, p. 468.
[3] *Phil.*, O.C. iii. 63.

But the dramatic form, even with its non-theatrical purpose, allows the exploitation of physical setting. Gide makes full use of it here and in so doing distinguishes his *Philoctète* sharply from his *Prométhée*. Where the hero of the latter work is set against the most cursory of contemporary Parisian backgrounds, in café, lecture hall, cemetery, or unlocated prison, Philoctetes moves in a world of fantasy or dream. He is discovered under the grey sky on the icy plain of an island surrounded by icebergs. It can only be reached after a fortnight's arduous voyage from sunny Greece, as Neoptolemus tells us in a highly undramatic expository speech. And it is not to be found in any atlas. Climate, island, journey to reach it: the whole décor is symbolically drawn. It is the externalization of the hero's spiritual state, a pure 'paysage d'âme', in the Symbolist convention—although an experience known personally by the young Gide on a visit to Belgium: as he writes at the time: 'Le "paysage", au lieu de me distraire de moi-même, prend toujours désespérément la forme de mon âme lamentable.'[1]

Philoctetes' island, as he explains to Ulysses and Neoptolemus who have come to take his bow from him, that bow which will assure victory over Troy, is the land of Being, not Becoming: 'Ici, rien ne devient, Ulysse: tout est, tout demeure.'[2] The seed does not sprout in the frozen soil, the dead bird does not rot. The island has taken on the quality of its owner's state of mind, without hope, without dreams, without passion or desire. It is the expression of almost complete intellectual abstraction: 'le froid donne à l'eau même, gelée,' he says, 'la forme de mes logiques pensées';[3] and Philoctetes is both fascinated and appalled by the prospect of the completed process towards abstraction: 'Bientôt, vivant toujours, je serai tout abstrait. Le froid m'envahit, cher Ulysse, et je m'épouvante à présent, car j'y trouve, et dans sa rigueur même, une beauté.'[2] This polar land of pure intellectuality recalls the final stage of *Le Voyage d'Urien*, the fantasy so warmly welcomed by the Symbolist writers although less warmly by Paul Valéry, whose friendly commentary sounds a warning note about excessive symbolism. As he writes to Gide in 1893: 'Tu y

[1] *Journal*, p. 22, 22 juillet 1891.   [2] *Phil.*, O.C. iii. 38.
[3] Ibid., p. 37.

a usé de notations qui te sont dès longtemps familières, par exemple: glace, pureté, — ardeur, chaleur. Mais il ne faut pas trop y stagner ... pas plus que dans les jeux assez tristes du "paysage d'âme".'[1]

But the familiar polar landscape takes on a new meaning here by its association with the heroes of Greek mythology, however odd their presence may seem. For Philoctetes, when he describes his present attitude and the future he foresees, expresses himself in terms of his relationship with omnipotent Zeus. When all human feelings and failings have died within him, when he has been so cleansed of impurities that his spirit and his actions are as clear as frost crystals, then he may become simply a means of transmitting the divine light of Zeus: 'Je ne veux empêcher aucun rayon de Zeus,' he says; 'qu'il me traverse, Ulysse, comme un prisme, et que cette lumière réfractée fasse mes actes adorables. Je voudrais parvenir à la plus grande transparence, à la suppression de mon opacité, et que, me regardant agir, toi-même sentes la lumière...'[2]

His attitude of submission to divine authority is far greater than the respect shown by Prometheus but it is no longer lasting. For when he tries to tell the young Neoptolemus where the origin of virtue is to be found, and what the true object of human devotion may be, he, too, gropes his way towards a *credo* of individualism that sets the self above the gods. When the boy asks: 'Se dévouer à quoi, Philoctète? Au-dessus des dieux, qu'y a-t-il?', the hero tries desperately to clarify his own thought: 'Il y a ... (*Il se prend la tête dans les mains, comme accablé.*) Je ne sais plus. Je ne sais pas ... Ah! ah! Soi-même! ... Je ne sais plus parler, Néoptolème...'[3] And when he voluntarily drinks the drug that enables Ulysses and Neoptolemus to take away the bow he does not act to please them, nor even to please Zeus: he acts in accordance with his own nature alone: 'ne me remercie pas: c'est pour moi que j'agis, non pour toi.'[4] Nor does he consider the fate of Troy, nor his own return to the life of a warrior, when he renounces the bow. As he cries to Ulysses: 'Comprends: je me dévoue, mais ce n'est pas pour la patrie.' He

---

[1] *Correspondance*, p. 179 [janvier 1893].
[3] Ibid., p. 48.
[2] *Phil.*, O.C. iii. 38–39.
[4] Ibid., p. 58.

does not in fact fully understand why he acts as he does: 'c'est pour autre chose, comprends; c'est pour ... quoi? Je ne sais pas.'[1] He is less certain of his motives than Prometheus, whose burdensome eagle provides him with both a positive motive for rebellion and a means of expressing it. Philoctetes feels the need to set the young Neoptolemus an example of the virtue he cannot define; he says in despair: 'Enfant! Ah! si je pouvais te montrer la vertu ...',[2] and by his subsequent act of voluntary self-deprivation he does indeed perform the action of a virtuous man. His reasons may not be reasons of state, they may not immediately profit Neoptolemus, they may not even be clearly understood. But the self-chosen act results in satisfaction and a sense of fulfilment that has nothing to do with filtering the light of Zeus. When Philoctetes finds himself abandoned for the second time on his island it is not among the frozen forms of abstract thought; flowers pierce the snow, and the birds of the sky feed him.

He has turned away from his former ideal of submission to divinity, with its compulsory subordination of personality, to recover the opacity that the human being involved in a complex situation, and governed only by the obscure needs of self-realization inevitably possesses. Gide's use of the term 'opacité' is particularly apt for the innate confusion that underlies human decision and motives. Philoctetes passes through something of the same experience as Prometheus, that of liberation from outside forces in order to pursue the need of self.

There are differences of course: in detail, in general outline; but the line of development is basically the same. Philoctetes meets the temptation of intellectual aridity where Prometheus suffers from the demands of his conscience. Philoctetes must withstand the claims of the State, a powerful concept represented by Ulysses, where Prometheus must extricate himself from the demands of an ever-evolving society, an equally powerful concept that threatens his personal life. Each of them must throw off the domination of divine authority personified in Zeus; one simply forgets his earlier aspirations as he becomes involved in circumstances; the other consciously rebels against authority and its

[1] Ibid., p. 58.   [2] Ibid., p. 48.

agents. Each must learn to understand himself and his needs, although Philoctetes chooses the way of abnegation, Prometheus the way of affirmation.

Philoctetes' story consists in a double abandonment, the first when his infected wound, distasteful, distressing, and disruptive to his companions, forces them to leave him on the island against his will; the second, when by his own choice he allows Ulysses and Neoptolemus to rob him of his bow and leave him to defenceless solitude. The one event is inflicted upon him and almost destroys him; the second comes from his own decision and brings him fulfilment. The new elements in his experience appear in the two moral attitudes that clash with his own: the devotion to the State embodied in Ulysses; and the potential devotion to a person represented by Neoptolemus. The triangular conflict of values which in some ways recalls the tripartite pattern of Prometheus, Cocles, and Damocles is developed as the potential threats to self-realization that patriotism and personal affection may offer. Both themes will be explored more fully later but both are considerations that are foreign to Prometheus' experience.

Ulysses' position is refreshingly clear. When Neoptolemus asks him to define duty he can reply without hesitation: 'La voix des dieux, l'ordre de la cité, l'offrande de nous à la Grèce.'[1] His attitude is a simple preliminary sketch for the fuller philosophical explanation that Theseus is to furnish much later. Neoptolemus' moral stance is established when he allows affection to take preference over policy: 'C'est à toi que je me dévoue. M'aimes-tu? Parle, Philoctète. Est-ce que c'est là la vertu?'[2] What is presented here as a static point of view without influence or development is to be further examined in Gide's works of the immediate future, *Saül* and *Le Roi Candaule*.

It is perhaps the Sophoclean triad of *personae* that attracted Gide to this particular heroic story which he presents without chorus, merchant, and, naturally, the god Hercules who resolves the tragic *impasse* in Sophocles. Gide's modifications to the myth are characteristic, dictated partly by his personal interests and partly by his theme. Just as he could evoke Paradise in the legend of Narcissus,

[1] *Phil.*, O.C. iii. 25.   [2] Ibid., p. 56.

just as he could so soon treat Saul and the Lydian king, Candaules, almost simultaneously, so there are Biblical echoes in this Sophoclean subject. As the young Neoptolemus approaches the island where he expects to be sacrificed by Ulysses for the sake of his country he sees himself as another 'Iphigénie [qui] s'avança vers l'autel, simple, décente et non parée'.[1] But the reader is reminded by his youth and helplessness of Isaac with Abraham. Again, the final flowering of the desert island is clearly reminiscent of the divinely protected prophets of the Old Testament.

The character of Neoptolemus undergoes a double change, the one consequent on the other. Where the Sophoclean figure is a young hero, old enough to have sailed with the attacking fleet to Troy, and thus, almost a decade later, a veteran soldier capable of challenging the influence of Ulysses once he is convinced of its injustice, the Gidian figure is a much younger person. He speaks and acts like an affectionate child, his innocence touches us like Isaac's, and his final obedience to Ulysses in picking up the bow the man hesitates to take demonstrates his immature submissiveness. It is his very youth that touches Philoctetes as Ulysses' arguments could never do.[2] But his youth and simplicity diminish his role and change the whole focus of interest. As Faguet points out, the hero of Sophocles' *Philoctetes* is Neoptolemus:

M. André Gide a changé tout cela; mais il l'a très agréablement changé. *Il a transporté l'intérêt moral de Néoptolème à Philoctète.* Dans Sophocle, Ulysse et Philoctète sont rigides. Ils sont inflexibles, l'un engainé tout entier dans son patriotisme intransigeant et dans son principe: 'Le salut du pays est la seule loi'; l'autre engainé tout entier dans son ressentiment implacable et dans le sentiment de son droit et *du droit* violé en lui. Néoptolème seul va d'un point à l'autre. Chez M. Gide, c'est Ulysse et Néoptolème qui sont (à très peu près) tout d'une pièce, et c'est Philoctète qui évolue, du reste, d'une manière très intéressante et presque admirable.[3]

In Gide's version only Philoctetes undergoes the change of attitude

---

[1] Ibid., p. 18.

[2] Brée, *André Gide*, p. 125, compares Neoptolemus with David in *Saül* and Gyges in *Le Roi Candaule* as three versions of the young man welcomed by the older whom he must inevitably despoil and destroy.

[3] É. Faguet, *Journal des Débats*, 21 juillet 1902.

that he considers proper in a hero and it is shown entirely within a human perspective. Gide keeps the wonder-working bow, as indeed he must, but he eliminates Hercules as he does in the Promethean story.

The subject-matter thus undergoes considerable changes: of setting, of number and nature of the characters, of resolution. All are explained by the theme of self-realization as it is expressed in voluntary action, however unrewarding it may appear to be.[1] But this new version which is concerned with human nature (Philoctetes announces: 'Moi, dans cette île, je me suis fait, comprends, de jour en jour moins Grec, de jour en jour plus homme ...')[2] does not possess the humanity of the Sophoclean tragedy. The Greek Philoctetes is a man in his harshness, in his despairing anger when he feels himself betrayed by Neoptolemus, in his physical suffering, and in his reawakened hope. When physical distress causes him to relinquish his bow to Neoptolemus he is acting like a human creature; when he takes farewell of his rough and imprisoning island, almost with regret, he is undergoing the tormented, divided experience of a man. As Gide uses the story he raises problems of human behaviour; but he loses the man.

This should not be taken as a reproach. Up to this time Gide has not been concerned with *la bête humaine*, neither in the *récit* nor in the *traités*. Their intention is didactic, their method allegorical. Gide abstracts from the Greek myths an intellectual application that leaves their imaginative and emotional content quite untouched; his descriptive sub-titles define their deliberately limited intention. The whole subject of myth and allegory, their similarities and their differences, was one of considerable topical interest as a contemporary discussion makes clear. It is indeed so illuminating in respect to these early Gidian works that it is worth extended quotation:

Le mythe et l'allégorie ne sont que des symboles continués [writes Saint-Antoine in June 1894], mais pas de la même façon, ce qu'il importe de préciser.

Le mythe n'est pas seulement un trait fabuleux concernant des divinités ou des personnages qui ne sont que des divinités défigurées,

---

[1] Brée, *Gide*, pp. 109–10.   [2] *Phil.*, O.C. iii. 34.

c'est avant tout un récit à double sens, le trait fabuleux n'étant que la figuration transposée, soit d'un événement historique, soit d'une théorie cosmogonique ou théologique. . . . Si ce double sens manquait, il n'y aurait plus mythe mais légende; de même si l'un des deux s'oubliait. La religion grecque était dite *Légende* à une époque où le sens symbolique des mythes était perdu. Ce n'est donc pas la qualité humaine ou divine des personnages qui différenciera, comme on le dit communément, le mythe de la légende, ce sera son double sens. . . .

Mais l'allégorie aussi a un double sens, et il importe de la distinguer du mythe. Le mythe trouve sa fin en lui-même, tandis que l'allégorie s'impose un but étranger. Le mythe s'adresse à l'âme plus qu'à l'intelligence, il émeut au lieu de convaincre, se dérobe au lieu d'éveiller la curiosité. . . .

Au contraire l'Allégorie est toujours didactique; son double sens n'est qu'un voile de coquetterie; elle n'est point spontanée mais réfléchie, voulue, fille du raisonnement et non de l'inspiration, s'adressant à la pensée plus qu'au sentiment. Le mythe produit des épopées ou des chants lyriques; l'allégorie produit des apologies ou des paraboles.[1]

Such a description of the allegorical method seems more easily attached to *Philoctète* than to the irrepressible companion piece, *Le Prométhée*, where the world, however explosively odd, has its own internal validity. But the capacity to awaken curiosity is common to both. In the case of *Philoctète* and due perhaps to its early title of 'Le Traité de l'immonde blessure' its origin has been much debated. It has been seen in the Dreyfus case,[2] in the Wilde case,[3] or in Gide's own hint of 'le robinsonisme';[4] Prometheus' eagle has produced many different interpretations.

Certainly *Philoctète* seems more deliberately didactic than *Le Prométhée* and rendered dangerously vulnerable to us in some moods by its hero's constant solemnity. Without going so far as to appear caricature, as has been thought,[5] or as undergoing an

[1] Quoted by Michaud, *La Doctrine symboliste: Documents*, p. 49.

[2] See O.C. iii, L. Martin-Chauffier, 'Notices', p. viii.

[3] Y. Louria, 'Le contenu latent du *Philoctète* gidien', *French Review*, April 1952, pp. 348–54.

[4] See André Gide, *Théâtre complet*, T. 1, Neuchâtel and Paris, Ides et Calendes, 1947, R. Heyd, 'Notice', p. 184.

[5] René Schwob, *Le Vrai Drame d'André Gide*, Paris, Grasset, 1932, p. 239.

'unconsciously comic beatification',[1] Philoctetes does seem to take himself with excessive seriousness. His position of undeviating earnestness is precariously maintained and may easily topple into the ridiculous. It is his abstraction from humanity that renders his pose liable to reversal. However obstinate the Greek Philoctetes may be, the intensity of his passions controls the spectator's response. The Gidian *Philoctète* exposes the dangers implicit in the allegorical approach. The ironical tone of *Le Prométhée* protects it from the hazards of the single point of view. The chief impression given by the *récit* is one of spontaneity which, whatever incongruities it may produce, seems the expression of inspiration rather than reflection.

Nevertheless the two works appeared together and should be taken as expression of complementary attitudes to the same problem. If their simultaneous creation surprises at first, it is but one illustration of the Gidian 'état de dialogue' that he himself understood so well and so often discussed. Ten years later he was to write of the critics' opinions of *La Porte étroite*:

> Il leur reste malaisé d'admettre que ces différents livres ont cohabité, cohabitent encore, dans mon esprit. Ils ne se suivent que sur le papier et par grande impossibilité de se laisser écrire ensemble. Quel que soit le livre que j'écris, je ne m'y donne jamais tout entier, et le sujet qui me réclame le plus instamment, sitôt après, se développe cependant à l'autre extrémité de moi-même.
>
> On ne tracera pas aisément la trajectoire de mon esprit; sa courbe ne se révélera que dans mon style et échappera à plus d'un. Si quelqu'un, dans mon dernier écrit, pense saisir enfin ma ressemblance, qu'il se détrompe: c'est toujours de mon dernier-né que je suis le plus différent.[2]

Apart from the suggestions of complacency arising from the idea of literary hide-and-seek this passage is of the greatest interest. It indicates certain limitations in Gide's work that will be considered later,[3] while it stresses the simultaneity of his creative thought, naturally most noticeable in his youth and middle age.

---

[1] Brée, *Gide*, p. 108.

[2] *Journal*, pp. 275–6, septembre, octobre 1909. See also p. 436, 12 juillet 1914; p. 684, 5 octobre 1920.

[3] See ch. IX.

Philoctète and *Le Prométhée* are thus twin attempts to re-create the problems of living, problems that were not envisaged in the earlier *Traité du Narcisse*, although the figures of Narcissus and Adam suggested alternative answers to initial *ennui*. Where the Symbolist *traité* theorizes about 'manifestation' as human duty and sketches in two opposing forms of it, the *récit* and the later *traité* fill in further details of a similarly opposed response to the problems of living among men and in the situations and relationships of life. In both cases the solution can only be found in the freedom of the individual man from pressures and constraint. Admittedly the act of rebellion requires courage, but adaptation to new circumstances demands as much if not more. Prometheus' future is indefinite; Philoctetes' even more so. Logically, if we may allow ourselves such a criterion for a moment, he can only reach a death made glorious by serenity and self-chosen solitude. Inevitably Gide had to withdraw from this extreme position. Life must, after all, be confronted. In the evolution of his thought 1899 marks the stage of the desirability of revolutionary heroism. Philoctetes and Prometheus furnished him with symbols for the process of liberation. But freedom once attained, what then?

4

THE HUMAN TRAP

THE experiences undergone by Gide's next two heroes are completely different. Where Philoctetes and Prometheus follow their separate paths towards total independence, Gide's Saul and his King Candaules are trapped and destroyed by their emotional dependence on others. The two theatrical heroes could hardly provide a more striking contrast in experience and attitude as well as literary form with their immediate predecessors. Indeed, it is chiefly for convenience's sake that *Saül* may be considered to follow the *Philoctète* and *Le Prométhée* since it was being written in 1898, and was partly published in June of that year.[1] It is therefore, in part at least, contemporaneous with them although it was only published in full in 1903.[2] If we remember Gide's own remarks about the simultaneous presence of different works in his thought we need not wonder at the appearance of *Saül* among such other works. He himself recognized its extreme divergence from *Les Nourritures terrestres* of 1897 to whose dangerous doctrine, as he wrote later to a priest, *Saül* was to provide the antidote.[3] Its natural connexion, however, is with *Le Roi Candaule*, written and published in *L'Ermitage*, in 1899, not only in chronological time, but in theme, attitude, and dramatic form.

In *Saül*, for the first time, Gide was writing for the theatre itself and not for the study as in *Philoctète* although he had at the time no assurance of its production. As he wrote to Paul Valéry in March 1898: '*Saül* avance et j'en suis assez content aujourd'hui. Mais quelle va devenir son histoire? Ce n'est pas du tout fait pour être lu, mais bien strictement pour la scène. Et comment

[1] *La Revue blanche*, 1898. L. Martin-Chauffier assigns *Saül* to O.C. ii on the grounds that it was written in 1896.

[2] Paris, Mercure de France, 1903.

[3] 'Lettre au R. P. Victor Poucel' (27 novembre 1927), O.C. xiv. 407.

faire pour l'y porter?'[1] He had every reason for misgivings since, despite negotiations with Antoine who would have produced it if he could,[2] *Saül* had to wait nearly twenty years to be produced; Jacques Copeau presented it at the Vieux-Colombier in June 1922.

Le Roi Candaule, in some ways at least, was more fortunate. Gide found it slow and difficult to write, as he confessed to Valéry,[3] but once completed it was published at once,[4] and produced within two years.[5] Nevertheless, it was only performed twice in Paris, although revived three years later, and it received scant praise from the newspaper dramatic critics of the day. Gide took pleasure in adding their critical comments to his Preface to the second edition in 1904. When it was performed in Berlin in 1908 (translated by Franz Blei) it provoked, as Gide records in his *Journal*, a 'déchaînement de la presse'; it was promptly removed from the theatre's repertory.[6] With the refusal of one play and the failure of the second Gide's dramatic career started badly. He did not return to the theatre until some thirty years later with his *Œdipe* (1931) and the lyrical work, *Perséphone* (1934).

By rights *Saül* has no place in a study of Gide's use of the Greek myth. Its biblical subject sets it apart, if not in the direct opposition Gide saw in Christianity and its demands. Its form too, romantic in the Shakespearian sense, alienates it from the spirit of classicism. But *Saül* is so important in Gide's estimation, in his development, and in its relationship with *Le Roi Candaule* that it cannot be passed over without some discussion.

Gide himself discussed it at length in his letters to his friends, seriously when he wrote to Valéry, slightly ironically and hence protectively when he wrote to Francis Jammes.[7] It was to Valéry that he confided his long-standing interest in 'ce triste scandale

[1] *Correspondance*, p. 315.

[2] R. Martin du Gard, *Notes sur André Gide (1913–1951)*, Paris, Gallimard, 1951, p. 31 (1920).

[3] *Correspondance*, p. 349, 11 juillet [1899].

[4] *L'Ermitage*, septembre, novembre, décembre 1899; *La Revue blanche*, with Préface, 1901.

[5] A.-M. Lugné-Poë, Nouveau Théâtre, 9 mai 1901.

[6] *Journal*, p. 258, 15 janvier 1908.

[7] *Correspondance de Francis Jammes et d'André Gide, 1893–1938*, Préface et Notes par Robert Mallet, Paris, Gallimard, 1948. Gide alludes to *Saül* from July 1897.

de cour'.[1] He later described its origin as the inspiration the creative imagination may find in the phenomena of natural history: 'Les plus beaux sujets de drames nous sont proposés par l'histoire naturelle et particulièrement par l'entomologie', he writes in his *Journal* under the date of 28th April 1943, 'Mon *Saül* me fut inspiré par la singulière découverte que j'avais faite d'une chrysalide de sphinx. . . . Rien ne révélait au dehors sa consomption totale et la victoire parasitaire. Ainsi dirait, pensai-je, mon Saül: "Je suis complètement supprimé." ' Above all Gide continued to value his play highly, considering it one of his finest works. In 1931, for instance, he thought it 'une des meilleures choses que j'aie écrite, et peut-être la plus surprenante. On la découvrira plus tard et l'on s'étonnera sans doute qu'elle ait pu rester si longtemps inaperçue.'[2] He was always intimately involved with its fortunes, feared for its future after the failure of *Le Roi Candaule*,[3] and when it was coldly received by critical opinion in 1922, he took its public reception particularly to heart: 'Ne pouvez-vous donc reconnaître un sanglot que s'il a même son que le vôtre?' he inquires in his *Journal*.[4]

Without a doubt there was a moment at least in Gide's life when he identified himself with his tormented Saul. He describes his state of mind in a letter to Jammes of October 1897, in terms of his dramatic hero: 'Tous les démons de la Judée m'habitent, se nourrissent de moi, me tourmentent; si je ne les chérissais un peu, je serais beaucoup plus malheureux; mais je ne serais pas si malade. Je suis hanté.'[5] Such a colourful description could well have resulted from his absorption in his writing of *Saül* and might therefore be a simple carry-over of metaphoric thought were it not for the close interest he always showed in his unproduced play, 'dont sans doute on reconnaîtra plus tard l'importance', he writes in 1927.[6] When it did reach the stage at last Gide's advice to Jacques Copeau as to the proper interpretation of Saul is strongly reminiscent of his own younger self: '*C'est un chaste*', he

---

[1] *Correspondance*, p. 339, 22 octobre 1898.
[2] *Journal*, p. 1065, 15 juillet 1931.
[3] Ibid., p. 258, 15 janvier 1908.
[4] Ibid., p. 737, 15 juillet 1922.   [5] *Correspondance*, p. 125.
[6] 'Lettre au R. P. Victor Poucel', loc. cit., p. 407.

stresses. 'Au début de la pièce, il paraît même plein d'austérité. Il est chaste; mais sensuel. C'est-à-dire qu'il ignore encore son penchant.'[1] Who else is this character but the young man, not of 1898 but of 1893, about to leave France for the Algerian experience? Gide's interest in the story of Saul, as he told Valéry, went back to 1891–2, that is to the years that immediately preceded his first freedom. He did not express this interest in the dramatic work until some years after he experienced the formative impact of freedom, but when he returned to the subject he recreated much of his own early mental suffering in the tragedy of Saul, torn by his fear of an unknown future, by his secret knowledge, and by his love for David.

Saul's story is true tragic matter, the political situation holding within itself the personal disaster. That Saul should be driven to violence in his attempt to preserve the secret of his successor who will never be his son, Jonathan, but a stranger is the main thread of political interest. That the stranger should be David, beloved both by Jonathan and by Saul himself, brings about the tragic disintegration of Saul's will and his personality. Saul's experience answers Gide's description of proper dramatic material as he defines it to Valéry in 1898: 'Si je continue à faire du drame, j'en voudrais bannir les hasards extérieurs; je voudrais que tous les mouvements, péripéties, catastrophes naissent du seul caractère de chacun, de sorte que chacun fasse et défasse son histoire.'[2]

This is of course a Shakespearian concept of drama, not necessarily confined to works for the theatre. Gide later explored and developed the idea of a 'fatalité intime' which replaces the *Fatum*, the idea of a personal rather than philosophical destiny.[3] Nevertheless, however Gide may deny it,[4] this first play is strongly influenced by Shakespeare: 'Mr W. J. Shakespeare, M.A. . . . cet Anglais si gênant', as Valéry calls him.[5] Saul's divided and tortured spirit, despite Gide's comment: 'ce caractère étant, je pense, très

[1] 'Notes pour l'interprétation de *Saül*', *Revue d'histoire du théâtre*, iii, pp. 267–8 (added to a letter to Jacques Copeau, 20 June 1922, after the first performance of *Saül*).

[2] *Correspondance*, p. 339, 22 octobre 1898.   [3] See ch. v.

[4] *Correspondance*, p. 327 [27 juillet 1898].

[5] Ibid., p. 326 [26 juillet 1898].

peu shakespearien', the little cup-bearer as a type of Fool, the supernatural elements, madness, crowds, the theatrical business with the crown itself, and the funeral close: all suggest the influence of Shakespeare. As Gide himself acknowledged to Valéry: 'Si *Saül* rappelle la griffe de W. S. c'est par l'impossibilité d'imaginer toujours et partout d'autres *moyens* que les siens.'[1] He was by no means the only young dramatist to meet the same difficulties.

It is probable that the sparseness and dramatic reticence of *Le Roi Candaule* are due to Gide's deliberate attempt to avoid Shakespearian abundance. It follows immediately on *Saül* with which it shares so much in subject and in theme, yet it differs markedly in its method. Gide, in his Preface of 1901, admits the truth of some adverse criticisms of his play which condemn its qualities of 'la sécheresse, la rapidité, l'inextension', declares his intention to draw rather than to paint, and trusts that his very discretion in presentation may disclose virtues as well as weaknesses.[2] Naturally, he does not discuss the effect that his still unknown play, *Saül*, may have had on the writing of the more publicly acceptable second play. Yet the proximity of the two works in an experimental period of Gide's career may have brought about the change in dramatic presentation.

Le Roi Candaule is, as it were, a distillation of an experience that is fundamentally similar to *Saül*. In both plays, as Gide desired, the main action springs from the king's inner experience rather than from circumstances. Each brings about his own destruction; each welcomes the agent of that destruction,[3] although the manner and means differ. In Saul's case the conflict between love and fear of David produces a disastrous paralysis of the will that endows the legendary material and David's predestined victory with personal meaning, while Candaules' self-destruction may seem at first arbitrary and irrational. Both heroes suffer for their lack of self-knowledge; both learn finally, and too late, to understand their true nature. What is made explicit in Saul, his attachment to David, remains veiled and so mysterious in the history of Candaules. And Gide feels called upon to justify the

[1] *Correspondance*, p. 327 [27 juillet 1898].
[2] O.C. iii. 296.   [3] See Brée, *André Gide*, p. 125.

irrationality of Candaules' action, again in his Preface: 'Tous les sentiments sont dans l'homme, mais il en est certains pourtant que l'on appelle exclusivement naturels, au lieu de les appeler simplement plus fréquents. Comme si le fréquent était plus naturel que le rare! le plomb plus naturel que l'or! Tout ce que fait Candaule est naturel.'[1]

It may be natural but it is not customary. There is much in the versions of the myth which Gide gives as his sources that remains unexplained. Herodotus tells the story of the legendary king of Lydia, the last of the Heraclides, who hides his favourite guard, Gyges, in the queen's bedchamber to prove the supremacy of her beauty. The queen discovers the trick and forces Gyges to choose between his own death or the king's. His choice is only too natural, and the king is assassinated. Herodotus' cryptic comments: Candaule 'ne pouvait éviter son malheur', 'Nul moyen pour Gygès de s'échapper. Il fallait qu'il pérît, lui ou Candaule',[2] suggest an inescapable destiny but do not fully explain how it comes about. Again in Plato's version Gyges, the Lydian king's shepherd this time, finds the miraculous ring which renders him invisible. Plato is even more laconic in telling his story: 'on coming there he seduced the king's wife and with her aid set upon the king and slew him and possessed his kingdom.'[3] In both cases the situation takes precedence over motivation. Gide's fusion of the two versions allows him to present the extreme situation he reaches in Le Roi Candaule, while he is free to suggest the motives that produce it.

Probably Gide was also familiar with Théophile Gautier's elegant version, Le Roi Candaule, which is based, despite an ostentatious galaxy of authorities, on Herodotus' simple story.[4] Gautier uses the plot to contrast the artist's point of view held by Candaules and the man of action's. Gyges here is a warrior, an ambitious man, and a lover. The tale is governed by the concept of destiny which rules men's lives; its charm lies chiefly in the

[1] O.C. iii. 295–6. [2] Ibid., pp. 293–4.
[3] Plato, The Republic, translated by P. Shorey, Loeb Classical Library, 1937, vol. i, bk. ii, p. 119.
[4] T. Gautier, 'Le Roi Candaule', La Presse, 1–5 octobre 1844; Le Roi Candaule, Paris, Ferroud, 1893.

ironic tone playing over a luxurious oriental setting. The contrast between the two characters is one that may be readily seen in Gide's later version, although he reaches it in his own way.

He makes his changes in the story and draws attention to some of them in the note to his Preface; but not to the most remarkable of them, one of which is the extreme action in which Gyges, thanks to his magic ring and the king's express wish, finds himself not only in the presence of the naked queen but in her bed, the other, the character of Gyges. When Gide makes him a humble fisherman rather than the devoted royal guard of Herodotus or the warrior of Gautier, he reduces him to the lowest status. And when that fisherman is given a strong feeling of affection for the king, developed during childhood games and maintained during the long years of separation, the change is even more significant.

For *Le Roi Candaule* and its companion piece, *Saül*, are both concerned with love and with happiness. The emphasis may differ in the two plays but the themes are common to both. As Saul's unfortunate queen who meets the same hasty death as Gyges' wife declares: 'Les soucis d'amour sont plus durs, plus usants que ceux du royaume.'[1] Both plays explore the mysteries of human love in its varied manifestations. In one way they may be seen as the development of Neoptolemus' code of morality, but where his affection for Philoctetes was tentative, immature, and so unequal to the counter-claims of State or self, in the plays human affection takes the central position. And it is never simple, never easy. When Saul asserts: 'Ma valeur est dans ma complication',[2] he could also be speaking for Candaules. Within a common triangular pattern (Saul, David, Jonathan; Candaules, Nyssia, Gyges) which again recalls the *traité*, *Philoctète*, the terrible intricacies of human desire and love are dominant. Indeed, from our point of view today Saul's feeling for David seems more straightforward, more directly realized, and so more dramatically successful than the indirect and summarily motivated history of King Candaules. Gide was, however, writing in 1899, and he had to run the dramatic risks entailed in deliberate discretion, if such was the cause of his play's ambiguity.

[1] *Saül*, O.C. ii. 261.   [2] Ibid., p. 398.

His principal explicit concern in *Le Roi Candaule* is to examine the nature of happiness. It is not a new idea in Gide's work. Prometheus freed himself to find it, Angela set off to Rome in search of it, Philoctetes believed he had found it in total abnegation. Saul, that most unhappy of men, recalls past happiness when he found himself alone in the desert, searching for lost donkeys he never found. Happiness, he might have said to the boy, Saki, if he had carried his recollection into analysis, lies in the search not in the success. The Witch of Endor, close to her own death, is the only one who can admit the fugitive nature of happiness: 'Et les hommes ne m'ont pas aimée', she says, 'car ils eussent voulu que je prédisse des choses heureuses, et car je prédisais au delà du bonheur. Et maintenant je pense qu'il n'est pas bon que l'homme sache l'avenir, car aucune joie de l'homme n'est durable plus que le temps de dire: je suis heureux, et qu'il faut se hâter de le dire, car pour dire: j'étais heureux, on a bien tout le temps qui reste, et que le bonheur de l'homme est aveugle... .'[1]

Gide's Candaules, of all people, has barely time to say how happy he is before he thrusts onward to his deposition and death. He is exceptionally endowed with all the possibilities of happiness, a lovely and beloved wife, infinite riches and the power they bring, the pleasures of the senses, the interests of the mind; nevertheless he must still ask questions. Not content with simple enjoyment, he must demonstrate his happiness and so lose it. In so far as he is capable of understanding himself, he makes two main discoveries about his own form of happiness. He can never know happiness alone as Saul once did; he must have others around him whose belief in his happiness and good fortune guarantees their existence for him. As he confesses in his cups:

> Mon bonheur semble
> Puiser sa force et sa violence en autrui.
> Il me semble parfois qu'il n'existe
> Que dans la connaissance qu'en ont les autres,
> Et que je ne possède
> Que lorsqu'on me sait posséder.[2]

Happiness, according to Candaules, is to be found indirectly,

[1] Ibid., p. 332.   [2] *RC*, O.C. iii. 332.

reflected by others, rather than directly experienced by the individual man.

Again, at the end of the banquet when his queen has unveiled herself before his friends so that they should in some way share the beauty he delights in, he goes on to define the particular pleasure he experiences in experiment rather than in enjoyment:

> — Chaque bien nouveau que l'on possède
> Entraîne son nouveau désir de l'essayer —
> Et posséder, pour moi, c'est expérimenter.[1]

Logical within his limits, he carries his argument still further to claim that the man already rich in every sense may find his happiness in risking all he possesses:

> Risquer! c'est l'autre forme du bonheur; celle des riches...
> C'est la mienne.[2]

This is the reasoning Candaules presents to account for his subsequent extravagant actions. It is curiously reminiscent of the epilogue to the story of Narcissus where the young Gide condemns the profanation of mysteries. Presumably, in the context of the *Théorie du symbole*, he is condemning the scientific spirit of the nineteenth-century investigations when he writes: 'Quelques mythes d'abord suffisaient. Puis on a voulu expliquer; orgueil de prêtre qui veut révéler les mystères, afin de se faire adorer, — ou bien vivace sympathie, et cet amour apostolique, qui fait que l'on dévoile, et qu'on profane en les montrant, les plus secrets trésors du temple, parce qu'on souffre d'admirer seul et qu'on voudrait que d'autres adorent.'[3]

But what is expressed here in sacerdotal terms may well clarify the story of Candaules' progress towards disaster. However unconscious his motives may be he, too, offers to share his riches with his courtiers, and then with the lowly fisherman so that he may be adored; he, too, unveils and profanes his secret treasure, the beauty and the love of his wife, because he cannot endure to admire her alone. He, too, makes the grave error of seeking to explain the mystery of his happiness as he transgresses by disclosing

---

[1] *RC*, O.C. iii. 334. [2] Ibid., pp. 334–5.
[3] *Narc.*, O.C. i. 218–19.

it to the sight of others. His queen, Nyssia, who identifies herself with Candaules' happiness, warns him of the dangers he runs in exposing her and her beauty to the world: 'je crains', she says of her unveiled beauty and so of her husband's disclosure of his happiness, 'qu'il ne fane à rester découvert...'.[1]

Throughout the play Gide reiterates the need for secrecy if happiness is to be experienced. It is stated in the opening verses of the play when Gyges delivers his long expository monologue:

> Que celui qui tient un bonheur, — qu'il se cache!
> Ou bien qu'il cache aux autres son bonheur.[2]

It is repeated by the queen in the minor key when she speaks in an aside to Philebus:

> Qu'il est certains bonheurs que l'on tue
> Plutôt que de les pouvoir partager.[3]

It is symbolized in the magic ring both in its two oracular words meaning, 'Je cache le bonheur', and by its power to render its fortunate bearer invisible. It is played out in the action, once when Nyssia's happiest experience of sexual love is gained in the dark of night and with Gyges hidden by the magic ring, and again when, in the final reversal of fortune, Gyges as king and master violently re-covers the naked face of his new queen. His triumphant accession to power and his possession of the queen are demonstrated in his brutal domination of Nyssia and his determination to restore her to the position of hidden intimacy she had formerly held with Candaules. He at least realizes the caution and the essential selfishness a happy man must exercise if he is to maintain his precarious state. He understands the need for secrecy that the misguided Candaules learns at last, but too late:

> Et Nyssia ... [says the king]
> Et Nyssia, tu sais: maintenant je l'enferme
> Dans l'ombre, loin de tous, pour moi seul;
> Comme un parfum subtil, indiscret, qui s'évente...[4]

Gyges' hostile words to Nyssia as they lead the courtiers in to feast again and his rough gesture in veiling her face are natural

[1] RC, O.C. iii. 332. [2] Ibid., p. 299.
[3] Ibid., p. 320. [4] Ibid., p. 393.

enough, for the possession of the queen has cost him dear; it has lost him his friend.

Friendship is as integral to the play as is the theme of secrecy. It is the subject of the courtiers' discussion: Candaules' lack of a friend is the only possible flaw in his happiness, despite his lovely wife: '. . . ce n'est pas la même chose', says Philebus.[1] It is demonstrated by the pair of friends, Phaedrus and Simmias, in their self-sufficiency, their peace of mind, and their precious contentment which Candaules envies them; he asks:

> de combien de trésors, beau Simmias,
> N'achèterais-je pas la tienne?[2]

But when Gyges appears to cap the wish Candaules does not recognize the past and future loving friend. As he elevates the fisherman to the companion, showering luxuries upon him, he is no more capable of understanding friendship's nature than he is of understanding himself. For the king, the newly made courtier, splendidly dressed and fêted in intimacy as we see Gyges with Candaules in Act II, provides yet another experiment in the search for happiness. The change in Gyges' situation comes about through a royal whim; his role is to be recipient of infinite benefits, giver of none.

This scene, which is crucial in the dramatic action since Candaules offers both ring and wife to Gyges, is one of the most successful in its exploration of human relationships. It is essentially concerned with the failure in communication between two mutually well-meaning people. And that failure is inevitable when each man holds so different a set of values. Candaules' concept of friendship is based uniquely on the benefits bestowed whether they are simple material gifts, pleasure of the refined senses, or the sharing of beauty. Gyges' idea of friendship is based on love. He is consistently governed by his human affection: first by his feeling for Candaules as a beloved friend; later, when indeed sorely tried, by his sexual attraction to the queen so freely offered by Candaules. The different views of friendship are exposed in the exchange between the two men when Candaules

---

[1] RC, O.C. iii. 311.   [2] Ibid., p. 335.

praises his own wine and possessions; Gyges asks, as he lifts his
head from his hands:

> Roi Candaule, pourquoi tiens-tu tant
>   A ce que je connaisse ta fortune?
> *Le Roi Candaule*: Pour que te réjouisse l'amitié
>   Qui te fait profiter de ces biens.
> *Gygès*: Je pensais que l'amitié que tu voulais
>   N'était pas celle de tes biens, mais de toi-même...
> *Le Roi Candaule*: Laisse ton ironie, Gygès,
>   Et ne résiste plus au bonheur.[1]

When two characters are at such cross purposes mutual understanding is impossible. Gyges, whose restlessness and perplexity
in the earlier part of the scene grow from his sense of the super-
ficiality of Candaules' friendship, sees clearly enough where the
flaw in their relationship lies. Asked if he still doubts the king's
affection, he replies:

> Tant que ce sera toi qui donneras toujours,
> Oui...[2]

The magic ring offered to him by the king seems at last to
symbolize true friendship: 'Quoi! je serais vraiment ton ami, cher
Candaule?' he exclaims.[3] Candaules considers him a simple man
and contrasts such simplicity with his own implied complexity.
But Gyges shows an emotional maturity the king does not possess
when he recognizes the eternal truth of giving and receiving in
human relationships.

Indeed Candaules' obtuseness alienates sympathy just when the
rashness of his acts requires a sympathetic audience if they are to
be thought tragic rather than foolish. The king is of course carried
away by wine but he has already said that:

> L'ivresse ne manifeste en nous
> Que ce que nous portons en nous-mêmes.[4]

What drunkenness reveals in him is such rashness of behaviour
that it cannot be explained on rational grounds. Is it to assert his
generosity that he offers his wife to his friend? Is it to demonstrate

[1] Ibid., p. 352.   [2] Ibid., p. 358.
[3] Ibid., p. 359.   [4] Ibid., p. 321.

his absolute power? Or is Candaules driven by an unrecognized desire for vicarious sexual pleasure? Or the equally unrecognized need to destroy himself? It is in the presentation of Candaules' character that we feel the need for further and fuller exploration than the play provides.

Gyges is antithetical not only in his simplicity or his loving heart but in his predominantly active nature. Throughout the play he appears as a character of instinctive and violent action. When he learns of his wife's infidelity he punishes her mortally, without hesitation or regret; when he is forced by the impatient Nyssia to resolve the intolerable situation of adultery in which she finds herself against her will Gyges, despite sorrow and remorse for the loss of his friend, kills the king, his rival. In his opening monologue he counts his four blessings: 'Ma hutte, mon filet, ma femme et ma misère.' The play demonstrates their loss, one by one. But he adds a fifth attribute:

> ma force
> Avec quoi j'ai construit ma hutte et ma fierté.[1]

In some ways *Le Roi Candaule* contains the same antithesis of character as *Le Traité du Narcisse*, where Adam and Narcissus react so differently to the same initially tedious circumstances. It is not only the pontifical epilogue to the Narcissus story that throws light on the later play; the contrast of character, although it is in juxtaposition in the *Traité*, opposition in the play, is similar. Gyges's violent action, repeated in his two emotional crises, has much in common with Adam's way of releasing himself from the intolerable strain of perfection by a destructive act. Candaules bears an even closer resemblance to Narcissus. He is drawn irresistibly to the reflection of his own life and happiness provided by the courtiers' approval or his friend's admiring gratitude. Incapable of directly experiencing joy himself, he lives in the mirror-image of his actions thrown back by others.

The tragedy of Candaules, if the tragedy is his rather than that of the passion-torn Gyges, lies in the fact that his ineffectual reflective bias of nature involves the lives of others, of a man and a woman of more conventional needs whose fulfilment must

[1] *RC*, O.C. iii. 299.

inevitably eliminate reflection. Narcissus was fortunate in his opportunity for undisturbed contemplation. Candaules has to live among men and women.

André Gide, too, had to live among the men and women of his time. As suggested before, the uncertainties of *Le Roi Candaule* may well have resulted from Gide's concessions to public opinion. The legend of the Lydian king offers a more conventional triangle of characters than that of the wholly masculine triangle of *Saül*. King Candaules, once his experiment passes beyond his control, undergoes a belated change of heart in his behaviour towards his wife. But the emotional centre of the play which lies in the relationship between the two men does not coincide with the pattern of the plot built on the rivalry between two men for a woman. It is only too easy to sympathize with the exasperated Nyssia when she cries out to Gyges, tormented by his conflicting loyalties:

Oh! mais il faut pourtant que l'un de vous deux soit jaloux![1]

Whatever the cause of the ambiguous impact of *Le Roi Candaule*, whether discretion or dramatic inexperience, the uncertainties have provoked many interpretations. Gide himself provides alternatives in his discussion of its origin in the Preface and defines the play as 'une invite à la généralisation'. The answers to that invitation have been plentiful. One critic sees the opposed characters as typical of men and artists: 'Il y a toujours eu des Candaule et des Gygès. Un grand Candaule ce fut Hugo; un vrai Gygès, en dépit de ses idées républicaines, ce fut Stendhal. Un Candaule, l'auteur de la *Neuvième Symphonie*.'[2] Another interprets the plot philosophically: it illustrates 'l'éternel et inexorable jeu de l'âme et de l'histoire humaine: égoïsme, altruisme: force, justice; action, contemplation; les deux côtés de la sphère qui tourne, tantôt à l'ombre et tantôt au soleil.'[3] Another takes it as the conflict of abstractions: 'The defeat of Candaule by Gygès does not symbolize the political conquest of capitalism by a communist proletariat. It represents, rather, the defeat of

[1] Ibid., p. 392.
[2] R. Kemp, *Lectures dramatiques*, Paris, La Renaissance du Livre, 1947, p. 247.
[3] L. Dumur, *Mercure de France*, juin 1901, pp. 801–2.

abstraction and illusion by reality'.[1] Yet another judges it from the moral viewpoint: 'le dénuement total est sans pareil quand on le réalise en soi-même, barbare dès qu'il entraîne à sacrifier les autres';[2] while another interprets it from the psychological angle, as the expression of an 'obsession homosexuelle'.[3]

All such interpretations are illuminating and applicable to the play. But perhaps their very variety and the ease with which such generalizations can be related to the drama suggest a weakness in it. Gide in his Preface reluctantly discusses 'la part des idées' which, as he says, should be subordinate to the beauty of a work of art. The readiness of critical opinion to find intellectual applications and analogies would seem to emphasize the ideas rather than the experience of human beings caught up in the essential conflict of dramatic situation. For Le Roi Candaule (and Saül too) by its concern with happiness and with sexual love as a major means of attaining it is presenting subject-matter which is more conventional, which is more customary, more generally acceptable, in short more popular, than that of any of the preceding works. And the theme of happiness is one that personally concerned Gide himself. The Journal entries of 1893-4 allude often to his need to experience happiness: 'C'est un devoir que de se faire heureux', he writes.[4] But just as his interest in Saul's story took some six or seven years to express itself in his play so his youthful preoccupation with individual happiness did not externalize itself in his second drama until some years later. Gide was shortly to acquire a new way of evaluating happiness whereby it appeared to him less an end in itself and more as the means of self-realization. The Witch of Endor sees beyond happiness but her knowledge is entirely pessimistic; Gide similarly but more affirmatively looked beyond happiness when he wrote in 1905: 'Est-ce jamais le bonheur que nous cherchons? Non; mais le libre jeu de ce qui est le plus neuf en nous-mêmes.'[5]

[1] J. C. McLaren, The Theatre of André Gide: Evolution of a Moral Philosopher, Baltimore, Johns Hopkins Press, 1953, p. 32.

[2] M.-J. Durry, 'La poésie d'André Gide', Hommage à André Gide, p. 104.

[3] Brée, André Gide, p. 125.

[4] Journal, p. 34, avril 1893; also p. 44, septembre 1893; p. 56, 1895.

[5] Ibid., p. 155, 16 mai 1905.

Nevertheless if Gide's own thought developed beyond the range of his dramatic characters' concepts of happiness, their relative failure to convince us should not be traced back to the immaturity of their personal philosophies. In part their weakness may be due to the particular difficulties of dramatic writing where a principal character of whatever complexity is not sufficient matter. Drama requires the creation of a convincing human world in which the hero, whatever his dilemma, may effectively take his place. And in neither of Gide's early plays did he succeed in establishing his heroes among creatures of apparent flesh and blood. Saul moves in a world of shadowy figures whether they are of supernatural or human origin; Candaules and, possibly, Gyges, play out their roles among courtly puppets. Interesting as their personal sufferings may be, they move in rarefied air that is not the natural element of the greatest drama.

Gide's creative imagination changed direction as did his philosophic comments on human happiness. He turned away from drama as literary vehicle in the great creative period of his career upon which he entered with the new century. Writing for the theatre had entailed valuable discipline in clarifying and controlling the presentation of human crises, but Gide was to find other and more congenial forms of literary self-expression. And he was to set those crises in other and more intimately known *milieux* when he moved on to the new examinations of love and happiness. He left the pagan world for the world of Christian belief, Protestant in his serious works, Roman Catholic in his *sotie, Les Caves du Vatican*; and he abandoned antiquity for the contemporary age. His interest in hellenism endured, but it offered him other pleasures besides the provision of skeletal plots.

5

PROJECTS AND THEORIES

A STUDY which examines any single aspect of a writer's work is liable to contain the grave fault of distortion. If it is true to say that for some thirty years André Gide seems to have found no use for the Greek myth (between *Le Roi Candaule* of 1901 and *Œdipe* of 1931) the statement needs qualification, since his interest in hellenism persisted, though manifesting itself in other than imaginative ways; it also presents a biased view of his career. For the period of his life that opens with the century and closes with his departure for the Congo is that of his maturity and of the richest creativity of his whole long literary life. Within it appeared novels such as *L'Immoraliste* (1902), *La Porte étroite* (1909), *Isabelle* (1911), *Les Caves du Vatican* (1914), *La Symphonie pastorale* (1919), and *Les Faux-Monnayeurs*, published in 1926; memoirs including the two volumes of *Si le grain ne meurt* (1920–1); a great deal of critical writing of which the most important is the study of Dostoevsky (1923). These are the works that established Gide's literary reputation, and through which he is generally known today. And although Greek allusions are frequent in the critical writing and in *Les Faux-Monnayeurs*, for instance, they have little, but not nothing, to do with the mythology of Greece.

Three fragmentary works alone are directly concerned with it: 'Proserpine' (1912), 'Ajax' (published in 1921), and 'Considérations sur la mythologie grecque' (1919); yet it would be wrong to take them as evidence of a lessening interest in the subject. Indeed Gide's concern with hellenism increased although his major imaginative works were otherwise inspired. But his interest changed direction. Up to this time he had drawn on Greek myth chiefly for his overall plot which he then treated with the greatest liberty; his ideas of the Greek spirit, the meaning contained in the myths, the qualities of 'classicism', had remained nebulous and unexplored. But he never lost his delight in the great heroes of myth, as the many allusions to possible subjects and themes scattered throughout his *Journal* testify.

Some of the projected subjects were never realized; for instance, the three-act play, 'Scylla', announced in *L'Ermitage* in 1901. Gide's single reference in the *Journal* (8 August 1905) to 'mon *Sylla*' also suggests a play but it does not indicate whether it will treat the mythical Scylla who betrays her father for love of Minos,[1] or the historical Roman general, Sylla, described by Plutarch.[2] In the one case the heroine would have resembled Ariadne; in the other far more probable case, the historical hero would have approached the subject of Alexander. There may even have been two projected works but neither saw the light.

'Alexandre aux Indes', however, although equally unrealized, was at least planned in some detail. In the *Journal* Gide works out the points of resemblance between his own personal situation in his forty-third year: 'Ai-je atteint l'extrémité de l'expérience? Et vais-je savoir me ressaisir à neuf maintenant?'; and the experience of historical conquerors: 'Danger de vouloir illimiter son empire. En conquérant la Russie, Napoléon dut risquer la France. Nécessité de relier la frontière au centre.' And he goes on to draw the conclusion common to both situations:

> Il est temps de rentrer.
> (Ce sera le sujet d'*Alexandre aux Indes*.)[3]

The analogy between historical adventure and the lifetime of an individual man is easily drawn and the subject seems so potentially symbolic that it is perhaps a pity that Gide never carried out his intention. One writer so regretted the unwritten work that he offers a reconstruction from Gide's comments and an interpretation of his own.[4] However, it is more than likely that Alexander's withdrawal from India only attracted Gide briefly, as a possible

[1] See Mallarmé, *Les Dieux antiques*, p. 199.
[2] Plutarque, *Les Vies des hommes illustres*, traduites par Amyot, Paris, Janet et Cotelle, 1818, T. IV.
[3] *Journal*, p. 358 [janvier], 1912.
[4] J. Guéhenno, 'Alexandre aux Indes', *Europe*, no. 145, 15 janvier 1935, pp. 109-12.

incarnation of a passing mood. Nothing that we know of Gide's later life would suggest that he had reached the extreme point of his experience in January 1912; and with *Les Faux-Monnayeurs* still to come there is more reason to be thankful than to regret that Gide did not set the limits to his ambition at that stage of his life and consolidate his gains rather than conquer new literary territory. Be that as it may, Alexander the Great slipped out of his thought like Sylla.

Ajax stayed with him a little longer but, despite Gide's long-held interest in the Sophoclean *Ajax*,[1] he could not carry his own version beyong a single scene written in 1907 and finally published as a dramatic fragment in 1921,[2] after an earlier proposal to publish it in *Vers et Prose* in 1912 with his 'Proserpine'.

'Proserpine' itself had an erratic career. It was announced in 1893 with the alternative title of 'Le Traité des grains de grenade'.[3] 'La Ronde de la grenade' appeared in the first edition of *Le Centaure* (1896) with its epigraph: 'Certes, trois grains de grenade suffirent à faire s'en souvenir Proserpine'; and it was incorporated in *Les Nourritures terrestres* (1897). Gide published 'Proserpine' as a poetic fragment in *Vers et Prose*, T. xxviii, in 1912, and reworked it twenty years later to provide the text for the opera, *Perséphone* (1934).

And there was always the recurring figure of Theseus: in the 'Ballade des plus célèbres amants' of *Les Nourritures terrestres*; as principal illustration of Gide's interpretation of mythological meaning in 'Considérations sur la mythologie grecque', and over and over again in the *Journal*. The character who was to provide Gide's last imaginative hero moves through the thought of a lifetime.

These abandoned projects and partial publications might seem of more biographical than literary interest were it not that they indicate, by implication more than statement, the qualities of hero Gide thought admirable and, thus, necessary. The very fact that some characters prove unrewarding, some actions unworthy

---

[1] *Correspondance d'André Gide et de Paul Valéry*, p. 170 [août 1892].

[2] *Les Écrits nouveaux*, T. viii, octobre 1921; *Morceaux choisis*, Paris, N.R.F. 1921.

[3] See A. Naville, *Bibliographie des écrits d'André Gide*, Paris, Matarasso 1949, p. 216.

of examination, makes these tentative projects and incomplete performances more revealing than their achievement warrants. As Gide conceived the hero, in this middle phase of his own life,[1] he is, above all, independent and free from any domination either by a superhuman force or by his human situation. Gide's analysis of Orestes (Racine's, not Aeschylus') emphasizes the need for self-sufficiency, for full personal responsibility. He judges him as 'un faux mâle, tout à fait dominé par sa destinée. Il a besoin du crime pour motiver ses remords.

Il est de ceux sur qui pèse une fatalité, c'est-à-dire qui se sentent une mission à remplir. Un saturnien, évidemment.'[2] The true male is therefore one who does not feel compelled to accept a ready-made mission, who consequently feels free to choose his own destiny, even to accept remorse if it comes to him without justifying it, as it were, by crime. Orestes is a character trapped in two fashions, first by the destiny that imposes the murderous act upon him, secondly and irretrievably, by the onset of madness: 'Et *brusquement* la folie et la crise de haut-mal le saisissent au moment où il veut sortir, où il veut échapper à lui-même. C'est un rideau qui tombe autour de lui, un rideau d'ombre et qui l'enserre à la façon dont le filet de Clytemnestre enveloppa son père Agamemnon. Il ne s'en échappera pas.'[2]

The overthrow of human reason presumably because it goes beyond the bounds of the intelligent man's explicable experience is as enslaving a factor as any supernaturally directed destiny. Both of these forms of shackling the human being enter into Gide's idea of Ajax and his story; they force him to abandon his projected drama: 'J'ai voulu me remettre à *Ajax*', he writes in his *Journal* of 1907, 'mais, examinant mieux le *sujet*, je crains de ne pouvoir expliquer, excuser même le geste d'Ajax sans intervention de Minerve ou de la folie; il faudrait les deux à la fois: pratiquement absurde (il l'est suffisamment) et, idéalement, admirable (il ne l'est point). — Rien à faire.'[3] Gide's dismissal of the unhappy Ajax echoes his judgement on Orestes and his sense of mission: 'Et il n'y a rien à faire à cela.'[4]

[1] See ch. VIII.   [2] *Journal*, pp. 146–7, 1905.
[3] Ibid., pp. 241, 22 avril 1907.   [4] Ibid., p. 146, 1905.

Three elements of experience at least are capable of dominating the unheroic character: madness (ironically enough for the author of *Les Cahiers d'André Walter*); supernatural direction of whatever form (Orestes is 'un saturnien', Ajax is only tolerable if controlled by Minerva), an influence which the author of *Philoctète* and *Le Prométhée* cannot accept; and innate stupidity.

The Gidian Ajax is driving to disaster, like his Greek predecessor. His story starts before his frantic act, Sophocles contemplates him after it, but the end must be the same. All possibility of choice is admittedly forbidden him once Minerva collaborates with Ulysses, but he is also predominantly stupid. Ulysses, describing him to the goddess, speaks of him with open contempt. He is physically powerful but his strength is 'sans mesure, irréfléchie, [elle] ressemble plus souvent à l'impétuosité qu'au courage; c'est une élémentaire fureur qui se satisfait d'elle-même et l'enivre, car sa tête est à la merci de son cœur'.[1] As Ulysses says, he and Achilles represent 'deux forces inéduquées' which the more subtle man exploits with ease. In the dramatic fragment it is Ulysses who appears admirable in his intellectual power and consequent control of other lives. In *Philoctète* the same figure seems overcalculating, too ready to subordinate individual needs and human feeling to the concept of the State. But his creator is nearly ten years older and the power of human reason appears greater, its need more urgent.

Gide's view of the importance of human love was also modified between 1901 and his *Journal* note on Theseus written some time after 1911. Where Candaules thought his whole happiness embodied in Nyssia, his fortune lost with her, Theseus, in Gide's later opinion, must have been more encumbered by Ariadne than his well-being was enhanced by her presence. He links Ariadne with Creusa and Lot's wife, and with Racine's impassioned Phèdre too, as examples of the retarding, restricting, by implication destructive, influence women can exercise on the heroic man. 'Dans le *Thésée*', he writes, 'il faudra marquer cela — le fil à la patte, soit dit vulgairement. Il voudrait, après avoir dompté le Minotaure, continuer. — Il est tenu — contraint de revenir.'[2] In

[1] 'Ajax', O.C. iv. 372.   [2] *Journal*, p. 347, Feuillets (after 1911).

a brief entry he does not analyse the cause of this restraining influence but it is clearly the woman's love. The duality of love that Gyges recognized in *Le Roi Candaule* is still disturbing: the giving and taking, the pleasures and the duties, the privileges and the limitations. As Gide discusses the *Thésée* he was not to write for another thirty-five years, all these elements of close human relationship appear to him more in the nature of shackles than satisfactions. Ariadne, like her sisters, raises one more obstacle in the hero's path towards self-fulfilment. It can be overcome, as Theseus is to find when he discards her, but the loving woman is potentially dangerous and represents a threat to heroic freedom. He who escapes from supernatural direction, madness, the enslavement of stupidity has still other monsters to conquer.

However, the Greek myth had more to offer Gide at this stage than the unsatisfactory characters and situations which he did not care to develop. The twin figures of the Dioscuri furnished him finally with a theory of aesthetics as well as many important ideas brought to light before that end was reached. The origin of his interest in Castor and Pollux preceded the publication of Pierre Louÿs's *Lêda* (written, as Louÿs says, in 1893, published in 1898). Gide suggests such an origin when in his *Journal* of 1918 he discusses his work in progress on '*Castor et Pollux ou le Traité des Dioscures*, que je porte en moi depuis près de vingt ans. Si j'en suis assez satisfait, je le dédierai à Pierre Louÿs sans doute, en souvenir de sa *Léda* qu'il me dédiait jadis.'[1] Certainly Gide's final view of the Tyndarides owes much to Louÿs's little work which in its turn answered Gide's *Le Traité du Narcisse*; but this relationship did not become clear for another ten years. Writing in 1918, Gide realized how his work was changing its shape: 'Je ne sais absolument pas ce que vaut ce que j'écris à présent. C'est, sous une forme un peu différente de celle que je pensais lui donner d'abord. . . .'[1] The whole question of Gide's use of the Dioscuri is complicated. He worked many years on it, from about February, 1912, as *Journal* entries indicate, in broken spells, naturally, and he changed his intention and approach more than once. In 1914, for instance, he wrote: 'l'enchevêtrement de mes idées est extrême

[1] Ibid., p. 644, 17 janvier 1918.

et chacune d'elles à son tour me paraît pouvoir servir d'exorde, de clef de voûte ou de conclusion.'[1] It was probably on account of the complexity of his matter that he abandoned his earlier idea of including his ideas in a novel planned as successor to *Les Caves du Vatican*,[2] and decided to publish the 'Fragments du *Traité des Dioscures*' in 1919 as 'Considérations sur la mythologie grecque.'[3]

The ideas contained in this essay are original and stimulating but they have little to do with the mythological twins. Gide recognized this when he wrote to André Rouveyre in 1928: 'ce petit livre [*Le Traité des Dioscures*], que je n'ai pas écrit, habite encore les limbes de mon esprit, avec maints autres beaux projets qui ne verront jamais le jour.'[4] It is this letter which finally reveals the symbolical use Gide had planned for Castor and Pollux. It explains why Gide had originally intended to dedicate his version of the myth to Pierre Louÿs, since the two young friends of twenty had shared a passionate interest in the myth of Leda. It was thanks to Louÿs that Gide learnt about the curious birth of the two semi-divine figures and their relationship with their sisters, Helen and Clytemnestra, which were to provide him with the basis for his theory of the artistic nature. Pierre Louÿs's *Lêda* indeed contains the prophecy of the birth of Helen, eternal symbol of Beauty, when the river god speaks to Leda after her union with Zeus: 'Tu es la nuit [he says]. Et tu as aimé le symbole de tout ce qui est lumière et gloire; et tu t'es unie à lui.

Du symbole est né le symbole et du symbole naîtra la Beauté. Elle est dans l'œuf bleu qui est sorti de toi. Depuis le commencement du monde on sait qu'elle s'appellera Hélène; et celui qui sera le dernier homme connaîtra qu'elle a existé.'[5] Although Louÿs denies the family relationship between the brothers, Kastor and Polydeukes, and Helen, his identification of Helen with Beauty, conventional as it is, reappears in Gide's exposition of the myth.

[1] *Journal*, p. 432, 7 juillet 1914.   [2] Ibid., p. 363, février 1912.

[3] *Nouvelle Revue Française*, septembre 1919; *Morceaux choisis*, 1921; *Incidences*, N.R.F. 1924.

[4] 'Lettre à André Rouveyre', 11 avril 1928, *Divers* [Paris], Gallimard N.R.F. 1931, p. 183.

[5] Pierre Louÿs, *Lêda*, Paris, Mercure de France, 1898, p. 18.

Gide's letter tells the legendary story in his own way and develops it into a discussion of the artist's character:

Léda pondit deux œufs. L'un contenait Castor; l'autre Pollux. Mais l'un contenait aussi Clytemnestre; l'autre, pareillement gemellé, contenait, avec Castor, Hélène. [Gide notes his simplification here.] Partant de ce renseignement, je me plus à imaginer qu'il restait à chacun des deux frères quelque chose de ce confinement, l'un avec la passion — Clytemnestre; l'autre avec Hélène, la beauté. J'y vis aussitôt la raison de cette immortalité partagée qui faisait l'un mourir de la vie de l'autre, . . . l'un disparaître à l'horizon lorsque l'autre, à l'autre extrémité du ciel, se levait; non par fuite, mais tout au contraire, par un égal désir désespéré de se rejoindre. J'imaginais le poète-artiste, docilement soumis à leur double influence, sentir se conjuguer en lui les rayons de ces deux astres *opposés*.[1]

But, Gide continues, the stellar influences need not be uniform; they may be responsible for the variations of the poet's nature: 'Il m'eût plu d'établir, à la faveur de cette fable, que . . . le créateur, poète, peintre ou musicien, peut être plus ou moins près d'un des deux astres, jusqu'à ne plus sentir que très peu le rayonnement de l'autre.'[1] One kind of creative spirit will therefore be influenced by the Pollux–Clytemnestra combination; the other by the Castor–Helen force. But the brothers are twins (presumably fraternal and not identical), and their equality prevents competitive rivalry between the creative artists affected by their separate spheres of influence. We may prefer one type of artist to the other; we should not therefore judge him to be better than his peer.

The aesthetic theory that develops from the myth starts by examining the individual creative artist but it leads to a new assessment of European writers. Gide reconsiders great writers in the light of his own definition of character and, incidentally, classifies himself as an artist 'd'extrême milieu'.

His treatment of the Castor and Pollux myth is chiefly interesting for a variety of secondary reasons. That part of the originally planned *Traité* which appears as 'Considérations sur la mythologie grecque' holds more provocative and more valuable ideas than the

---

[1] *Divers*, pp. 183–5.

somewhat laboriously pursued theory he finally produces in the letter. To distinguish one type of creative mind from another is valid enough. What else has the long debate about Romanticism and Classicism attempted to do? To distinguish them on the basis of the predominance of 'passion' or of 'beauty' is more questionable. Gide's employment of the general and time-worn terms of 'artistes' to describe the writers in whom passion dominates, *poètes* for those who are governed by 'beauty' (presumably the concern with form and style) is too personal and too imprecise to be particularly illuminating. Nevertheless, the long period of gestation is itself worth attention. And the new use of the myth employed here to carry aesthetic theory and intellectual discussion is even more remarkable.

It is in his prolonged contemplation of the Dioscuri that Gide evolves his ideas of what, in a wide sense, he calls 'le classicisme'. Within this general descriptive term he groups together various, although related, concepts. They may as readily arise from the narratives and myths of classical antiquity as from their formal qualities or from their philosophical bases.

In the first instance Gide considers the meaning he discovers in Greek mythology. In 1919 he rejects outright the earlier, widely held interpretation of the myth as symbol of physical phenomena. Such rejection entails the re-examination of the mysterious force of antiquity, the *Fatum*, and Gide brushes aside the power of Fate as he rejects the natural explanation: 'Or je dis que plus on réduit dans la fable la part du Fatum, et plus l'enseignement est grand. Au défaut de la loi physique la vérité psychologique se fait jour, qui me requiert bien davantage.'[1] His belief in the psychological truth of the myth and, therefore, in a 'fatalité intérieure' which replaces external forces is the natural outcome of his earlier versions. Hercules, as we saw, was eliminated from the experiences of Prometheus and Philoctetes, Zeus reduced to an irresponsible banker (if such there be). Minerva in the fragmentary 'Ajax' is simply instrumental in exteriorizing Ulysses' inner conflict. She describes her role as an aid to the clarification of confused thought: 'Parle, Ulysse!', she advises him. 'Les paroles n'exagèrent les

---

[1] 'Myth. grecque', O.C. ix. 149.

perplexités que des fous. Le sage qui demande conseil n'attend pourtant point du dehors l'inspiration de sa conduite; mais, exposant les motifs de son incertitude, il trouve la leçon qu'il quêtait, à les développer clairement.'[1] Ajax's madness ultimately depends on the decision Ulysses must reach; Minerva plays her subordinate part in the formation of that decision as she would no doubt have done in its execution. She personifies in fact Ulysses' moment of indecision. And it is the state of doubt offered by the Ajax myth that interests Gide. Once physical action becomes necessary he drops the subject.

His re-reading of mythology is therefore undertaken in the light of this belief in an inner fate. It is a belief that enters deeply into his own self-examination. When he discusses his preference for natural history, for example, rather than the political history of men he bases it on the laws of necessity which govern the one whereas the other is subject to fortuitous, non-recurring events. The opposing views can be summed up as 'Fatalité extérieure — fatalité intime'.[2] Again, his belief in a psychological fate seems to be confirmed by his own experience. His *Journal* notes the illumination the forgotten past can throw on a moment of immediate crisis, how a characteristic pattern of behaviour can be observed in the records of the past:

X. se prend un jour à relire d'anciennes lettres de lui qu'il retrouve (à sa mère morte) [he writes (presumably of himself)], stupéfait de reconnaître que, précédemment, il a traversé déjà une crise exactement semblable à celle qu'il traverse présentement . . ., et qu'il a agi alors exactement de même, aussi stupidement; — c'est-à-dire qu'il se rend compte qu'il ne peut agir autrement — et il se souvient qu'il s'était pourtant promis de ne plus y être pris. . . . Il songe que chacun refait toujours le même geste; ou que, plus exactement, il y a, dans le caractère de chacun, une propension à tel geste particulier, qui détermine l'allure de toute la vie.[3]

His independently acquired belief is astonishingly close to the findings of scientific psychology as he himself observes in 1922: 'Le freudisme... Depuis dix ans, quinze ans, j'en fais sans le

---

[1] 'Ajax', O.C. iv. 369.   [2] *Journal*, p. 717, Feuillets (after 1921).
[3] Ibid., pp. 718–19.

savoir.'[1] In his psychological explanation of the myth's inner meaning he adopts something of the same approach as Jung (never mentioned in his *Journal*) and, for instance, Kerényi were to do.

His opinions of the aesthetic aspects of 'classicism' are equally definite and equally personal. The classical method, he argues, is inclusive not exclusive, and he roundly condemns the negativism of an 'excluding' writer: 'Le seul classicisme admissible c'est celui qui tienne compte de tout. Celui de Maurras est détestable parce qu'il opprime et supprime, et rien ne me dit que ce qu'il opprime ne vaut pas mieux que l'oppresseur. La parole aujourd'hui est à ce qui n'a pas encore parlé.'[2] He was to demonstrate the effects of this principle of inclusiveness on subject-matter, approach, and tone in his version of the Sophoclean tragedy, *Œdipe*, but that did not appear until 1931. As it stands, this statement of 1921 seems to abuse the patient term of 'classicism' by making extravagant claims for it. It can certainly mean a great deal but not everything. Gide is perhaps forced into excess by his personal dislike of a reputedly 'classical' author's writing.

When a 'classical impersonality' is attributed to his own works he takes the description as an accusation which he most indignantly refutes: quoting a critic's phrase ' "Impersonnalité classique que M. Gide peut envier à son élève" ', he replies vigorously: ' — Mais je ne l'envie pas du tout, cette qualité! et n'ai jamais considéré l'impersonnalité comme une vertu particulièrement classique.' He goes on to claim that he has always sought 'le caractère le moins impersonnel possible, le moins objectif, le plus *entrant*'.[3] His indignation arises perhaps from confusion between the two possible meanings of the debated 'impersonality'. In its sense of detachment, he denies its application to his work, whether rightly or wrongly we will consider later; he very properly admires the author who is wholly committed to his work. But impersonality, as an avoidance of an excessive display of individuality or of idiosyncrasy, he would not have found an offensive trait. Indeed such impersonality had long been one of his ideals of classical

[1] *Journal*, p. 729, 4 février 1922.   [2] Ibid., p. 689, 14 janvier 1921.
[3] Ibid., p. 965, janvier 1930.

style. As early as 1893 he praised 'cette banalité supérieure' that Goethe possesses;[1] in 1921 he maintained the same criterion in judging the classical writer: 'le grand artiste classique travaille à n'avoir pas de manière; il s'efforce vers la banalité. S'il parvient à cette banalité sans effort, c'est qu'il n'est pas un grand artiste, parbleu! L'œuvre classique ne sera forte et belle qu'en raison de son romantisme dompté.'[2] There is nothing controversial in such a declaration. The expression of passionate experience in disciplined form and the primacy of that experience with the consequent self-effacement of the creative artist are essential elements in the classical work of art. So, too, is the style which conveys more than it declares. Gide, in praising disciplined emotion and its economical expression, concurs with general opinion: 'Le classicisme — et par là j'entends: le classicisme français — tend tout entier vers la litote. C'est l'art d'exprimer le plus en disant le moins.'[3]

Where he goes further than conventional opinion is in his deduction of a moral code from stylistic qualities. Economy, reticence, understatement in expression derive from a fundamental reserve in the artist's character: classicism 'est un art de pudeur et de modestie. Chacun de nos classiques est plus ému qu'il ne le laisse paraître d'abord. . . . Faute de savoir les pénétrer et les entendre à demi-mot, nos classiques dès lors parurent froids, et l'on tint pour défaut leur qualité la plus exquise: la réserve.'[4] These are the natural judgements of 'un protestant scrupuleux et d'un esthète raffiné, qui attribue une haute valeur morale à la réserve, à la sobriété, à la mesure, c'est-à-dire à un certain idéal artistique', as Henri Peyre writes. But the generalizing thought is not without its weaknesses. As Peyre points out, does the 'immorality' of some romantic writers necessarily follow from their use of three epithets instead of one?[5]

If we admit that 'classicism' to André Gide involves all these different aspects of subject-matter, literary aesthetics, even ethics,

---

[1] Ibid., pp. 42–43.   [2] 'Billets à Angèle', O.C. xi. 36 (mars 1921).
[3] Ibid., p. 39.   [4] Ibid., pp. 39–40.
[5] H. Peyre, *Qu'est-ce que le classicisme?* Essai de mise au point. Deuxième tirage, Paris, E. Droz, 1942, p. 82.

we can still employ the term to make some assessment of his thought in his middle age and his maturity. It does at least serve to isolate one section of his multiple interests; we may therefore legitimately ask what it means to him.

It seems obvious that temperamentally Gide was attracted to the classical attitude. As his comments show he is always drawn to the literary works possessing the qualities he so painstakingly distinguishes. But he is equally attracted to the same qualities in the sister arts. He prefers Pope to Shelley,[1] but he also sets Mozart infinitely above a Wagner or a Richard Strauss. Indeed, he writes so violently about Strauss's *Salomé* that his diatribe carries him far beyond a simple criticism of an opera:

Exécrable musique romantique, d'une rhétorique orchestrale à vous faire aimer Bellini. Seules les parties de pittoresque comique . . . ou morbide, . . . attestent un remarquable 'savoir faire'. Lasserre remarque de même l'excellence de la truculence comique chez Hugo; — de même *les Maîtres-Chanteurs* — mêmes causes. Et mêmes causes des défauts: indiscrétion des moyens et monotonie des effets, fastidieuses insistances, insincérité flagrante; mobilisation indiscontinue de toutes les ressources. De même Hugo, de même Wagner, quand les métaphores lui viennent en tête pour exprimer une idée, ne choisira pas, ne nous fera grâce d'aucune. Inartistisme foncier de cela. Amplification systématique, etc... Défaut qu'il n'est même pas intéressant d'examiner. Mieux vaut condamner l'œuvre en bloc, et attendre les baïonnettes, parce que, cet art-là, c'est vraiment *l'ennemi*.[2]

If his outburst may seem excessive in expressing an aesthetic preference it arose, no doubt, from a fundamental antipathy of temperament. For a man who saw himself as a Dorian and, therefore, incompatible with Ionians such as Pierre Louÿs,[3] or such outright Asiatics as Pierre Loti and Jules Lemaître;[4] for whom the devil himself presented himself in classical guise;[5] for whom the admirable traits were *pudeur* and *modestie*, the threat presented by the violent, rhetorical, and reiterative artists (as he judged them) seemed really that of the enemy.

With his current interests and his innate disposition inclining

[1] *Journal*, p. 979, 31 mars 1930.   [2] Ibid., p. 246, 22 mai 1907.
[3] Ibid., p. 232, janvier 1907.   [4] Ibid., p. 1134, 27 juin 1932.
[5] Ibid., p. 561, 19 septembre 1916.

him towards the classical spirit it is only natural that Gide should turn back to the source of classical inspiration. When he did so during this middle period of his life he found himself opposing his closest friends. Paul Valéry, for instance, was frankly hostile to Greek art; as he wrote to Gide in 1894: 'Je n'ai rien vu de plus ennuyeux que les frises du Parthénon. Je me promets de me payer la tête du premier chrétien qui m'en parlera.'[1] And he continued to be equally frank, equally sweeping, in 1907, at the time of Gide's greatest interest in hellenism: 'Qui est-ce qui s'occupe aujourd'hui des Grecs? Je suis convaincu que ce que nous appelons encore aujourd'hui "langues mortes" va tomber en putréfaction. Il est impossible désormais de comprendre les sentiments des héros d'Homère.'[2] Such frank hostility in an admired friend is a force to be reckoned with and Gide's *Journal* proves his anxiety: 'La conversation de Valéry me met dans *l'affreuse* alternative', he writes: 'ou bien trouver absurde ce qu'il dit, ou bien trouver absurde ce que je fais.'[3] Nevertheless Gide continued his explorations into the spirit of Greek antiquity. Where Valéry saw a schism between past and present Gide came to believe that France was the natural heir to Greece: 'A présent', he writes in 1914, 'je sais que notre civilisation occidentale (j'allais dire: française) est non point seulement la plus belle; je crois, je sais qu'elle est la *seule* — oui, celle même de la Grèce, dont nous sommes les seuls héritiers.'[4]

In acknowledging the legacy from antiquity Gide makes a comparison between the two great formative influences on Europe: Christ's teachings and hellenism. 'Je . . . sais qu'il y a deux enseignements dont jamais l'homme n'épuisera la vertu', he writes in 1923: 'celui du Christ, et celui de la "fable grecque".'[5] The association of the two forces, so influential in his own intellectual development, might suggest that he has found a means of reconciling them. But it would not yet be true; there is still a choice to be made between the two traditions. In the same year, during an argument with Maritain about the publication of 'certain

---

[1] *Correspondance*, p. 206.   [2] *Journal*, p. 238, 9 février 1907.
[3] Ibid., p. 237.   [4] Ibid., p. 416, 'La marche turque', 1914.
[5] Ibid., p. 754, 23 janvier 1923.

livre' (presumably *Corydon*), an argument which Gide records in his *Journal*, he frames the nature of the choice as lying between 'l'équilibre grec et le déséquilibre chrétien'.[1] There is no question as to where Gide's preference lies. Indeed the idea of Greek equilibrium which echoes his youthful ideal of the equilibrium, the plenitude, and the health of 'classicism' is at the centre of Gide's concept of hellenism.

The Greek civilization of the great period seemed to him to hold the secret of individual and social happiness as it has never been known since: 'Nul peuple n'eut plus le sens et l'intelligence de l'harmonie que le peuple grec. Harmonie de l'individu, et des mœurs, et de la cité.'[2] Harmony is the key word. And harmony results from the combination of essentially independent sounds, not from sound in unison. The Greek equilibrium was produced by the acceptance of diversity.

In the individual man harmony is achieved by frank recognition of his own nature. Where diversity is smiled upon by society individual honesty is possible and the free development of the self is desirable: 'le païen ne croyait pas devoir être différent de ce qu'il était', Gide announces in a lecture of 1904. 'L'être ne se banalisait pas, par contrainte, mais se poussait à bout, par vertu; chacun n'exigeait de soi que soi-même . . .'.[3] A permissive social attitude simplifies existence. Difficulties and obstacles have to be met and overcome, but since in the Greek world they were external, brought about only by the impact of the outside world, they were less menacing than subjective restraints: 'Le paganisme heureux ne considérait point d'ennemi qui ne fût extérieur à l'homme. . . . Radieuse matinée du monde; forces de l'homme non divisées.'[4] (It would be impertinent to interrupt Gide's argument by recalling the Persians or the Peloponnesian war.) This ideal and uncomplicated way of living, in Gide's opinion, was brought to a close when Christian morality imposed a single ideal of character to which every man must aspire whether it was congenial to him or not. It may bring about the 'déformation

---

[1] *Journal*, p. 773, 21 décembre 1923.   [2] Ibid., p. 996, 8 juillet 1930.
[3] 'L'évolution du théâtre', O.C. iv. 211.
[4] *Journal*, p. 375, février 1912.

chrétienne' he observed in his own upbringing; it certainly encourages hypocrisy: 'Oui, l'homme devient ce qu'il prétend être; mais prétendre être ce que l'on n'est pas, c'est une prétention toute moderne; précisons: c'est proprement la prétention chrétienne.'[1]

Gide holds this morality responsible for the inhibiting of full self-development. It is more dangerous to personal happiness since less easily recognized than external threats. The battlefield is now the human spirit where the demands of the ideal conflict with the inclinations of nature: 'Le christianisme = l'opération intérieure', Gide writes in 1912.[2]

Let there be no misunderstanding. Gide does not reproach Christianity for having directed man's attention to his spiritual state. On the contrary, he admires the new emphasis and its understanding: 'L'admirable révolution du christianisme est d'avoir dit: le royaume de Dieu est au-dedans de vous. . . . C'est *en nous* que sont les écuries d'Augias, les hydres, les marais à nettoyer. C'est en nous que doit œuvrer Hercule.'[2] What he does reproach the Christian morality for is the imposition of an ideal uniformity on the multiplicity of human nature which may well produce imbalance of the personality. 'L'opération intérieure' in itself does not mean unhappiness; but the repression or suppression of natural instincts in order to conform to the ideal may well result in it. The Greeks, understanding the needs of the well-balanced man, practised a happy inclusiveness of all such instincts. Gide again draws on his own interpretation of the myth's validity when he defines his own ideal of human nature: 'Les Grecs qui nous ont laissé de l'humanité, non par le peuple de leurs statues seulement, mais par eux-mêmes, une image si belle, reconnaissaient autant de dieux que d'instincts, et le problème pour eux était de maintenir l'Olympe intime en équilibre, non d'asservir et de réduire aucun des dieux.'[3]

The well-balanced 'inner Olympus' is only possible in a society which permits diversity to flourish in freedom. For the offended

[1] 'L'évolution du théâtre', O.C. iv. 210–11.
[2] *Journal*, p. 375, février 1912.
[3] Ibid., p. 777, Feuillets (after 1923).

gods, or the frustrated instincts they symbolize, can be dangerous: the gods may take vengeance, 'comme il advient terriblement pour Penthée, dans les *Bacchantes* d'Euripide'.[1] Only a society that admits and approves the infinite variety of human nature can be without hypocrisy, which is not inevitable in a community of men: 'L'hypocrisie des mœurs n'a donc pas toujours existé.'[2] For the admirably honest society was again one achieved by the Greeks particularly by their intelligent acceptance of homosexuality: 'Harmonie de l'individu, et des mœurs, et de la cité. Et c'est par besoin d'harmonie (intelligence autant qu'instinct) qu'ils donnèrent droit de cité à l'uranisme. C'est ce que j'ai tâché de faire voir dans *Corydon*', he writes in 1930.[3]

At this point the question of Gide's reasons for pursuing and praising the characteristics of Greek antiquity inevitably arises. Is his admiration for things Greek based on a genuine understanding of the classical age or does that illustrious civilization authorize his own sexual inclinations? We must leave the first part of that question for later discussion but we may well ask how true the latter part seems. When he recalls his state of mind before setting off for Algeria in 1893, with his desire for 'équilibre . . ., plénitude . . ., santé', he himself describes it as the impulse towards 'classicism'. Theoretically that meant freedom from the puritan restraints of his home. In practice, as he frankly confesses later, it meant chiefly sexual freedom. Even later he recognizes the relationship between homosexuality and hellenism in his thought (in *Corydon* and elsewhere).[4] It is therefore certainly possible to explain the interest of Gide, 'un Grec né hors de saison', as Charles du Bos describes him, in this way. Du Bos takes care, however, to distinguish the two aspects of Gide's character, the philosophical and the physical: 'il va de soi que je ne veux pas dire que Gide ne soit *grec* parce que pédéraste, mais seulement que la donnée grecque en son ensemble n'est pas chez lui *native*: envisagée en

[1] 'L'évolution du théâtre', O.C. iv. 211.
[2] Ibid., p. 210.
[3] *Journal*, p. 996, 8 juillet 1930.
[4] See *Journal*, p. 671, Feuillets (after 1918): 'Socrate et Platon n'eussent pas aimé les jeunes gens, quel dommage pour la Grèce, quel dommage pour le monde entier'!

son ensemble, elle est non pas une donnée, mais un *problème* et une *aspiration* d'abord, puis une graduelle *conquête*.'[1]

However, the motivation of Gide's original interest in Greek mythology and civilization is less important surely than the use he personally can make of the myth, both in his imaginative works and in his critical theories. His discovery of the essential truth of mythological incident is original and valuable: judgement of his imaginative writings does not yet concern us.

A similar qualification should be made when considering the attraction Gide felt for 'classicism' in its aesthetic sense. Henri Peyre suggests that extra-literary motives encouraged Gide's wide and international reading: 'Il est clair que toute une partie de ses goûts littéraires (sa curiosité pour Winckelmann, pour Walt Whitman, pour les Grecs eux-mêmes, pour le *Hero and Leander* de Marlowe) s'explique par le même souci de justifier son anomalie physiologique qui lui fit, dans *Corydon*, accumuler les preuves empruntées à l'histoire naturelle.'[2] But Gide read and admired Robert Herrick for the purest of artistic reasons. When he links Herrick with Marlowe as the most pleasing of his readings in poetry, his judgement is surely unaffected by biographical detail.[3]

It would seem therefore prejudiced not to recognize a temperamental predisposition towards the classical artistic approach, whatever hostile opinion may say of Gide's adoption of classicism as 'une feinte suprême pour masquer la révolte de son âme où les démons assemblés se disputent'.[4] Something in the method and expression of the classical creative spirit in whatever art, some essential element of order or discipline, answered the needs of his nature. If those needs found satisfaction in their contraries does that matter? Is it not enough to record that this man of unusually wide literary interests and of unusual erudition was more strongly drawn to the classical works than to others? When he discusses the work of Racine and of Shakespeare (where biographical

---

[1] Charles du Bos, *Le Dialogue avec André Gide*, p. 244.

[2] H. Peyre, 'André Gide et les problèmes d'influence en littérature', *MLN*, November 1942, p. 564.

[3] *Journal*, p. 657, 15 juillet 1918.

[4] H. Massis, 'L'influence de M. André Gide', *Revue universelle*, T. XII, no. 16, 1921, p. 502.

criteria might possibly incline him to the sonneteer) he bases his preference for Racine on purely aesthetic reasons: 'J'ai aimé les vers de Racine par-dessus toutes productions littéraires', he writes in 1933. 'J'admire Shakespeare énormément; mais j'éprouve devant Racine une émotion que ne me donne jamais Shakespeare: celle de la perfection. . . . précisément me plaît [chez Racine] cette limitation exacte, ce non-débordement du cadre, cette précision des contours. . . . Homme et nature, dans ses pièces ouvertes aux vents, toute la poésie rit, pleure et frémit dans Shakespeare; Racine est au sommet de l'art.'[1] Would it not be sophistical to deny the validity of such reasons? A recent writer, Henri Morier, studies the relationship between style and the writer's character and sets out to prove that 'le style est une affaire de caractère, et qu'adopter une manière d'écrire c'est opérer une sélection parmi les procédés d'expression. Or, c'est ce choix-même, et lui seul, qui révèle le goût et livre les secrets de la personnalité.'[2] Since Gide's own writings are not at the moment our concern could the same not be said of his preferred reading? Morier criticizes a weakness of Taine who had not realized that 'l'esthétique, étant affaire du goût, était fonction du tempérament'.[3] Gide's attraction to 'classicism' in art can be convincingly explained by his individual nature.

[1] *Journal*, p. 1187, 27 octobre 1933.
[2] H. Morier, *La Psychologie des styles*, Genève, Georg, 1959, p. 20.
[3] Ibid., p. 70.

6

THE HERO AND HUMANITY

With the publication of *Œdipe* in 1931, followed in 1933 by the opera, *Perséphone*, Gide's interest in hellenism, like his cyclical Chthonian goddess, comes to the surface again. He turns to Greek mythology for two works designed for the stage, very different in dramatic form and intention and belonging essentially to two different periods of his life. Nevertheless, in his reworking of much earlier material for the opera he makes some suggestions that only belong to his attitudes of the 1930's. Both the theatrical works pursue the examination of happiness that so largely provided the subject-matter of *Le Roi Candaule*; both, like the preceding plays rather than the earlier *traités* or the *récit*, are concerned with human relationships; and both, within the given outline of the myths, contain Gide's personal interpretation of the characters' behaviour.

Despite the later appearance of *Perséphone* and its production by Ida Rubinstein and Jacques Copeau in 1934 it really belongs to an earlier phase of Gide's career, whereas *Œdipe* wholly expresses Gide's thought at the time of its writing and publication. In dedicating *Perséphone* to Madame Ida Rubinstein 'dont la ferveur a su ranimer un projet endormi depuis plus de vingt ans',[1] Gide acknowledges the dependence of the opera book on the early poetic fragment, 'Proserpine', published in 1912,[2] and indeed most of the poetic text is incorporated in the later and more ambitious version. In its first form, of a single scene set within a prose account of the projected action, it treats the contrast between the joy and fecundity of the earth that precedes the abduction of Proserpine and the desolation that follows it. The myth naturally provides the contrasted seasons and situations but they also seem excellent

---

[1] *Théâtre* [Paris], Gallimard, 1942, 8ᵉ éd., p. 305. This collection includes both *Perséphone* and *Œdipe* to which following notes will refer.

[2] See p. 86.

'paysages d'âme' after the fashion of Gide's earliest work. As Proserpine exclaims:

> . . . Que la terre était belle
> Quand l'amoureux éclat de nos rires mêlait
> Aux épis d'or, des fleurs, et des parfums au lait;[1]

and this state of happiness is set against the desolation of winter and loss when all nature mourns:

> Des rivières figées;
> Cesser la fuite en pleurs des ruisseaux, et leur voix
> S'étouffer sous le gel.[1]

There is the equally natural contrast between the existence led by the dead in the underworld, inconsolable even by the hope of an end to misery in death, and man's life on earth where he can watch the summer renew his fields and where the expectation of death can comfort him in times of dearth and trouble.

The narcissus links the two worlds. Gide's use of the traditional flower is his own, as is his later symbolism of the pomegranate. In the myth, Proserpine, 'gathering flowers', plucks the narcissus sacred to the god of the underworld which causes him to rise and snatch her away. The narcissus summons Hades. In Gide's version, the flower at first draws Proserpine towards the underworld and from there allows her to see within its cup the effect of her absence on 'la terre désenchantée'.

As they stand the verse fragments of the unfinished work suggest the love between Proserpine and Ceres as an example of the filial love which Gide developed so much later in *Œdipe* and the growth of the Demophoon–Triptolemus figure whose labours will release her from the underworld, a resolution of her dilemma which he used again in the opera. The prose account anticipates the outcome of the action as Proserpine's equal commitment to her two loves, 'le terrestre Triptolème et l'infernal Pluton', and hence her divided life. Gide's plan presents the traditional Kore in his first act; Proserpine is still an anxious young girl, attached to her mother and the lost earth. When she voluntarily returns to the underworld she makes her final appearance on Pluto's arm,

[1] 'Pros.', O.C. iv. 353.

splendidly clad, fully conscious of her dominant role as Persephone, Queen of the underworld, Proserpine, the implacable goddess of Homer.[1] She has fully accepted her destiny and proposes in some way to reconcile the unhappy shades to their melancholy fate. The complexity of the mythological Proserpine is suggested but is not fully developed in a work which for so long remained unfinished.

When Gide returns to the myth, however, he is further from the concept of the double nature of Persephone. That aspect which represents the 'avenging deity' described by Walter Pater[2] has been completely lost in the ideal young goddess who willingly returns to Pluto, governed by her pity for the inhabitants of the underworld, 'Où non point tant la loi que mon amour me mène'.[3]

In the same way the sad, if not tragic, figure of the bereaved Demeter, 'the *mater dolorosa* of the Greeks', in Pater's phrase,[4] is never directly shown in the opera but is left in the less affecting, less effective perspective of narrative report. Thanks to the narcissus Persephone has carried with her to the underworld she can see the wintry earth where her mother 'errante et de haillons vêtue' seeks despairingly for her lost daughter. But the audience never sees her.

The figure of Demophoon–Triptolemus undergoes a similar simplification. Indeed, the 'patron of the plough', as Pater calls him, who plays his part, it is believed, in the Eleusinian mysteries is reduced here to the mute, ritual role of Persephone's earthly bridegroom whose agricultural labours release her from the underworld. Certainly Persephone glimpses her mother's experiment with the child, Demophoon, whom she hopes to immortalize through fire. Watching the events of earth from the underworld Persephone says:

> Au-dessus d'un berceau de tisons et de flammes
> Je vois... Je vois vers lui Déméter se pencher.

[1] Gide uses both names for the goddess without attaching any special significance to them. Her mother also appears as Demeter or as the Roman Ceres.

[2] Walter Pater, 'The Myth of Demeter and Persephone', *Greek Studies*, 2nd ed., London, Macmillan, 1901, p. 143. (Two lectures given in 1875, published in the *Fortnightly Review*, January–February, 1876.)

[3] *Pers.*, p. 327.   [4] *Greek Studies*, p. 144.

and Eumolphe points the moral:

> Au destin des humains penses-tu l'arracher,
> Déesse? D'un mortel tu voudrais faire un dieu.[1]

But in the myth Demeter's attempt to purge the child of human weaknesses is unfortunately interrupted. Gide himself is to retell the story of the interrupted and imperfect experiment in his prologue to his *Retour de l'U.R.R.S.* in 1936; but in the opera we are led to believe that the ordeal by fire is successful since the child 'prospère et sourit à la vie' until he reaches perfect manhood, and total abstraction.

The operatic text is a simplified version of one of the oldest and richest of myths. (It is, of course, unfair to judge the text without Stravinsky's music but since Gide published it alone it must be included in his dramatic works.) Its action is confined to three continuous tableaux: Persephone's descent to the under-world; her sojourn among the shades in the *Champs Élysées*; her release into the upper world thanks to Triptolemus' labours, her betrothal to him; and her departure for the world of shades again. It allows the inclusion of three choral groups of women and children; it requires the personage of Eumolpe as Presenter and as commentator; and its only dramatic interest lies in the spoken role of Persephone.

Persephone's choice to be made between the two worlds is legendary but the motives provided here for her choice are Gide's alone. She is governed by her feelings and she acts by her own free will. This is no story of rape and release but rather of the oscillation between the desire for joy and sunlight and the strong movement of compassion that draws her to the world peopled by shades. 'Radieux Triptolème' calls her to the earth but 'ténébreux Pluton' offers her the opportunity to console the unhappy shades. As Eumolpe interprets her first movement towards the dark world:

> Déjà ta pitié te fiance
> A Pluton, le roi des Enfers.
> Tu descendras vers lui pour consoler les ombres . . .;[2]

---

[1] *Pers.*, p. 321.   [2] Ibid., p. 313.

so he explains her return:

> Ton lot est d'apporter aux ombres
> Un peu de la clarté du jour,
> Un répit à leurs maux sans nombre,
> A leur détresse un peu d'amour.[1]

Pity is a new explanation for Persephone's descent into Hades, but so too is her reason for desiring to return to earth. Gide suppresses the intervention of Zeus in her release, replacing it partly by Triptolemus' human, if superhuman, efforts partly by the pomegranate offered to her by the mute dancer, Mercury. For the pomegranate Persephone tastes should guarantee her return to Hades, but in Gide's version it revives her desire for the earth and incites her to watch, through the magic narcissus that now reveals the earth as it had previously revealed the underworld, her mother's search and the fostering of Triptolemus. Gide is therefore reversing the symbolic use of the pomegranate as he doubles the symbolic direction of the narcissus. The latter leads both away from and back to the earth, but the taste of the pomegranate restores the taste for earth's physical pleasures only. Gide uses it in the same sense elsewhere: in the epigraph to the 'Ronde de la Grenade', for instance, which, if traditionally interpreted, would contradict the poem's meaning: 'Certes trois grains de grenade suffirent à faire s'en souvenir Proserpine';[2] and again in *Le Retour de l'Enfant prodigue*.[3] Even in this lyrical little work chiefly concerned with 'le monde ombrageux où . . . l'on souffre' the sensuous pleasures of the earth should not be forgotten.

The re-presented myth clearly carries a second meaning which demands the special attention of allegory. It is probable that Gide, in adopting the allegorical approach to his earlier poetic subject, was influenced by Walter Pater (whose *Greek Studies* he read with great admiration in 1922 and with equal enthusiasm in 1930), who analyses the three evolutionary phases through which the myth may pass. Pater remarks on the 'half-conscious, instinctive, or mystical phase' of 'unwritten legend' which contains 'primitive impressions of the phenomena of the natural world'. This is

---

[1] Ibid., p. 327. [2] *Les Nourritures terrestres*, O.C. ii. 126.
[3] O.C. v. 25.

followed by the 'conscious, poetical or literary, phase' in which
the poets fix the outlines of popular material and simplify or
develop its situations (Gide's 'Proserpine' fragment might possible
be considered here). But Gide's *Perséphone* more deliberately
aspires to the third and 'ethical phase in which', as Pater writes,
'the persons and the incidents of the poetical narrative are realised
as abstract symbols, because intensely characteristic examples, of
moral and spiritual conditions'.[1]

The allegorical meaning of the opera has generally been accepted
as the expression of Gide's interest in Communism which arose
and fell in the 1930's, although critics differ as to the degree of
social conscience Gide demonstrates. One, for example, considers
that the opera holds 'rien de nouveau dans la pensée de Gide: tout
au plus un vague geste esquissé du côté de la "misère" '.[2] Another
judges the Prosperpine theme as 'vehicle for a wholly social
preoccupation that never entered [Gide's] mind in the years
before the First World War'; *Perséphone* was thus written 'at the
height of his fervor for Communism, not many months after he
had proclaimed that he would willingly give his life "to ensure the
success of the USSR" '.[3] This reading of the opera text can be
supported in various ways. Gide's social application is indeed so
deliberately sought that it produces Persephone's curious declaration that in returning to the world of the dead, of the suffering
immortal shades, she wishes to descend 'jusqu'au fond de la
détresse humaine'. More important than such a slip is its similarity
in subject and its proximity in time with the prologue to *Retour
de l'U.R.R.S.*, where Demeter's attempt to immortalize Demophoon is told in some detail. The operatic figure who grew from
child to represent human labour now illustrates an abortive
social experiment in Gide's opinion: 'J'imagine la grande Déméter
penchée, comme sur l'humanité future, sur ce nourrisson radieux',
Gide writes. 'Il supporte l'ardeur des charbons, et cette épreuve
le fortifie. En lui, je ne sais quoi de surhumain se prépare, de
robuste et et d'inespérément glorieux. Ah! que ne put Déméter

[1] *Greek Studies*, p. 91.   [2] Brée, *André Gide*, p. 324.
[3] J. O'Brien, *Portrait of André Gide*, a critical biography, London, Secker and
Warburg, 1953, pp. 316–17.

poursuivre jusqu'au bout sa tentative hardie et mener à bien son
défi! Mais Métaneire inquiète, . . . faussement guidée par une
maternelle crainte, repoussa la déesse et tout le surhumain qui se
forgeait, écarta les braises et, pour sauver l'enfant, perdit le dieu.'[1]
Finally and more significantly still, Gide's concept of Communism
and the identification of its system with the teachings of Christ
which for a time he made, shape his expression of the myth and
reveal his conscious inner meaning. The closing verses of the opera
directly echo the Gospel according to St. John:[2]

> Il faut, pour qu'un printemps renaisse
> Que le grain consente à mourir
> Sous terre, afin qu'il reparaisse
> En moisson d'or pour l'avenir.

Much later, in a discussion of the New Testament, Gide clarifies
his earlier expectations of Communism and its deceptive suggestions of creating a Christ-like society. He writes in 1946 of the
Gospels as a text 'qui contient meilleur conseil qu'aucun autre
livre au monde. Et même j'ai dû vite comprendre que tout ce que
je cherchais naguère dans le communisme (en vain, car [là] où
j'espérais trouver de l'amour, je n'ai trouvé que de la théorie),
c'était ce que le Christ nous enseigne, nous enseigne avec tout le
reste en surplus.'[3]

Perséphone may seem too slight a literary work to merit so
detailed an examination; a recent writer assigns it to 'the world of
Dresden shepherdesses not to that of Dionysus'.[4] Nevertheless
it takes its place in Gide's own *œuvre* and possesses, despite the
exceptional medium, much that is characteristic of him: familiar
symbols of the narcissus, the pomegranate, and the 'grain'; a
central figure who acts affirmatively as other Gidian heroes do
and, as has been noted, 'accepte jusqu'au bout son destin, . . .
parachève son geste';[5] a plot without Zeus; and an interpretation

---

[1] *Retour de l'U.R.R.S.*, Paris, Gallimard, 1936, pp. 9–10.
[2] Ch. XII. 24.
[3] *Deux Interviews imaginaires* [Paris] Charlot [1946], pp. 25–26.
[4] Leo Aylen, *Greek Tragedy and the Modern World*, London, Methuen, 1964, p. 265.
[5] Brée, *André Gide*, p. 324.

of the myth that expresses Gide's particular and current pre-occupations.

There are obvious suggestions in the earlier and far more ambitious *Œdipe* that herald the controllingi dea of *Perséphone*. The pity that motivates the goddess is already present in the Theban princess whose decision to enter the life of contemplative religion is made in order to intercede for the sick and unhappy people of her father's city; the love that Persephone feels for the shades is a more general, more dispersed and vague form of the love for her blinded and helpless father that impels Antigone to dedicate her life to caring for him and so to heed, as she says, 'le seul enseignement de ma raison et de mon cœur'.[1] Oedipus himself professes a love for humanity when, on hearing the prophecy that the land of his burial will be blessed, he refuses to confine that privilege to his own Theban folk. He replies to the self-interested Chorus that strangers may as well benefit from his death as Thebans: 'Quels qu'ils soient, ce sont des hommes. Au prix de ma souffrance, il m'est doux de leur apporter du bonheur.'[2] This declaration and the whole character of Antigone link *Œdipe* to the later operatic text.

Gide's interest in the Sophoclean *Oedipus* was long standing. As early as about 1911 he joined *Oedipus* with *Prometheus* as the most solemn drama bequeathed by antiquity.[3] Since he had already reworked the one it is not surprising that he should be drawn to the other great myth for reasons, as we shall see, that were not confined to its acknowledged supremacy. His own *Œdipe* had a long gestatory period. Indeed self-mockery caused him to write in 1930 of '[les] lenteurs de végétation de mon *Œdipe*'.[4] He discussed it so often in its projected form that we are able to trace the modification of his intention as he actually worked on the given legend. In 1920, as his friend Roger Martin du Gard reports, Gide had a clear idea of the interpretation he would give to Oedipus' crucial situation. He was to be an 'Œdipe rayonnant, fier de sa réussite, actif, ignorant tout souci: un Œdipe "gœ-théen"'. And he was to be ousted from his happiness by a

---

[1] *Œd.*, pp. 302–3.   [2] Ibid., p. 304.
[3] *Journal*, p. 342, Feuillets (after 1911).   [4] Ibid., p. 1000, 29 juillet 1930.

Christian Tiresias. At this stage Gide explained the reversal of Oedipus' fortunes as entirely due to the influence of Christian morality on a happy life. His theme was to lie in the fact that *l'optique chrétienne aurait remplacé l'optique païenne*. This is the familiar opposition of Christian morality and pagan: its dramatic use was to prove that the situation which produced happiness became, when seen by other eyes, both immoral and untenable. Gide's idea was indeed so positive that he declared that nothing in Oedipus' situation changes except the new light thrown upon it by the priest, Tiresias. When he continued, 'Et puis, sans qu'aucun événement nouveau ne se produise . . .' even such a devoted friend as Roger Martin du Gard could not fail to comment, 'Aucun événement? Il apprend qu'il a tué son père, épousé sa mère, etc. ... Peu de choses, en effet!'[1]

The change in attitude as a principal element in Oedipus' fortunes is a persistent Gidian idea. As he notes elsewhere, the reversal of Oedipus' situation should undoubtedly come about through this changed viewpoint: 'Simple changement d'éclairage sur les conditions mêmes de son bonheur. Les raisons de sa félicité vont devenir une occasion de calamité.'[2] And, although the emphasis of the final work has altered, Gide expresses the same idea when his Oedipus is forced to reconsider his murder of the stranger who, he now fears, was his father: 'Mais à présent je ne me reconnais plus dans mes actes. Il en est un, sanglant, pourtant bien né de moi, que je voudrais désavouer... tant il a changé de visage. Ou du moins mon regard a changé; et tout m'apparaît différent.'[3]

The conception of his *Œdipe* haunted Gide's mind but he delayed in defining it. In 1927 he writes: 'J'ai raconté la pièce à Martin du Gard. J'aurais mieux fait de l'écrire.'[4] The *Journal* entries of 1927 show how constantly he contemplated the subject; the suggested titles indicate his floating ideas for its orientation. His first proposal is for a 'Nouvel Œdipe' (a retelling such as in *Le Prométhée*?) which would need to be accompanied by a 'Dialogue

[1] Martin du Gard, *Notes sur A.G.*, pp. 21–22.
[2] Fonds Gide, Bibliothèque littéraire J. Doucet, MS. γ 906, p.9.
[3] *Œd.*, p. 296.   [4] *Journal*, p. 837, 7 mai 1927.

avec Dieu'.[1] The next, 'Œdipe, ou le triomphe de la morale', would
have been most proper for the plan he outlines to Roger Martin
du Gard.[2] 'La Conversion d'Œdipe' follows as a possible title for
the play which was to end with Oedipus' entry into the 'palais
de la foi'.[3] But we are not shown such an Oedipus until he comes
into the experience of *Thésée* nearly twenty years later. In the end,
Gide settled for the traditional and non-committal title of *Œdipe*,
shorn of his kingly rank, after a period of actual writing that
lasted from the 17th of June 1929 to the 9th of November 1930.
On this day he records with some satisfaction: 'Je crois bien avoir
achevé *Œdipe*; et je crois l'avoir bien achevé. C'est-à-dire que
j'ai fait entrer à peu près tout ce que je m'étais proposé d'y mettre.'[4]

The work as completed had undergone many changes. The
antagonism between the conventional religious point of view and
heroic humanism remains but it is complicated by other, equally
important themes. The conclusion foreseen by Gide in his early
description had been one of essential defeats: Oedipus was to welcome his blindness as an escape from his ruined happiness: 'entrer
dans cette nuit, peuplée de souvenirs heureux, qui seule peut lui
rendre sa vision optimiste du monde, et le goût de vivre.'[5] This
is not the state of mind of Gide's dramatic figure as he ultimately
presents him.

Once published and performed Gide's *Œdipe* continued to
concern him. He seemed as anxious about its interpretation as he
had been about the proper understanding of his earlier *Saül*; his
Journal entries return to it again and again. *Œdipe* was a work that
he felt profoundly compelled to write,[6] and once written equally
compelled to explain and defend. He defines its theme, for instance, as being the struggle between individualism and submission
to religious authority rather than, as some thought it, the opposition of free-will and predestination. The latter impression is

---

[1] *Journal*, p. 833, 7 mars 1927.   [2] Ibid., p. 837, 7 mai 1927.
[3] Ibid., p. 840, 10 mai 1927; p. 837, 7 mai 1927.
[4] Ibid., p. 1016, 9 novembre 1930. Éditions de la Pléiade, 1931, produced by
G. Pitoëff, Antwerp, 10 December 1931, and elsewhere; Paris, 18 February
1932.
[5] Martin du Gard, *Notes sur A.G.*, p. 22.
[6] *Journal*, p. 978, 31 mars 1930.

possible, he concedes, but while it describes a problem that concerned him in his youth he no longer considers it important, either for himself or for the time. The conflict that he chooses to present, between individualism and authority, is on the contrary of the greatest immediacy and general interest: 'ces problèmes sont étroitement, inextricablement liés', he writes. 'N'importe: on peut ne plus s'inquiéter du déterminisme (soit qu'on l'accepte, soit qu'on le nie), le drame reste pourtant le même et l'opposition entre le perspicace antimystique et le croyant; entre l'aveugle par foi et celui qui cherche à répondre à l'énigme; entre celui qui se soumet à Dieu et celui qui oppose à Dieu l'Homme.'[1]

It is certainly true that the theme of predestination runs through the play. It can hardly fail to do so in the story of Oedipus, trapped by his inescapable fate. The Gidian Oedipus recognizes the trap he has fallen into: 'Crime imposé par Dieu, embusqué par Lui sur ma route. Dès avant que je fusse né, le piège était tendu, pour que j'y dusse trébucher. Car, ou ton oracle mentait', he says to Tiresias, 'ou je ne pouvais pas me sauver. J'étais traqué.'[2] But he goes on to claim freedom of action when he blinds himself. He acts, as indeed we must all continue to do, as if he is free to choose his own action. Whether freedom is illusory or not does not matter to the man whose only criterion is his own desire: 'Sans doute cette offrande de moi était-elle prévue, elle aussi', he says, 'de sorte que je ne pusse pas m'y soustraire. N'importe! C'est volontiers que je m'immole.'[3] As Gide treats this aspect of the situation he has it as it were both ways: freedom within predeterminism. And since these abstractions are personified in the figures of Oedipus and the high priest, Tiresias, where personal antagonism supports the clash of ideas, the chief thematic conflict undoubtedly takes places between 'le perspicace antimystique et le croyant', as Gide claims. Oedipus' contemptuous dismissal of the credulous populace: 'Le peuple préfère toujours à l'explication naturalle l'interprétation mystique: rien à faire à cela',[4] echoes Gide's earlier dismissal of the untreatable subjects of Orestes and a divinely led or lunatic Ajax: 'Rien à faire.'

---

[1] Ibid., pp. 1106-7, 22 janvier 1932. [2] Œd., p. 295.
[3] Ibid., p. 301. [4] Ibid., p. 261.

Oedipus therefore embodies that part of Gide's thought which opposes Christian dogma. He is an example of the 'sacrifice du meilleur', as Gide describes the action of his third act, the sacrifice of the strong to the weak for which he reproaches Christianity. But he continues in a way that seems curiously orthodox: 'Mais c'est dans ce don de soi, cet holocauste, que lui-même s'affirme le mieux et se prouve son excellence. Cette abnégation qui accompagne toute noblesse, ce ruineux besoin de se sacrifier à ce qui ne vous vaut pas.'[1] We are entitled to ask, nevertheless, to whom the Sophoclean Oedipus sacrifices himself. The implacable forces which pursue him leave him very little choice and the triumphant weakling can hardly be seen in Creon. The Gidian Creon, the pompous conformist, and Tiresias are clearly his butts in his own version.

What Gide does not consider in his many discussions is the play's contemplation of human happiness. For the word happiness is on Oedipus' lips as often as on King Candaules'. His introductory monologue declares his satisfaction in the attainment of it: 'Par la force de mes poignets, j'atteins au sommet du bonheur', he announces.[2] Candaules in his turn exclaims on his first appearance: 'O plénitude de mon bonheur!' And the Chorus points out Oedipus' overstatement, as the courtiers had noted it in Candaules': 'Que toi, tu sois heureux', they say, 'encore que tu le dises un peu trop, nul n'en doute. Mais nous ne sommes pas heureux, nous, ton peuple, ô Œdipe.'[3] He is thus in the same initial situation of confident happiness as Candaules, the more content since he has achieved it by his efforts: 'Le bonheur ne me fut pas donné; je l'ai conquis.'[2] But where the earlier plot concerned the king's risking and losing his happiness and his life, Oedipus' experience is that of voluntary destruction of his personal happiness in the search for the true situation it has successfully masked for him for twenty years. Where *Le Roi Candaule* established by its examples of failure and success the thought that happiness can only be possessed and held in secrecy, Oedipus despises a happiness that needs protection, that thrives in privacy and the dark, and that cannot

---

[1] *Journal*, p. 1006, 10 août 1930.   [2] *Œd.*, p. 253.
[3] Ibid., p. 255.

stand the disclosure of truth and the light of public day. When
he is on the verge of discovery (characteristically enough without
the help of messenger or shepherd) Jocasta makes one last appeal
for restraint and prudence: 'N'auras-tu pas pitié de ton bonheur?'
Oedipus defines his own concept of happiness in replying: 'Pitié
de rien. Un bonheur fait d'erreur et d'ignorance, je n'en veux pas.
Bon pour le peuple! Pour moi, je n'ai pas besoin d'être heureux.
C'en est fait! Toute la nuée de cet enchantement doré se déchire.'[1]
While the early play demonstrated the simple substitution of one
man for another in the position of happiness, *Œdipe* examines the
foundation of happiness itself and if it is not based on awareness
and truth it is judged to be not worth the holding. This decision,
too, is made without reference to the point of view of religious
orthodoxy, as Tiresias expresses it. For Tiresias is, on the one hand,
ready to accept the inequalities of individual fortune as God's
will: 'Entre la prospérité de quelques-un et la misère du plus grand
nombre, Dieu tisse un lien mystérieux', he says;[2] and, on the other,
ready to deny the desirability of any earthly happiness at all.
When Oedipus extends his blessing to the men of the future,
Tiresias' last sanctimonious words are: 'Ce n'est pas leur bonheur
qu'il faut vouloir, mais leur salut.'[3]

Yet Oedipus, who has known great happiness, who judges it
to be wrong once he finds it to be based on falsehood and so
voluntarily destroys it, passes beyond to what may seem another
form of happiness. For in the end he is governed by the attitude
Gide had expressed so much earlier: 'Est-ce jamais le bonheur que
nous cherchons? Non; mais le libre jeu de ce qui est le plus neuf en
nous-mêmes.'[4] In one sense Oedipus may be trapped by his destiny;
in another, he has been trapped by his long period of tranquil
happiness. There is a feeling of relaxation and relief that comes
after his self-blinding when he says: 'J'étais parvenu à ce point que
je ne pouvais plus dépasser qu'en prenant élan contre moi-même';[5]
a feeling which is confirmed when he sets off once again to an
unknown destination. When Antigone asks him where she is to
lead him, he says, echoing his earlier pleasure in leaving Polybus,

[1] Ibid., p. 293. [2] Ibid., p. 259. [3] Ibid., p. 304.
[4] *Journal*, p. 155, 16 mai 1905. [5] *Œd.*, p. 301.

the kingdom of Corinth and its responsibility which is no longer
his, 'Je ne sais. Droit devant moi... Désormais sans foyer, sans
patrie...'.[1] What should be a scene of desolating exile becomes
within its immediate pathetic context and within the contextual
meaning of the whole play a scene of welcome liberation from
yet another burdensome past.

For this Oedipus is the Gidian hero who, as it were, subsumes his
predecessors. There is so much in his nature and his opinions
that is already familiar in Gide's work. The myth, of course,
provides the ambivalence in Oedipus' origins, his apparently
orphaned state, his self-imposed exile from the kingdom of
Corinth, and the terrible discovery of his real parentage. Gide uses
the triple disinheritance of Oedipus to express his characteristic
view of the independence of the individual and exceptional
man. (For women are never free—if we except the special case
of Alissa in *La Porte étroite*—and are, on the contrary, forces of
retardation, as Oedipus realizes in Jocasta who pulled him back,
or are themselves motivated by the desire to return to the past.)
But the hero should be free and rejoice in his condition, as Oedipus does in his outcast childhood: 'Enfant perdu, trouvé, sans état
civil, sans papiers, je suis surtout heureux de ne devoir rien qu'à
moi-même.'[2] Again, when Oedipus recalls the ostracism of his
childhood to Creon, that mouthpiece of convention, he counters
the description of bastard by a catalogue of the privileges of the
bastard's state. Not only does the child without a father escape
from the ties of family (as in *Les Nourritures terrestres*, Bernard of
Les Faux-Monnayeurs, Lafcadio of *Les Caves du Vatican*) but he is
freed from the demands made by his circumstances, by his *cul-
ture*: 'Personne à qui ressembler, que moi-même' as he says
triumphantly to Creon. 'Que m'importe, dès lors, si je suis ou
Grec ou Lorrain? O Créon! si soumis, si conforme à tout, comment comprendrais-tu la beauté de cette exigence? C'est un appel
à la vaillance, que de ne connaître point ses parents.'[3]

At this moment of confounding the unfortunate Creon with his
concept of life as a challenge to which only the full man can reply,
Gide returns to an idea of over thirty years before, expressed in a

---

[1] *Œd.*, p. 303.   [2] Ibid., p. 253.   [3] Ibid., p. 272.

literary debate with Maurice Barrès. Gide's three articles were grouped under the title of *Autour de M. Barrès* but it is the first, 'A propos des "Déracinés" ' (published in *L'Ermitage* of December 1897) which is particularly drawn on so much later. In it Gide emphasizes his idea that 'le déracinement peut être une école de vertu',[1] a hard school in which only the strong can prosper. The weak, and the women, must stay where they are: 'Aux faibles l'enracinement, l'encroûtement dans les habitudes héréditaires qui les empêcheront d'avoir froid.'[2] The old clash of ideas is personified in Oedipus and Creon: Creon, who is above all 'conservateur', as he says; whose character is to respect tradition, customs, and established law; whose role in society is to represent 'cette force d'inertie et de cramponnement', which is needed to restrain the daring of Oedipus' 'esprit novateur';[3] and whose function is to provide 'interim' government in moments of disaster. His dramatic function, caricature as he is made, is to throw into relief the totally contrasted and wholly admirable ideas of Oedipus who accepts life's challenges and thrives on uprootings. Oedipus, in fact, embodies Gide's early concept of the man, strong in spirit as he must be in body, who can be judged by his adaptability. As Gide writes in 1897: 'Et peut-être pourrait-on mesurer la valeur d'un homme au degré de dépaysement (physique ou intellectuel) qu'il est capable de maîtriser. — Oui, dépaysement; ce qui exige de l'homme une gymnastique d'adaptation, un rétablissement sur du neuf: voilà l'éducation que réclame l'homme fort, — dangereuse il est vrai, éprouvante; c'est une lutte contre *l'étranger*; mais il n'y a éducation que dès que l'instruction modifie. — Quant aux faibles: enracinez! enracinez!'[2]

The myth thus provides two figures whose contrast naturally illustrates this early theory of 'instruction, dépaysement, déracinement',[2] and adds yet another basic opposition in the complexity of themes woven into the plot. As Tiresias represents organized religion and its attempt to control man through his fear and suffering: 'Dans la crainte de Dieu gît mon pouvoir', as he says; as Jocasta represents the restraining power of family and also of

---

[1] O.C. ii. 440.   [2] Ibid., p. 442.   [3] *Œd.*, p. 269.

sexual love; so Creon incarnates the conservative restraints of
society on its members. And against them all Oedipus asserts the
value of the individual man. As he explains to his sons, the only
password in the dangerous situations of life, whether external as
in his own encounter with the Sphinx or in crises of mental
conflict that may hinder development, is 'Man'. His advice to
his sons, using mythological matter yet again to express subjective
experience, carries his creator's central message: 'Car, comprenez
bien, mes petits, que chacun de nous, adolescent, rencontre, au
début de sa course, un monstre qui dresse devant lui telle énigme
qui nous puisse empêcher d'avancer. Et, bien qu'à chacun de nous,
mes enfants, ce sphinx particulier pose une question différente,
persuadez-vous qu'à chacune de ses questions la réponse reste
pareille; oui, qu'il n'y a qu'une seule et même réponse à de si
diverses questions; et que cette réponse unique, c'est: l'Homme;
et que cet homme unique, pour un chacun de nous, c'est: Soi.'[1]
It is a far more articulate expression of the attitude which caused
Prometheus to eat his eagle and Philoctetes to set, however
tentatively, the self above the gods.

But then Oedipus himself is more articulate than any of the
preceding myth-based heroes. He may see himself as simple and as
straight as an arrow, as a man governed by intuition and not
logical thought, as, in fact, a man of action not of words: he is
nevertheless a great debater, ever-ready to thrash out a point of
difference with Tiresias, Creon, or his two sons. He is over-ready,
indeed, to plunge into argument, never at a loss for a telling
point. The outstanding example of this occurs, of course, at the
climax of the action when Jocasta has taken her life and Oedipus
gouged out his eyes off stage then returns on stage to continue,
after a brief touching exchange with Antigone, the unending
controversy with Tiresias: 'A présent que me voici plus calme et
que s'apaise ma douleur avec mon irritation contre moi, je puis
discuter avec toi, Tirésias,' he says. 'J'admire que cette proposition
de repentance vienne de toi.'[2]

That the blinded Oedipus, blood on his cheeks, his intellectual
powder kept dry, should be able to renew his running debate

[1] Œd., pp. 283–4.   [2] Ibid., p. 301.

with Tiresias is shocking to our expectations formed by Sophocles. But Gide protects himself from such a comparison by declaring that he has quite other intentions for his *Œdipe*: 'vous avez la pièce de Sophocle', he writes in his *Journal*, 'et je ne me pose pas en rival; je lui laisse le pathétique . . . c'est à votre intelligence que je m'adresse. Je me propose, non de vous faire frémir ou pleurer, mais de vous faire réfléchir.'[1] The myth contains, as he believes, a meaning for the twentieth century that an earlier age would not have perceived: and he, as man of his own age, has the right to present his own reading of it: 'mais voici ce que lui, Sophocle, n'a pas su voir et comprendre et qu'offrait pourtant son sujet; et que je comprends, non parce que je suis plus intelligent, mais parce que je suis d'une autre époque.'[1] In this idea of the continual reinterpretation of the myth, Gide touches on the mystery of its perennial attraction. If each age demands its own translation of the classics, each age may make its own interpretation of the mythologem. Jean Cocteau, in his Preface to his own *Œdipe-Roi* and his *Roméo et Juliette*, makes this claim for the modern author. His method of using the myth, as he writes, is 'de retendre un vieux chef-d'œuvre, le dérider, déblayer ses matières mortes, enlever la patine qui donne le change à la longue sur une œuvre médiocre mais n'ajoute rien aux chefs-d'œuvre, quoi qu'on en dise', and Cocteau goes on to claim that he has set both his *Œdipe* and his *Antigone* 'au rythme de notre époque'.[2] It is perhaps on account of their awareness of changing tastes and ideas that the modern authors distinguish themselves from their predecessors who similarly made use of the ancient myths. Where the earlier writers modified their given matter they did so without discussion. When the twentieth-century writer appears to be deliberately conforming to the taste of his age, he takes care also to express his personal point of view. Gide, for instance, declares that he now wishes to expose 'l'envers du décor' of Oedipus' story, even if such a view diminishes the emotional impact.[1] But the new light thrown on the Theban palace is familiar to us; it has already been projected on Prometheus and Philoctetes.

[1] *Journal*, p. 1151, 2 janvier 1933.
[2] J. Cocteau, *Œdipe-Roi*, Paris, Plon, 1928, pp. 1–2.

Gide returns over and over again to this treatment of the myth in his *Journal* entries; he seems often on the defensive, even in his solitude. For when Roger Martin du Gard, to whom he had told his original plan, criticizes the play for its 'peu d'ampleur et de développement', Gide hastens to thank him for his frank letter but confides in his *Journal* that the play satisfies him personally: 'j'accueille très volontiers les critiques', he writes; 'mais, décidément, celles de Roger ne m'apparaissent pas bien fondées. Tel qu'il est, je crois que mon drame est ce qu'il devait être et ce que je voulais qu'il soit (qu'il *soit*, non qu'il *fût*). Il répond à mon exigence; me satisfait. Une fin plus ample l'eut déséquilibré.'[1] But the criticism was levelled at the whole play, not only its end, and it would seem a valid comment. Gide recognizes that the austerity of his method, deliberately adopted in order to focus all attention on the conflict of ideas which provides its chief interest,[2] runs certain risks. He describes it as a voluntary suppression of 'les résonances amplificatrices',[1] by which, presumably, he means not only the deliberately flat expression but also the universalizing comments of the Chorus. He supplies no indications of scene or staging and makes little or no use of dramatic spectacle (even so Oedipus *must* return to the stage mutilated). The original production of the Pitoëffs was set with curtains and drapes on a bare stage with only lighting effects to help the actors to create the dramatic illusion.[3] A later production, which pleased Gide, represented the play's anachronisms physically by the columns of a Greek temple placed against a backdrop of Notre Dame de Paris, and by the mixture of tragic and modern costumes: 'L'illusion scénique, dès lors, était nulle', Gide notes with satisfaction; 'mais ma volonté de ne point chercher à l'obtenir devenait du coup évidente.'[2]

With no scenic illusion, no spectacle, very little physical movement, 'le combat des idées' that Gide intended as the whole dramatic experience must carry the weight of the performance. And whether it can is open to question. Certainly the character of Oedipus himself, his formulation of a personal philosophy,

[1] *Journal*, p. 1030, 5 février 1931.   [2] Ibid., p. 1129, juin 1932.
[3] R. Derche, *Quatre Mythes poétiques*, p. 53.

the oppositions into which he is thrown, hold our attention. But surely the episode of his sons, Polynices and Eteocles, those far from admirable versions of the Dioscuri twins, is over-contrived and indeed simply a means of filling out the action without extending or advancing it. They may show, in their incestuous desires for their sisters, a transposition of the incest theme which is integral to the Oedipus myth, as one writer suggests,[1] thus providing concrete examples of hereditary taint; but the same discussion may alternatively be thought a somewhat perverse variation playing over the tragic subject. Admittedly their readiness to quarrel over their sister, Ismene, forecasts their future war; again, each in turn echoes his father's opinions, Eteocles with his belief that the only remaining monsters are subjective, Polynices with his faith in heroes rather than in gods, and so stresses those Gidian views by reiteration; and their delinquent attitudes authorize Oedipus to deliver them a long and unusually grave disquisition on the future of men and the value of Man. They are, however, neither interesting in themselves nor essential to the action.

Martin du Gard's critical opinion of the 'peu d'ampleur et de développement' has thus much to be said for it. And Gide himself feared as much. He first questions the effect of his matter-of-fact prose: 'Ma volontaire exclusion de toute image, de toute amplification oratoire ne devait-elle pas nécessairement aboutir à ce rétrécissement? Je ne sais si je dois le regretter.'[2] But such a stylistic limitation need not prove a handicap to an author. We need only remember what can be done with impassioned prose and non-metaphoric poetry to realize that the weakness may lie elsewhere. And Gide conscientiously and anxiously returns to the subject. In an afterthought, added as a footnote, he admits honestly: 'Je crois pourtant que j'aurais pu, dans le IIIe acte, me laisser aller davantage. Sans doute ma raison intervient-elle trop. Rien qui n'y soit voulu, motivé, nécessaire. Ce que j'appelais jadis "la part de Dieu", réduite à rien, par inconfiance, incroyance en l'inspiration, qui me fait ne plus oser écrire que la tête froide. Il faudrait accepter d'écrire sans plus trop savoir ce que l'on dit, ni surtout ce que

[1] Ibid., p. 57.   [2] *Journal*, p. 1030, 3 février 1931.

l'on va dire.'[1] It is, of course, fact that Gide did not approach the awe-inspiring myth of Oedipus until he was over sixty: thirty years separate it from *Saül* where he allowed his inspiration full sway. It is also fact that he was by then a figure of literary eminence with a reputation to maintain or increase, a situation which perhaps engenders caution. But there is also in the deliberate restraint of his version of Oedipus a suggestion of a fundamental temperamental deficiency that must be discussed later.

The other major criticism of *Œdipe* which Gide had to meet, the condemnation of its facetious style, left him quite impenitent. He might make allowance for the provincial audience of Antwerp and write an explanatory preface to the programme; he might regret the inclusion of that preface in the Paris programme, considering it redundant for a sophisticated audience; but if, as he records, 'Les plaisanteries d'*Œdipe* déplurent, en général, et rebutèrent même certains des mieux disposés',[2] he never allows public disapproval to affect his own opinion of decorum: 'Non, je n'ai pas à regretter les plaisanteries plus ou moins incongrues qui émaillent mon *Œdipe*',[2] he writes firmly; and he provides his own rationalization for their presence: 'Il y a, dans les plaisanteries, trivialités et incongruités du mien, comme un besoin constant d'avertir le public: vous avez la pièce de Sophocle et je ne me pose pas en rival.'[3]

That is, as far as it goes, perfectly true. Oedipus' opening monologue which reveals his own image of himself as the hearty, happy man of action sets a tone which is far removed from the tragic anxiety of the Sophoclean opening. His bluff colloquialisms, his irritation when Ismene faints on hearing her brother's recital of the city's horrors; his contempt for Tiresias' persistence which is designed to raise laughter: all are explicable in the character Gide presents, of a hero who is also capable of the greatest solemnity in delivering his advice to his erring sons on the value of Man. But the jarring effect of incongruous tone comes chiefly in Act III where the character of Creon, hitherto a pompous, well-meaning bore, becomes a caricature of himself. The revelation of Oedipus'

---

[1] *Journal*, p. 1030, 5 février 1931.   [2] Ibid., p. 1129, juin 1932.
[3] Ibid., p. 1151, 2 janvier 1933.

unconscious sins against nature is interspersed by the fatuous comments which pursue the trivial at the expense of the tragic. When Oedipus, on the verge of disclosure, says: 'Je veux d'abord descendre au plus bas du gouffre. Ce roi que j'ai tué, dis . . . Mais non; ne parle pas. Je comprends tout. J'étais son fils'; Creon finds nothing better to do than twitter: 'Ah! par exemple!... Comment! Qu'apprends-je? Ma sœur serait sa mère! Œdipe, à qui je m'attachais! Se peut-il rien imaginer de plus abominable? Ne plus savoir s'il est ou mon beau-frère ou mon neveu!'[1] The timing of Creon's interjections, both here at the moment of discovery and again at the time of Oedipus' exile when Creon, on learning of possible future benefits to be bestowed on the country where the king will die, is quite prepared to reconsider the verdict of exile: 'On pourra toujours s'arranger', is so manipulated that the trivial comments produce their maximum deflationary effect. They control the audience's response with skill; they destroy the developing emotional charge; they diminish the impact of the whole situation. Whether Gide's deliberate avoidance of rivalry with Sophocles is an adequate explanation of such incongruity of tone and mood is again something to consider later. It is hard at this point not to judge Gide's defence of such heterogeneity of tone as rationalization of the play, 'tel . . . qu'il *soit*'.

Whatever our total impression of *Œdipe* may be (and a modern critic describes it as a 'relatively dull' presentation of an essentially gripping experience[2]) there are some innovations that are worth noticing. There are technical devices which play their part in distancing the myth, in preventing the audience's total absorption in the experience by reminding them of the theatrical medium. When Oedipus steps forward to make his opening expository address he draws attention to his dramatic role and to the illusion engendered by drama: 'Me voici tout présent, complet en cet instant de la durée éternelle; pareil à quelqu'un qui s'avancerait sur le devant d'un théâtre et qui dirait: Je suis Œdipe.' The Chorus, too, defines its role: 'Nous, Chœur, qui avons pour mission particulière, en ce lieu, de représenter l'opinion du plus grand

[1] *Œd.*, p. 294.
[2] L. Aylen, *Greek Tragedy and the Modern World*, p. 266.

nombre, nous nous déclarons surpris et peinés par la profession d'une individualité si farouche.'[1] But so willing are we as audience to suspend disbelief that these introductory remarks are quickly absorbed into the play's action. However, we are never allowed total empathy, for even Jocasta steps out of her experience to point out earlier misreadings of the myth. When Oedipus realizes that, in order to fulfil the prophesied marriage with Jocasta that was to crown the victor of the Sphinx, the king Laius had still to be killed, that Jocasta, offered as a reward, was not at that moment free to remarry, she warns him: 'Mon ami, mon ami, n'attire pas l'attention là-dessus. Aucun historien ne l'a jusqu'à présent remarqué.'[2] Once again this dislocation of the dramatic illusion comes at a moment of rising intensity when Oedipus is about to identify himself with the king's murderer; the reminder of the given subject-matter thus shifts the perspective and jolts the growing emotion in much the same way as Creon's disruptive interjections. Such a double perspective, of the given plot and the present performers of it, seems a kind of Brechtian 'alienation' device *avant la lettre* and it plays its part in controlling the emotional impact of the whole work.

There is also the idea new to Gide, as we noted above, of the future freedom of humanity. Oedipus' declaration of individual value is familiar but his concern for the anonymous multitude, 'une humanité désasservie', is less so. More effective still is the presence of Antigone who, older than her Greek prototype, plays a Cordelia-like role to her degraded, ostracized father. In some ways she seems a fuller development of Neoptolemus and his tentative morality of love, and of those, like Saul, Candaules, and Gyges, who are controlled by their feelings; but in Antigone the love is filial, selfless, and full of compassion. Oedipus who so readily renounces his past and his surroundings is none the less thankful to commit himself to his daughter's guidance and care. So complete is his submission to Antigone that Malraux's comment, as Gide reports it, is to the point: 'Oui, me dit-il en riant, Œdipe échappe au Sphinx; mais c'est pour se laisser bouffer enfin par sa fille....'[3] Antigone and her dedicated human love in some

[1] *Œd.*, p. 254.   [2] Ibid., p. 292.   [3] *Journal*, p. 1021, 18 janvier 1931.

measure redeem the play's austerity; her religious attitude expresses itself in action in a way that is contrasted with the detachment, almost the malevolence of Tiresias. She is the embodiment
of human affection, and her final domination thus relates *Œdipe*
to the earlier plays, as it announces the concept of *Perséphone*.

Nevertheless she is but one element in a play preoccupied with
ideas rather than the experience of human suffering. Gide's concern with the 'combat des idées' is made manifest but it is hard to
decide what positive values he establishes. His antagonism to
organized religion is clear, his mockery of the convention-bound
equally clear; Oedipus' profession of faith in future humanity is
nebulous, his belief in the value of individual man and his self-
fulfilment is positive but undefined, while his own assertion of
total independence is contradicted by his ultimate reliance on his
daughter.

Œdipe and the later *Perséphone* are better seen as works of
transition than as wholly satisfactory ends in themselves; they are
too tentative and too general to express a definite philosophy.
And indeed Gide's thought was to move on to *Thésée*.

7

THE LAST HERO

Thésée was Gide's last important work of imagination. Between *Œdipe* (1931) and Gide's death in 1951 memoirs, criticism, works such as *Geneviève* (1936), *Le Treizième Arbre* (1942) appeared, but *Thésée* (1946) dominates them all both as personal document and as an artistic success. Gide describes it in his dedication as 'ce dernier écrit' and this is certainly how it should be regarded. According to Roger Martin du Gard, Gide's intention of treating the Cretan myth as his final subject was in his mind in 1938; as Gide's friend writes: 'De toutes les heures passées ensemble émerge pourtant un souvenir précis: l'émotion avec laquelle il m'a parlé, le dernier soir, de ce *Minos* qu'il veut écrire, et qui pourrait être le grand œuvre de sa vieillesse: un testament. Onze heures avaient sonné. Il s'était levé de son fauteuil, il arpentait fébrilement la pièce, dans un sursaut d'enthousiasme, avec un regard de visionnaire, transposant à sa façon, d'une voix inspirée, les grands mythes de l'antiquité, les légendes de Pasiphaé, de Déméter, de Thésée; il était intarissable.'[1]

But, as always, the project took time to mature and find its satisfactory form. As early as 1931, immediately after the completion of *Œdipe*, Gide had planned the confrontation of Oedipus and Theseus that was to provide so much later the culminating experience of his *Thésée*: 'Et j'imagine', he writes in his *Journal* of the 18th of January 1931, 'en manière d'épilogue, un dialogue entre Œdipe et Thésée. Je songe à une vie de Thésée (oh! j'y songe depuis longtemps) où se placerait ... une rencontre décisive des deux héros, se mesurant l'un à l'autre et éclairant, l'une à la faveur de l'autre, leurs deux vies.' He does not say just how long he has thought of a life of Theseus but the persistence of his

[1] Martin du Gard, *Notes sur A.G.* (1938), pp. 135–6.

interest and his many allusions to the Cretan episode at least date
from his youth. Theseus, in *Les Nourritures terrestres* (1897) plays
the role of the passionate pilgrim whom Ariadne cannot hold:

> Ariane, je suis le passager Thésée
> Qui vous abandonne à Bacchus
> Pour pouvoir continuer ma route.[1]

Pasiphaë's explanation of the birth of the Minotaur provides the
epilogue to *Le Prométhée mal enchaîné* (1899); and his references
to 'le fil à la patte', always related to Theseus' adventure in the
labyrinth of Cnossus, are frequent.

An account of Theseus' whole life would allow the inclusion
of youthful adventures as well as much else. And Gide continued
to record plans, some of which were carried out, for instance,
'Dédale et Icare' as a possible chapter of *Thésée* (a project of the
16th of September 1931), some of which were forgotten. In 1940
Gide proposed a treatment of Minos that never came to light.
Instead of the single figure of Minos that he ultimately presented
in an ironical fashion he considered a pair of brothers, like
Dioscuri of the underworld, who would provide subsidiary
conflict: 'Dans ma *Vie de Thésée*', he writes, 'Minos et Rhadamante, ces deux frères, les futurs juges des enfers, ne seraient
jamais du même avis sur personne. Éaque et Rhadamante, lorsqu'il
se serait agi de faire passer en jugement Pasiphaé, par délicatesse,
s'entendraient pour profiter d'une "absence" de Minos, et pour la
gracier.'[2] Presumably this incident was dropped in order to focus
all attention on Theseus himself. For the notes show an increasing
concentration on the central figure to whom the accumulating
related episodes may be attached. They also indicate the way in
which Gide's imagination worked, episodically and argumenta-
tively. Nevertheless they might well have remained in note form
had it not been for external circumstances.

For the creation of *Thésée* is more intimately connected with
Gide's physical situation than was ever the case before. It was
completed on the 21st of May 1944, in Algiers. Gide had passed
the war years partly in the South of France (1939–42) and partly

[1] O.C. ii. 134.   [2] *Journal 1939–1949*, p. 54, 9 septembre 1940.

in North Africa. The outbreak of war, the second in his adult life, therefore meant enforced displacement for the prophet of 'dépaysement' and it is hardly surprising that Theseus expresses a changed attitude to such uprooting when he finds himself in Crete and homesick: 'Je ne suis pas du tout cosmopolite', he declares. 'A la cour de Minos, pour la première fois, je compris que j'étais hellène, et me sentis dépaysé.'[1] Once safely returned to Athens, Theseus is content to remain there. Indeed Gide suppresses the legendary exile of Theseus in order to allow his hero to await his death quietly in his own city.

It is no more surprising that Gide's ideas of personal liberty should undergo alteration during the disastrous years for France, as we shall see later, although his estimation of the value of literature to himself and to others never faltered. In the dark days of September 1939 he consoled himself by committing to memory long passages of *Phèdre* and *Athalie*,[2] and, a fact of some relevance to his own creation of *Thésée*, he published 'Notes sur l'interprétation du rôle de "Phèdre" ' in 1942,[3] thus demonstrating his constant admiration for Racine and his continued interest in the Theseus myth. His opinion of the public function of literature and aesthetic criticism is shown by the foundation of *L'Arche* in 1944 in Algeria which was intended to replace the *Nouvelle Revue Française*, now suspected of collaboration. And the renewal of hope in a European future no doubt influenced the revival of creative energy which Gide experienced in 1944. As he observed so much earlier, there is a propitious moment in which the encounter with a new work meets the personal needs of the reader so that the work has an immediate and lasting impact on him; so, too, there may be a propitious period for creation when the rising enthusiasm of public opinion is paralleled by personal aspirations and conviction.

Be that as it may, Gide set to work on his long outstanding task in early 1944 and accomplished it with spontaneity and ease. Indeed he himself was astonished by his creative drive: 'Depuis un mois', he writes on the 21st of May 1944, 'j'y ai quotidiennement,

---

[1] *Thésée*, Paris, Gallimard, 1946, 68ᵉ éd., p. 40.
[2] *Journal 1939-1949*, p. 9, 11 septembre 1939.
[3] *Interviews imaginaires*, Paris, Gallimard, 1942.

et presque constamment, travaillé, dans un état de ferveur joyeuse que je ne connaissais plus depuis longtemps et pensais ne plus jamais connaître. Il me semblait être revenu au temps des *Caves* ou de mon *Prométhée*.'

But Gide was no longer thirty, nor even forty-five, he was in his seventy-sixth year and the upsurge of enthusiam that carried him through to the completion of *Thésée* left him exhausted. As he writes in June 1944: 'Sans trop d'impolitesse, je voudrais prendre congé de moi-même. Je me suis décidément assez **vu**.' The state of exhaustion persisted to such a degree that he writes on the 1st of December 1946: 'Je renonce avec une facilité déconcertante. Je renonce à tout et à n'importe quoi: plaisirs, voyages, gourmandises, et sans efforts, sans regrets. J'ai eu mon suffisant. "Au suivant de ces messieurs." Je me retire.' Everything confirms the impression that *Thésée* should count as Gide's last imaginative work, as his 'dernier écrit'. That position alone would justify the closest of attention for, as Simone de Beauvoir writes of a dying person's last wish, it sums up a life: 'C'est pourquoi sans doute on attache tant d'importance à la dernière volonté d'un mourant: elle n'est pas seulement une volonté parmi d'autres, mais c'est en elle que le mourant a ressaisi toute sa vie.'[1] Certainly in literature a writer's last work takes on a special meaning, *Samson Agonistes*, for instance, *The Tempest* and, particularly, *Oedipus at Colonus*, for Gide has drawn on the Sophoclean tragedy for the climatic meeting of Oedipus and Theseus. And *Thésée* is worthy of its position, for it carries within its apparent lightness and ease the final stages of Gide's thought. It codifies as it were earlier statements and incorporates them in a philosophy that, though it may seem pragmatic to some, does attempt to provide answers to the problems of living from a humanist point of view.

When Gide finally undertakes his 'Vie de Thésée' the autobiographical stance adopted offers him the most effective means of self-expression. It allows him to include all the projected scenes, providing they touch the hero's own life. They must be abandoned, like the Minos–Rhadamante episode, if they threaten distraction. Nevertheless, all the early plans share the common nature of

[1] Simone de Beauvoir, *Pyrrhus et Cinéas*, Paris, Gallimard, 1944, p. 122.

human opposition: Theseus set against Oedipus; Theseus resenting and escaping from the 'fil à la patte' and Ariadne; Minos and Rhadamante in intellectual conflict; the difference in character and behaviour in Daedalus and Icarus. Gide's imagination is set in motion by the clash between opposing opinions and attitudes. We need only recall the complex structure of oppositions that shapes and guides *Les Faux-Monnayeurs* (Bernard–Olivier, Édouard–Passavant, Bronja–Ghéridanisol, Laura–Lady Griffiths, etc.) to realize how characteristic this matter and this pattern, once again 'le combat des idées', are of his thought. Generally, he thinks dramatically and in dialogue; more particularly, he is inspired by antitheses rather than by syntheses. The single name of Proust is enough to throw into relief the alternative way in which Gide's imagination works. Solitude, self-analysis, prolonged meditation, an infinitely subtle pursuit of truth: all are alien to the Gidian Theseus. He moves through a series of encounters (for instance, in the Cretan phase of his story, with Pasiphaë, Ariadne, Daedalus, Icarus, pp. 43–77), and defines himself in his positive speech and actions.

Since Theseus himself tells the story of his life, a story which can no longer instruct his son, Hippolytus, as he had hoped, but may illuminate others, it is only natural that the events of a lifetime should seem episodic and self-oriented. What might appear perhaps an over-simple narration of more or less chronological incidents—the occasional forecasting, such as the death of Hippolytus or of Egeus, effectively suggests the spoken tale—is justifiable in the autobiographical method. The first-person narration thus protects the work from the possible charges of structural simplicity, thinness of plot, or of egocentricity. A man remembers the events and the people who have made him what he is.

By treating the whole lifetime of Theseus Gide considerably extends his early symbolic view of the hero of the labyrinth and the reluctant lover of Ariadne. To place Theseus in some sort of continuous narrative the whole Cretan adventure must be filled out and the Minotaur episode established in place and time. As indeed Theseus, the builder of a city, must similarly be established. Gide acknowledges his scholarly debt in the construction of his

fable: 'Je dois beaucoup aussi aux beaux livres de Charles Picard; à ceux de Glotz, d'une si sensible intelligence (pour ne parler que des modernes)';[1] but a critic makes other suggestions as to his sources:

Il est, sans doute, parti de cette *Phèdre* racinienne qu'il admire. . . . Il a sans doute parcouru dans l'édition de 'La Pléïade', *Plutarque*, mais n'en a pas gardé grand-chose. Pour la plongée de Thésée au fond de la mer, il a accommodé ce me semble et transposé dans le ton de l'ironie, l'ode exquise de Bacchylide . . ., *Les Adolescents ou Thésée*. Je dois avouer que l'antique poète ionien garde la supériorité de la foi, de la fraîcheur et d'une indicible grâce. Le miracle de Thésée rencontrant, au fond de la mer, de la pleine mer, des Néréides qui le fêtent et couronnent sa jeune tête, est remplacé par une tête piquée, du haut du rivage, et la feinte d'un onyx que Thésée cachait dans sa main, et présente comme un don de Poséidon.[2]

However, while the change in tone and explanation of the diving episode may disappoint some readers Gide's presentation of the Theseus myth makes little attempt at poetic or archaeological accuracy. The labyrinth, for example, is part building, part garden and situated outside the House of the Labrys, while the palace of Cnossos itself can only be reached after a long and exhausting journey from the coast, a journey which puts Theseus to sleep for thirty-six hours of recovery. Gide's only concern is with the human experience, and the detailed description of setting and circumstances can thus be minimal. The embroidered skirts worn by Ariadne and Phaedra are described for their revelation of character and the festival that calls forth such finery takes place in 'un vaste hémicycle ouvert sur la mer'. There is thus a considerable shift in focus in the author who had earlier been reproached for his symbolic 'paysages d'âme', but it is understandable in the light of Gide's predominant interests in the problems of living and heroic behaviour, in the light, also, of the explanations that satisfy him.

[1] *Journal 1939–1949*, p. 270, 21 mai 1944. His allusion is probably to G. Glotz and R. Cohen, *Histoire ancienne*, Deuxième partie, 'Histoire grecque', Paris, Les Presses Universitaires de France, 1925. T. I, ch. II: La Crète préhellénique, especially II: La civilisation crétoise, pp. 36–58.

[2] R. Kemp, Review of *Thésée*, *Les Nouvelles littéraires artistiques et scientifiques*, 19 septembre 1946, p. 3.

Although some critics have thought that the ideas contained in *Thésée* are reiterations of earlier and over-familiar concepts, they are given new vitality and application here. This comes about in two ways: the ideas are either transformed by their narrative context; or they undergo modification within that context. For *Thésée* is the only work, among those based on the Greek myth, that has temporal duration. The earlier presentations of mythological subjects were either treated without regard to time (as in *Le Prométhée* or *Le Narcisse*) or at moments of crisis (as in *Philoctète*, *Le Roi Candaule*, the proposed 'Ajax', 'Alexandre aux Indes,' *Œdipe*). But *Thésée* treats a whole lifetime and thatsubject alone permits, even demands, the inclusion of many phases of experience and changes of attitude. It is a poor and limited creature who holds the same views throughout a long life. It would be particularly repugnant to a Gidian hero who owes it to himself not to be enslaved by his earlier opinions.

The *récit* thus forms a document of human development wherein phases succeed one another, sometimes in contradiction, sometimes in amalgamation, to produce the final contented, if not exuberantly happy, human being. The concept of the developing man shapes the whole account: Egeus drives his son, Theseus, on his way, saying as he hands him the ritual arms: 'Le temps de ton enfance est passé. Sois homme.'[1]

Daedalus sets the immediate Minoan adventure in perspective, and outlines a human life when he counsels Theseus: 'sache qu'il te reste à faire de grandes choses, et dans un tout autre domaine que tes prouesses du passé; des choses près desquelles ces prouesses, dans l'avenir, ne paraîtront que jeux d'enfant.'[2] So when Theseus recalls his carefree adolescence with its pleasures of the senses he speaks in the tone of *Les Nourritures terrestres*: 'O premiers ans vécus dans l'innocence! Insoucieuse formation! J'étais le vent, la vague. J'étais plante; j'étais oiseau. Je ne m'arrêtais pas à moi-même, et tout contact avec un monde extérieur ne m'enseignait point tant mes limites qu'il n'éveillait en moi de volupté. J'ai caressé des fruits, la peau des jeunes arbres, les cailloux lisses des rivages, le pelage des chiens, des chevaux, avant de caresser les femmes.'[3]

[1] *Thésée*, p. 12.   [2] Ibid., p. 75.   [3] Ibid., pp. 10-11.

The final phrase, however, belongs to Theseus alone for the phase of sexual experience which in some ways recalls the subject-matter of *Saül* and *Le Roi Candaule* now follows in his account. Since he is telling it at the end of his life he can view such experiences with Olympian detachment, partly brought about by the perspective of age, partly by his own nature. He realizes that the experience of love can be a means to self-knowledge but he places it firmly where, in his opinion, it belongs, as an element in the process of maturation. His attitude is thus far removed from the passionate disturbances and disasters that overwhelm Saul and Candaules. As he says of his *amours*: 'Celles-ci n'ont du reste eu d'importance que dans la première partie de ma vie';[1] and he relates them, in a fashion that is at once amusing, malicious, and self-revelatory, to the heroic conquest of monsters: '[celles-ci] m'ont appris du moins à me connaître, concurremment avec les divers monstres que j'ai domptés.'[1] For Theseus, the legendary philanderer, the casual affairs and the sexual relationships formed in Crete with Ariadne and Phaedra are simply means to an end. And that end, as he used to describe it to his son, Hippolytus, includes two connected states: '"il s'agit d'abord de bien comprendre qui l'on est . . .; ensuite il conviendra de prendre en conscience et en mains l'héritage." '[1] The need to know oneself means first the definition of oneself in relationship with one's surroundings; the boy has to learn to distinguish himself from the winds and waves, from the plants and birds of his idyllic childhood, as indeed Adam in his Paradise had to assert himself even to the point of destroying its overwhelming harmony. Next, learning involves the understanding of one's own nature that comes through the testing experiences of love and fear. When Theseus remembers his achievements he summarizes to some extent the subject- and thematic-matter of *Œdipe*, where the hero frees himself from monsters and from terror: 'je crois avoir rendu quelques notoires services', Theseus declares; 'j'ai définitivement purgé la terre de maints tyrans, bandits et monstres; balayé certaines pistes aventureuses où l'esprit le plus téméraire ne s'engageait encore qu'en tremblant; clarifié le ciel de manière que l'homme, au front

[1] Ibid., pp. 9–10.

moins courbé, appréhendât moins la surprise.'[1] If, as Theseus
admits, an ignorant populace living in a physically uncultivated,
socially uncivilized country feel constantly threatened they are
the more ready to explain their inexplicable terrors in terms of the
supernatural (just as, Gide contends, imperfectly understood
mythology allows too much power to the *Fatum*). They must be
enlightened by the hero who challenges physical and psychological
terrors alike: 'Tout paraissait divin', Theseus says of his inherited
country, 'qui demeurait inexplicable, et la terreur s'épandait sur la
religion, au point que l'héroïsme souvent semblait impie. Les
premières et les plus importantes victoires que devait remporter
l'homme, c'est sur les dieux.'[2]

The episode of Pasiphaë's appeal to Theseus to spare her monstrous offspring, the Minotaur, is a brilliant and amusing variation on the same theme of the special pleading of ignorance. Gide
revives his earlier idea of the Dioscuri when he works it into his
witty denunciation of hypocritical awe. Exceptionally, Pasiphaë's
appearance is described in some detail: 'Elle avait les lèvres gour-
mandes, le nez retroussé, de grands yeux vides, au regard, eût-on
dit, bovin.'[3] This we remember as she draws the over-feasted,
squeamish young hero on to the divan to hear her confidences:
'Comprenez-moi, je vous en prie', she urges him: 'je suis de
tempérament mystique. J'ai l'amour exclusif du divin. Le gênant,
voyez-vous, c'est de ne point savoir où commence et où finit le
dieu. J'ai beaucoup fréquenté Léda, ma cousine. Pour elle, dieu
s'était caché dans un cygne. Or, Minos avait compris mon désir
de lui donner comme héritier un dioscure. Mais comment
distinguer ce qui peut rester d'animal dans la semence même des
dieux?'[4] Gide has told the same story before (in the Epilogue to
Le Prométhée) but it is admirably exploited here, expressed by the
extravagant Minoan queen to the sceptical hero and related to
the advancing action.

When Theseus finally encounters the Minotaur, with all provision made for his safety by Daedalus' advice about the thread
that Ariadne must hold (not her own idea, incidentally), it is no

surprise to us to discover that the fabulous monster is stupid and therefore deserves his death. The labyrinth, as Daedalus describes his creation to Theseus, with its fatally seductive, perfumed vapours that diminish the will to return in every visitor by trapping each man in his own peculiar illusory pleasure, leads Theseus into its centre where he is subject to a double attraction. There, in a garden which he remembers afterwards as being 'si capiteux que je pensais ne pouvoir m'en distraire',[1] he sees the monster as beautiful, as harmonious as a centaur, with the charming grace of youth, all attributes which, as Thesesus admits, are 'armes . . . plus fortes que la force',[2] and against which he must summon all his remaining energy of will-power: 'Mais il ouvrit un œil', Theseus recalls. 'Je vis alors qu'il était stupide et compris que je devais y aller...'[2] Weakness of will may be regrettable, as Theseus considers his friend's surrender to fantasies, but stupidity, as Theseus and the author of the 'Ajax' fragment believe, is unpardonable.

It is the will to survive that brings Theseus out of the labyrinth, helped certainly by Daedalus' warnings and the co-operation of Ariadne, and the adventure closes the period of his individual development. As Daedalus sums up Theseus' character to him, he possesses 'une sorte de dévouement à la tâche, de hardiesse sans recul, et même de témérité qui vous précipite en avant et triomphe de l'adversaire après avoir triomphé de ce que nous avons en chacun de nous de couard'.[3] The same summary might have been made of Prometheus, of Saul, of Candaules, even of Adam, certainly of Oedipus. Such character traits and code of behaviour find their admirable symbolic expression in the journey into the dark, towards the unknown and the monstrous, and in the difficult return to the light of day.

Theseus' life divides sharply into the two stages of individual development and of social conscience. They are represented by Cnossos and Athens, and the transition between them is partly accomplished by Daedalus' prophecies that the hero will become the 'vaillant rassembleur de cités',[4] partly by Theseus' recognition

[1] Ibid., p. 84.   [2] Ibid., p. 83.
[3] Ibid., pp. 56-57.   [4] Ibid., p. 75.

of middle age and stability when he returns to Athens with Phaedra: 'J'épousai la femme et la cité tout ensemble', he says. 'J'étais époux, fils du roi défunt; j'étais roi. Le temps de l'aventure est révolu, me redisais-je; il ne s'agissait plus de conquérir, mais de régner.'[1] What he later says to Pirithous of society may be equally applicable to the life of an individual man: 'Il est un temps de vaincre, . . . de purger la terre de ses monstres, puis un temps de cultiver et de porter à fruit la terre heureusement amendée.'[2]

Theseus' total devotion to his State, to the founding of his City and the political reforms that create its proud citizens and his own glory, is the final outcome of the concepts of Ulysses in *Philoctète* and in 'Ajax', just as his economic reforms, the equal opportunities he provides for every citizen, the welcome he extends to immigrants, are developments of the humanitarian ideas of *Œdipe* and *Perséphone*. But in both the political and the economic aspects of Theseus' ideal Athens the concepts are developments from earlier ideas, not mere echoes of them. For the ideals of political equality are impractical and cannot be maintained; as Pirithous points out, there will always be 'une plèbe souffrante, une aristocratie'. And Theseus admits natural differences of aptitude and energy in men and, therefore, the inevitable ascendancy of an *élite*. He is prepared to accept inequality under certain conditions: 'je ne vois pas pourquoi cette plèbe serait souffrante', he answers Pirithous, 'si cette aristocratie nouvelle, que je favoriserai de mon mieux, est, comme je la désire, celle non de l'argent, mais de l'esprit.'[3] As his city grows he is forced to accept a hierarchy, as he says, for the better functioning of the State. His aspirations for absolute equality must compromise with the reality of human endowment; he must rationalize the compromise by offering equal opportunities for all and by the acceptance of an emerging domination by an intellectual *élite*. How such domination can fail to produce economic inequalities and thus, by rights of inheritance, open the way to unearned privilege in the future is of course the problem to be met by all those many who hold such humanist ideals. However, Gide's *Thésée* is not a sociological treatise; his fictional

---

[1] *Thésée*, p. 100.   [2] Ibid., p. 107. Cf. Eccles. iii.
[3] *Thésée*, pp. 104–5.

hero is contented with his compromise, with the creation of his *peuple*, and with his sense of having fulfilled his destiny.

In something of the same way Theseus modifies his ideas of liberty. As a young hero of renowned exploits he enjoys total independence of others, and indeed can only realize himself in isolation, as he understands at the Cretan banquet: 'Moi qui n'ai jamais rien valu que seul', he thinks, 'pour la première fois j'étais en société. Il ne s'agissait plus de lutter et de l'emporter par la force, mais de plaire, et je manquais d'usage étrangement.'[1] Not only does he have to adapt himself to living in a social community but he comes to believe that no man is really free nor should he be. Theseus' personal adjustment has first to be made, his philosophy modified in the course of practical living. As ruler of his City he is aware that 'l'homme n'était pas libre, qu'il ne le serait jamais et qu'il n'était pas bon qu'il le fût'.[2]

The origin of this changed concept of human liberty undoubtedly lies in the Second World War, for Gide in enforced isolation reflected on the events that had led to the fall of France and he decided that freedom is a privilege that should only belong, once again, to a self-transcending *élite*:

L'humanité me paraissait mériter un peu l'esclavage [he writes on the 16th January 1941 in his *Journal*], et si seulement celui qui nous menaçait, qui nous menace encore, eût été soumission à des valeurs plus nobles, je ne dis pas que je n'eusse été jusqu'à le souhaiter. Me paraît mériter la liberté celui-là seul qui saurait en user pour une autre fin que lui-même, ou qui exigerait de soi tel développement exemplaire. La stagnation du plus grand nombre possible de représentants d'une humanité médiocre, dans un médiocre bonheur quotidien n'est pas un 'idéal' dont je puisse m'éprendre. Nous pouvons et devons tendre à mieux.

Three years later Theseus similarly disapproves of popular contentment and complacency: 'je n'admis pas que l'homme s'en tînt à lui-même, à la manière des Béotiens, ni qu'il cherchât sa fin dans un médiocre bonheur.'[2] As ruler he must allow his people at least the illusion of liberty, for their own good and for the good of their future. This may seem less a compromise, as in the

[1] Ibid., p. 41.   [2] Ibid., p. 107.

concept of equality, than the pragmatism of an efficient ruler. It can be reconciled with all of Gide's earlier ideas of self-realization in freedom only when we understand that he distinguishes the *élite* from *le peuple*, not on grounds of hereditary rank and power (though all his mythological heroes are, naturally enough, of royal or outstanding quality), but by virtue of intellectual comprehension which can grasp the relationship of the individual being with the whole of mankind.

Theseus is the hero most capable of such comprehension, with the additional qualities of energy, devotion to duty, and above all the sense of direction and purpose that Oedipus lacked. Theseus has the same forward-looking nature as Prometheus and Oedipus although he knows more clearly where he is going. As he says of himself when young: 'Ainsi fus-je toujours moins occupé ni retenu par ce que j'avais fait, que requis par ce qui me restait à faire; et le plus important me paraissait sans cesse à venir.'[1] This attitude is encouraged by his friends with their counsels to him to go forward, 'passer outre', although he has little need of such admonitions. This favourite Gidian phrase is used in two phases of Theseus' life. Pirithous offers his advice to the young philanderer each time he enters on a new affair: '"Vas-y, mais passe outre."'[2] At this stage it is used cynically, as one critic notes: he thinks it 'un appel à l'épicurisme, au donjuanisme, à la plus déplorable des lâchetés humaines: l'infidelité.'[3] But later Daedalus, looking far beyond the Cretan adventure that Theseus is immediately undertaking, repeats the same phrase with other and graver meaning: 'Passe outre', he says to the young hero. 'Considère comme trahison la paresse. Sache ne chercher de repos que, ton destin parfait, dans la mort. . . . Passe outre, va de l'avant, poursuis ta route, vaillant rassembleur de cités.'[4] Since Daedalus has the power to foresee a future as yet unimaginable to Theseus, his counsel bridges the two stages of his heroic achievement and announces his maturity. The same critic considers that Daedalus' advice,

---

[1] *Thésée*, p. 21.   [2] Ibid., p. 17.
[3] B. Guyon, 'Le testament d'André Gide', *La Vie intellectuelle*, juin 1951, pp. 53–54.
[4] *Thésée*, p. 75.

which orientates the hero 'vers le dépassement de soi, par la fuite des plaisirs faciles, vers l'incessante marche en avant, vers le mieux', is irreconcilable with the tone and attitude of Pirithous' frivolous advice.[1] However, within the story of a whole lifetime where two forms of heroism are distinguished the repeated phrase may rather throw into relief the modification of goals that comes about with maturity. Gide himself often uses the phrase as a kind of formula for self-realization. As early as 1918 he writes: 'Toute théorie n'est bonne que si elle permet non le repos mais le plus grand travail. Toute théorie n'est bonne qu'à condition de s'en servir pour passer outre.'[2] And looking back on his own life in 1934 he can see that the same formula carried him through complicated human situations as it had carried him beyond out-lived ideas.[3] Its importance to him personally is no doubt respon-sible for the urgency and authority of Daedalus' prophetic words.

The forward movement in the older Theseus is no longer a simple abandonment of the past but rather its consolidation in the present. The various symbolic meanings of 'le fil à la patte' represent a developing and maturing attitude in Theseus. Gide always used the symbol of the thread in an ambiguous way. In 1911, as in his earlier idea of 'le passager Thésée' of *Les Nourritures terrestres* taking his lighthearted leave of Ariadne, he judges the thread to be a bond on the hero which forces him to return against his will; he is 'tenu-contraint de revenir'.[4] Shortly afterwards, the same thread may appear to be protective and beneficial: the hero risks his life '*parmi* le labyrinthe, assuré par le fil secret d'une fidélité intérieure...'.[5] The thread may be either a chain or a safety belt. The same ambiguity persists in *Thésée* but here as in the case of the 'Passer outre' concept the thread takes on two consecutive and consequential meanings. On the plot level it is related to the cloying, encumbering Ariadne who represents once again an obstacle to freedom that the heroic male must over-come. Theseus' means of surmounting that obstacle may seem

[1] B. Guyon, loc. cit.
[2] *Journal*, p. 661, Feuillets.
[3] Ibid., p. 1210, 24 juillet 1934.
[4] Ibid., p. 347, Feuillets.
[5] Ibid., p. 375, 1912. See also 12 mai 1927 and 26 novembre 1931.

over-ingenious, with its complicated episode of pederastic customs
to explain the abduction of Phaedra instead of her little brother, but
its result is the decisive abandonment of Ariadne. But once again
it is Daedalus who, in instructing Theseus in the practical use of
the thread, declares its symbolic value of duty and the essential
interdependence of past and present; the thread that ties Theseus
to Ariadne is 'figuration tangible du devoir', he says. 'Ce fil te
permettra, te forcera de revenir à elle après que tu te seras écarté.
Conserve toutefois le ferme propos de ne pas le rompre, quel que
puisse être le charme du labyrinthe, l'attrait de l'inconnu, l'entraînement de ton courage. Reviens à elle, ou c'en est fait de tout
le reste, du meilleur. Ce fil sera ton attachement au passé. Reviens
à lui. Reviens à toi. Car rien ne part de rien, et c'est sur ton passé,
sur ce que tu es à présent, que tout ce que tu seras prend appui.'[1]
This is yet another transitional passage where Theseus, in understanding the relationship between past and present, present and
future, is moving towards his final conception of the continuity
of human life. In terms of his personal experience, he is to recall
his father's advice to him to abandon irresponsibility and accept
the duties of inheritance and later to recognize his wisdom; he is
also to regret the death of his own chosen heir, Hippolytus: 'Car
il ne suffit pas d'être, puis d'avoir été', he says at the end of his life:
'il faut léguer et faire en sorte que l'on ne s'achève pas à soi-même,
me répétait déjà mon grand-père.'[2] If he is never to immortalize
himself in his own flesh and blood, then he must do so through the
creation of his City. It is that work of the past which will guarantee his personal immortality but which will also benefit the men
of the future. 'Il m'est doux de penser qu'après moi, grâce à moi,
les hommes se reconnaîtront plus heureux, meilleurs et plus
libres', he says. 'Pour le bien de l'humanité future, j'ai fait mon
œuvre.'[3] At the end of his life Theseus thus understands and
accepts his place in the history of mankind fruitful in its past and
rich with the promise of its future. When we remember for a
moment the total rejection of the past by Prometheus, Philoctetes,
even Oedipus, the reconciliation of Theseus with his human condition is the more remarkable.

[1] *Thésée*, pp. 63–64.   [2] Ibid., p. 18.   [3] Ibid., p. 123.

Yet Gide had long understood the value of tradition in literature. It provided his theme for a lecture delivered in Brussels in
1900,[1] and he was often to return to it. *Thésée*, in fact, illustrates
the double application of the same idea to the story of a hero and
the history of a nation; it is therefore a natural enough though
delayed transposition of a familiar idea.

And Gide returns in this last imaginative work to one of his
earliest conceptions, that of the individual duty to 'manifest'
human truths. Gide had declared this obligation in *Le Traité du
Narcisse* in 1891; *Thésée*, in 1944–6, illustrates it; and Daedalus'
words summarize it: 'chacun de nous, dont l'âme, lors de la
suprême pesée, ne sera pas jugée trop légère, ne vit pas simplement
sa vie', he says. 'Dans le temps, sur un plan humain, il se développe,
accomplit son destin, puis meurt. Mais le temps même n'existe pas
sur un autre plan, le vrai, l'éternel, où chaque geste représentatif,
selon sa signification particulière, s'inscrit.'[2] Daedalus' own son,
Icarus, is the clearest example of such 'manifestation' since he was
before his birth and continues to be after his death 'l'image de
l'inquiétude humaine, de la recherche, de l'essor de la poésie, que
durant sa courte vie il incarne', as his father says. 'Il a joué son
jeu, comme il se devait; mais il ne s'arrête pas à lui-même.'[2] But
the actions of every hero, the lives of such doubtfully admirable
heroines as Pasiphaë and Ariadne will all develop their symbolic
value for others. Daedalus, within the fictional world, is addressing
Theseus as the conqueror of monsters, as the creator of a City
when he says: 'si insoucieux que tu paraisses et que tu te croies,
tu n'échapperas pas, non plus qu'échappait Hercule, ou Jason,
ou Persée, à la fatalité qui vous modèle.'[3] Within the plot these
achievements guarantee Theseus' heroic reputation. But we as
readers recognize the further symbolic value of Theseus' life as
a literary creation. For that life, as in all works of literature,
carries its own representative meaning over and above the con-
tributory and more or less coherent episodes. It does not simply
embody one aspect of human nature (if we may speak thus of

---

[1] 'De l'influence en littérature', conférence faite à la 'Libre Esthétique' de
Bruxelles le 29 mars 1900, O.C. iii. 251 sqq.
[2] *Thésée*, pp. 72–73.   [3] Ibid., p. 74.

Icarus' spirit), nor one aspect of human experience (as do Ariadne as mistress and Pirithous as friend), but it represents the evolution of a human being, from the unconscious pleasures of childhood to the evaluating consciousness of an old man. The autobiographical structure thus allows Gide full scope for his ideas, familiar ones modified by their narrative context, or undergoing natural change in a continuous experience, or new ideas emerging to resolve old problems.

But what is most remarkable perhaps is that this is the story of a satisfied man. Theseus may have lost lovers such as Antiope, friends such as Pirithous, a son like Hippolytus, and may find himself at last alone facing a solitary death; yet he is content. For he is one of the fortunate who complete their allotted task within their span of life. Not for them the punishment of the underworld that Daedalus describes as 'de recommencer toujours le geste inachevé de la vie'.[1] Theseus finds in his projected City a task that employs him fully and satisfies him as a creator. Its establishment was to be his destiny, its completion his glory and his particular legacy to mankind: 'Derrière moi', he says finally, 'je laisse la cité d'Athènes. . . . J'ai fait ma ville.'[2]

The City as symbol of human achievement is a singularly happy choice, involving as it does both the physical construction and the ordering of men in society of increasing civilization and complexity. It is no wonder that Gide chooses to close his account of Theseus with his accomplishment complete and thus omit his legendary death in exile from his own country. The City symbolizes the culmination of Gide's thought. For if we test his earlier heroes by their capacity to come to terms with their human environment, we see that Philoctetes and Candaules ignore it, Prometheus and Oedipus turn their backs on it, while Tityrus in Prometheus' allegory is increasingly overpowered by his newformed City with its growing social complexity until he abolishes it and returns to his solitary wastes. The symbol of the City, in fact, proves how far Theseus has developed from Prometheus, for he alone is capable of living in and through his City.

It is this capacity which gives him confidence in the encounter

[1] *Thésée*, p. 74.   [2] Ibid., p. 123.

with Oedipus that he describes as 'le sommet, le couronnement de [sa] gloire'.[1] For the first time Theseus meets a man of equal nobility, even one whose heroic exploits seem to surpass his own essentially human and inferior successes, one whose legendary reputation as victor of the Sphinx and champion of Man against the gods had unaccountably crumbled into defeat. Yet from this 'suprême confrontation' Theseus emerges unshaken in his own philosophy, indeed quite unaffected by Oedipus' opposing opinions.

The meeting of the two great heroes that Gide had so long planned ('Qui s'en est avisé depuis les Grecs?' he asks Roger Martin du Gard[2]) allows the exposition of two totally opposite views of life. On the one hand there is the mysticism of Oedipus whose lost sight of the physical world is replaced by the light of divinity. As he explains his experience to Theseus: 'Tandis que le monde extérieur, à jamais, se voilait aux yeux de la chair, une sorte de regard nouveau s'ouvrait en moi sur les perspectives infinies d'un monde intérieur, que le monde apparent, qui seul existait pour moi jusqu'alors, m'avait fait jusqu'alors mépriser. Et ce monde insensible (je veux dire: impréhensible par nos sens) est, je le sais à présent, le seul vrai. Tout le reste n'est qu'une illusion qui nous abuse et offusque notre contemplation du Divin.'[3] Theseus' answer is simple: 'Je reste enfant de cette terre . . .'.

The second fundamental incompatibility between them is revealed by their opposing interpretations of human nature. For Oedipus, man is innately sinful; his only hope of redemption can be found in God: 'je pense que quelque tare originelle atteint ensemble toute l'humanité, de sorte que même les meilleurs sont tarés, voués au mal, à la perdition, et que l'homme ne saurait s'en tirer sans je ne sais quel divin secours qui le lave de cette souillure première et l'amnistie.'[4] Oedipus' position is now so close to Tiresias' that he has undergone a reversal of role, although he is more sympathetically presented than the earlier high priest. Where before he argued as a humanist against Tiresias' religious views of original sin and divine redemption, now, as the representative of spirituality whose only reality is the contemplation

---

[1] Ibid., p. 115.   [2] Martin du Gard, *Notes sur A.G.*, p. 136.
[3] *Thésée*, pp. 118–19.   [4] Ibid., pp. 120–1.

of divinity, he is opposed by the intransigent humanism of Theseus. Theseus acknowledges the imperfection of human nature, sets aside any hope of divine redemption, and takes his stand on the responsibility, activity, and will-power of human beings when he declares: 'Je reste enfant de cette terre et crois que l'homme, quel qu'il soit et si taré que tu le juges, doit faire jeu des cartes qu'il a.'[1]

The supreme confrontation is, in fact, simply that. Neither speaker is affected by the other, as is only too natural, and although Oedipus might be said to have passed through and beyond Theseus' position, Theseus is merely reaffirmed in his philosophical stance by Oedipus' explanation. As he says later, he was quite unshaken by the meeting: 'son explication, il me faut bien l'avouer, ne me satisfit guère; ou c'est que je ne la compris pas bien.'[2] While Oedipus' experience is on a higher plane than Tiresias' dogmatic orthodoxy and he is presented with greater respect nevertheless Gide's exposition is slanted against him, although more subtly than in the earlier flippancy. There is the suggestion made by Theseus' deliberate pause before replying to him for the last time that Oedipus has been long-winded. Theseus' mistrust of all that he has been saying is indicated when he qualifies the points he picks up: 'cette sorte de sagesse surhumaine que tu professes'; 'sans doute as-tu su faire bon usage de ton infortune même' . . .; 'ce que tu nommes le divin.'[3] Theseus succeeds in diminishing the content of Oedipus' statements (which is admissible) but also, which is less admirable, his person and his presentation. Despite a deliberate attempt at objectivity Gide's preference is made abundantly clear: he stands with his Theseus as 'enfant de cette terre'.

His treatment of the myth is characteristically confined to the human level. Theseus exploits popular credulity and makes political capital out of the rumours about Ariadne and her new spouse, Dionysus. His own explanation is that she has now consoled herself with wine but he disarmingly confesses how useful such rumours were to him: 'On la prit même, raconte-t-on, pour Aphrodite. Je laissai dire et moi-même, pour couper court

[1] *Thésée*, p. 122.   [2] Ibid., p. 116.   [3] Ibid., p. 122.

aux rumeurs accusatrices, la divinisai de mon mieux, instituant
à son égard un culte où d'abord je pris la peine de danser.'[1] So,
too, are the accumulating tales of his own supernatural exploits:
'enlèvement d'Hélène, descente aux Enfers avec Pirithoüs, viol de
Proserpine', he recounts: all are means of gaining and maintaining
popular respect,[1] and so should not be denied. Nevertheless, Gide
must keep the intervention of Poseidon in Hippolytus' story.
Both antiquity and Racine require it. But he gives it a typical
twist, when we recall the irresponsible and cruel 'Miglionnaire'
of *Le Prométhée*, since the gods answer men's prayers, as Theseus
thinks, only to destroy them: 'Les hommes, lorsqu'ils s'adressent
aux Dieux, ne savent pas que c'est pour leur malheur, le plus
souvent, que les Dieux les exaucent.'[2] It would be unfair perhaps
to quibble over Gide's use of such a traditional element of the
myth but we may still ask if the gods exist or not, and, if they do,
are they always malevolent; or should they be seen simply as
agents of human will. Theseus blames himself for the death of his
son: 'Par volonté subite, irraisonnable, passionnée, je me trouvais
avoir tué mon fils', he says;[3] and by thus assuming total responsibility distracts our attention from the supernatural intervention
and leaves it focussed on the human and destructive passion of rage.

Gide's style plays its part in the humanizing of the legend. Just
as Prometheus expresses himself, although in a different timbre
from others, as a Parisian of the 1890's, so Theseus, in his mythological world, speaks with '[une] aisance familière du ton', as it has
been described, which unifies the *récit* and, by its contrast with
the fabulous world it presents, provides 'une source très pure de
poésie et d'humour'.[4] Another writer analyses the intermingling
of styles of diction: 'half-archaizing half-anachronistic, with a
strong admixture of colloquialisms' which produces a 'piquant
and ironical effect'.[5] But not every critic so approves. For one
mistrusts 'une sorte de désinvolture concertée et pour ainsi dire
d'application dans le sans-gêne' which, while it may deliberately
bring the fable closer to the reader and certainly possesses the

[1] Ibid., p. 99.   [2] Ibid., p. 114.
[3] Ibid., pp. 114–15.   [4] Brée, *André Gide*, p. 334.
[5] S. Ullman, *The Image in the Modern French Novel*, Cambridge U.P., 1960, p. 92.

virtue of being easily adopted, may not be artistically effective.[1] Gide himself found the tone difficult to establish; as he writes in 1944: 'Il me reste de grands morceaux à récrire; et, en particulier, le début, pour lequel je n'avais pu d'abord trouver le ton.'[2]

There is of course such disparity between the monumental world of antiquity as we commonly imagine it and the familiarity, lightness, often cynicism of Theseus' account that it naturally provokes strong feelings one way or another. But the fictional character of Theseus must not be forgotten. Nothing in the Theseus myth demands a particularly respectful treatment. Indeed Gide has only presented the more admirable episodes of a long and varied career, keeping only those that best illustrate Édouard's famous advice to Bernard in Les Faux-Monnayeurs: 'Il est bon de suivre sa pente, pourvu que ce soit en montant.'[3] Hence the relegation of the 'faits controuvés' to popular gossip; hence the elimination of banishment and exiled death. Again, it is Gide's Theseus himself who in his old age is looking back on his long life. This fact alone is enough to reconcile the subject-matter of heroic exploits and ironical description. He has the perspective given by age. Whether that is profit or loss is debatable; it is none the less natural in the fictional *persona* and need not be attributed to his creator's failure in taste. There may be deficiencies in the character of Theseus which reveal his creator's own attitudes; but his manner of expressing himself does not form one. He is representative of the heroic man: energetic, full of physical courage, without pity or remorse; at once large in conception and shrewd in execution; devoted to his task, indifferent and inadequate in his personal relationships; capable of assuming public responsibility but of shedding it in his private life; a man, in fact, who plays his representative role with *bravura* and conviction.

[1] G. Marcel, 'Le "Thésée" d'André Gide', *Érasme*, T.II, no. 16, avril 1947, p. 148. See also Étiemble, 'Le style du "Thésée" d'André Gide', *Les Temps modernes*, T. II, 1947, p. 1036 for an analysis of the style which he considers 'un *exercice d'atticisme*'.

[2] *Journal 1939–1949*, p. 269, 21 mai 1944.

[3] *Les Faux-Monnayeurs*, O.C. xii. 495.

8

THE HERO AND HIS WORLD

In a study of Prometheus, C. Kerényi discusses mythology as the expression of man's eternal relationship with his environment, re-creating the ancient cosmos in the '*world of men*, taking the form of mythological figures compounded of vision, dream, and poetry'.[1] In a general sense this relationship could be said to be the constant subject-matter of the artist, particularly, of course, of the artist working through language, just as it produces the myth. For, as Kerényi writes, 'The myth is the content . . . [which] is a fragment of the world that addresses us in human terms'.[1] Our present concern is Gide's choice of such fragments. Among the multiplicity of experiences that makes up the world of Greek mythology, which heroes, and what experiences kindle his imagination?

The intimate connexion between the myth itself and the men who create and respond to it has been generally accepted. Images, symbols, myths are never irresponsible creations of the human psyche, but are governed by necessity and their common function of illuminating human nature.[2] So, too, the myth is accepted and perpetuated if it expresses universal tendencies and experiences.[3] The myth arises from the human need for self-expression, survives because of the same need, and may be chosen by succeeding writers as means of self-expression, however individual motivation and presentation may vary. Gide himself was well aware of the self-revelatory nature of both subject and style. He discounts

[1] C. Kerényi, *Prometheus: Archetypical Image of Human Existence*, translated by Ralph Manheim, London, Thames and Hudson, 1963, p. 63. (Hamburg, 1959; earlier version, Zürich, 1946.)

[2] M. Eliade, *Images et Symboles: essais sur le symbolisme magico-religieux*, Paris, Gallimard, 1952, pp. 13–14.

[3] M. Delcourt, *Œdipe ou la Légende du conquérant*, Liège, Faculté de Philosophie et Lettres, Paris, E. Droz, 1944, p. 229.

Maurois's explanation of Oscar Wilde's aestheticism, for instance, and interprets it himself rather as an ingenious disguise, allowing glimpses of what cannot be openly shown, rather than as a fundamental character trait: 'Ici, comme presque toujours', he writes in his *Journal* of the 1st of October 1927, 'et parfois à l'insu même de l'artiste, c'est le secret du profond de sa chair qui dicte, inspire et décide.'

What Gide finds attractive in Greek mythology may well reveal his own attitudes and beliefs; how he chooses to present his chosen heroes may be equally revelatory. The choice of the hero as representative of different aspects of Gide's character is the method adopted by J. O'Brien in his earlier study of Gide;[1] the intention here is narrower since it must confine itself to what can be known of Gide's interests, achievement, and value from one part only of his total body of works. Yet it may be justified partly by the position of works based on the Greek myth, since they appear at the beginning, in the middle, and at the end of his career; partly by the importance he personally attached to them. As he writes to Francis Jammes of his *L'Immoraliste*: 'Je l'ai vécu pendant quatre ans, et je l'écris pour passer outre. Je fais des livres comme on fait des maladies. Je n'estime plus que les livres dont l'auteur a failli claquer.'[2] How he identified himself with *Saül*, *Œdipe* and, certainly, *Thésée*, we know from his own admission. We may well suppose that Adam's action in *Le Narcisse* and Prometheus' revolt, at least, come into the same category of books that must be written. They are, as has long been recognized, witness of the continual 'dialogue gidien de soi avec soi',[3] that 'état de dialogue' in which Gide discovered the source of his creativity.[4] They are also, as has always been acknowledged, totally concerned with Man: man alone, man among men, rarely, and only in a special sense, in his natural physical surroundings.

Environment, in Gide's imagination, is always the world of

[1] *Portrait of André Gide*, p. 7.

[2] *Correspondance*, p. 189 [mai 1902].

[3] H. Hell, 'A propos du théâtre d'André Gide', *Fontaine*, T. IV, no. 24, octobre 1942, p. 474.

[4] *Journal*, pp. 777–8, Feuillets.

men. Philoctetes' icy island and its final transformation symbolize a state of mind and its reconciliation with its situation; the Promethean Caucasus is nebulous, Tityrus' oak-tree illusion; while Theseus' rapturous sensuous pleasures of childhood and the labyrinth's spell are equally dependent on the experiencing mind. (Even the splendid use of garden and gate in *La Porte étroite* is only meaningful in the relationship of Alissa and Jérôme.) Nature is always subordinate to the central figure of man, known only through him. It is never dangerous, never threatening, never terrible to the heroic and rational mind, as Theseus describes the civilizing of his early savage country. The potentially destructive elements of flood, fire, ice, and storm play no part in the Gidian cosmos. Ice does not freeze Philoctetes, the sea is the giver of treasure in *Le Roi Candaule* and the playground of Theseus; even the vengeance of Poseidon on Hippolytus is passed over without description when Theseus takes the blame upon himself. Saul is the only sufferer from the storm. No divine thunderbolts are hurled at the Gidian hero; he stands firmly on the soil of which he is master.

The imaginative works have always established this relationship. When Gide, towards the end of his life, distinguishes 'le côté Zeus' of the natural laws, matter, forces, and energies of the cosmos from 'le côté Prométhée' (or 'le côté Christ') which is the aspiring, evolving, dominating human spirit,[1] he is reaffirming in an expository manner the separation he has always assumed between man and nature. He affirms yet again the pre-eminence of man and his efforts 'vers le bien, vers le beau, la lente maîtrisation de ces forces brutales et leur mise en service pour réaliser le bien et le beau sur la terre',[1] which he sees as the expression of 'le côté Prométhée' or 'le côté Christ' of mankind. His reconciliation of the two forces of paganism and Christianity as interchangeable terms for describing the noblest stage of human development, which is 'l'épanouissement de l'homme, et toutes les vertus y concourent',[1] is a late and rather didactic declaration of a life dedicated to the praise of man.

It is for this constant attitude, of course, that Gide is generally

[1] *Deux Interviews imaginaires*, pp. 35–36.

known. When Pirithous dares to question the amount of attention paid to men in the new City-State of Athens, Theseus replies
in an irrefutable fashion: 'Eh! de quoi s'occuper, que de l'homme?
. . . Il n'a pas dit son dernier mot.'[1] But if we ask ourselves just
what kind of man Gide has in mind we have two possible lines
of inquiry: either we may examine the Gidian heroes (from
Greek myth, naturally) to discover what they have in common:
in nature, in situation, and in action; or we may measure the
heroes against certain basic abstractions from complex human
nature in order to discover the nature of Gide's ideal man. There
is much to be said for both methods, since Gide's work consistently adopts both approaches: the treatment of an individual
experience and the generalizations about man. Indeed, although
it is not the usual way of approaching works of imaginative
literature, it may be more profitable to test Gide's heroes against
certain abstract categories of human disposition as a means of
discovering what he considers most admirable. We may distinguish, for convenience's sake, such abstractions from the 'mire and
blood' of human life as 'the man of action', 'the contemplative
man', 'the civic man', 'the man of feeling', 'the spiritual man'.
And our authority for so doing would come from Gide's own
constant preoccupation with 'Man', an abstraction if ever there
were one. From his first little book where Adam, the first Man
of all, breaks the harmony of Paradise and where Man's duty is
defined as 'manifestation', since 'Tout homme qui ne manifeste
pas est inutile et mauvais'[2] to Oedipus' much-quoted reply to the
Sphinx and to life: 'il n'y a qu'une seule et même réponse à de si
diverses questions; et que cette réponse unique, c'est: l'Homme;
et que cet homme unique, pour un chacun de nous, c'est: Soi',[3]
Gide's concern has been as much with Man as with men. If then
he is so much at home with the abstract concept of Man, we may
legitimately adopt an equally abstract approach to his *personae*,
which may well lead to a deeper understanding of his thought.

    In a provisional hierarchy of human types the man of action,
with his physical strength and his capacity to act impulsively and
energetically, should be considered first. For however desirable

---

[1] *Thésée*, p. 108.   [2] *Narc.*, O.C. i. 215 n.   [3] *Œd.*, p. 284.

physical strength may be it is in itself the simplest of attributes. Many Gidian characters, both central and secondary, possess such strength and openly glory, as do Gyges and Oedipus, in its possession. From Adam to Theseus, the hero is physically strong. But that strength is not enough in itself to create a hero, as the abandoned fragment of 'Ajax' makes clear. The ease with which Ulysses manipulates the two Greek champions, Achilles and Ajax, and the focus of attention on Ulysses' crisis of indecision suggest contempt for the simple and stupid men of war: 'Ainsi leurs deux vigueurs se pondéraient', as Ulysses says to Minerva; 'avec un peu d'habileté j'en maintenais l'élan en équilibre, les exaltant l'une par l'autre tant qu'ils servaient contre Ilios, l'un contre l'autre les usant, dès que le calme revenu dans le camp eût laissé chacun d'eux ne chercher plus de servir qu'à soi-même. Ces deux forces in-éduquées étaient d'un maniement presque commode pour qui savait ne les employer qu'à la fois.'[1] Ajax, like the Minotaur with his truly brute force, is too stupid for heroism.

What is very properly demanded of the active man is purpose-ful behaviour. The Gidian heroes increasingly understand them-selves, their needs, and the use to which physical strength may be put. Adam's act in breaking the branch of the sacred tree in Paradise is caused by an instinctive desire to affirm his individuality and define his own outline. Gyges, whose 'force' is the last blessing left to him before Candaules drives him into a situation of painful decision, must use his strength to gain the mistress and the Queen and so destroy the friend and the King; he is driven by sexual passion. When Oedipus, as a young man rejoicing in his energy and strength, moves towards the Sphinx he must draw his intelligence into successful action in order to answer the unan-swered riddle. Indeed, in his particular story, impulsive physical action in slaying the stranger at the crossroads destroys him as effectively as his power of rational thought in replying to the Sphinx advances him. His strength is his weakness, although he never recognizes it as such. It is his capacity to argue with Tiresias that frees him from fear of the gods and supports him, although blinded, again by his impulsive action, in his journey forward.

[1] 'Ajax', O.C. iv. 371.

When Theseus remembers his early physical strength he has the amused detachment of an old man for uncontrolled animal vigour. As he describes his search for Poseidon's weapons which were to initiate him into the heroic life, his father, Egeus, watches the enthusiastic adolescent: 'Il riait de voir, par cet entraînement, mes forces s'accroître assez vite. Et cet entraînement musculaire doublait celui de mon vouloir. Après que, dans cette recherche vaine, j'eus déplacé les lourdes roches d'alentour, comme je commençais de m'attaquer aux dalles du seuil du palais . . .', and Egeus stops him before he pulls the palace down. Egeus is given the last word on the value and proper use of physical strength: '"Les armes . . ."', he says to his son, '"importent moins que le bras qui les tient; le bras importe moins que l'intelligente volonté qui le guide.'"[1]

The concept of 'l'intelligente volonté' as the force governing heroic action is *Thésée*'s contribution to the increasingly complex presentation of the 'man of action'. For it is the intelligent exercise of will that ensures Theseus' continuing successes: it demands the devotion to the task in hand which he knows is necessary; it serves his desire of survival and victory in bringing him, thanks to thread and gag, warnings and a sense of purpose, safely out of the corrupting labyrinth; it authorizes his reforms of society and gives him the power to carry them through. Gide's treatment of the active man thus moves from instinctive and destructive self-assertion, at the bidding variously of passion and reason, to culminate in the combined and invincible forces of intelligence and will. It demonstrates an increasingly complex motivation which may not originally have been present in the given myth. As one critic writes: 'This is the fascination of the Greek myths for Gide: the great unreflective initiative of the demi-gods and heroes.'[2] If that fascination accounts for a rebelling Prometheus or even for the image Oedipus has of himself when he says: 'Dis simplement ce que tu as à dire et n'apporte pas à tes paroles ce gonflement que déjà tu prétends éviter dans ta vie. Tout est simple

---

[1] *Thésée*, p. 12.
[2] Van Meter Ames, *André Gide*, Norfolk, Conn., New Directions Books, 1947, p. 41.

et tout vient à point. Sois simple toi-même et direct comme la flèche. Droit au but . . . . Je raisonne mal; la logique n'est pas mon fort; je procède par intuition',[1] it does not explain all the heroes. Oedipus, as he really is, not as he thinks himself, Narcissus, and Philoctetes cannot be so described. And Theseus, as a boy, is taught to value reason and effort before his simple and sensuous pleasures.

The intelligent man, even the rational man, is not necessarily the same as the 'contemplative man'. And this too is a recurring type among Gide's *personae*. He first appears as Narcissus, the archetype of the self-contemplative nature. That there were external reasons for Gide's choice of the Narcissus myth for his first publication has been shown elsewhere in considering his participation in the Symbolist world; that there were essential personal reasons for his choice is the argument of Jean Delay's masterly study of *La Jeunesse d'André Gide*.[2] Gide's Narcissus, representative of the poet studying the world of symbols to find absolute Truth, is at the same time the mythological figure, absorbed by his own reflected image. But this Narcissus recognizes the risks involved in self-obsession and, long before Theseus' elevation of the will, voluntarily withdraws from the fatally attractive image. Once he understands the dangers of solipsistic illusion he is capable of avoiding it and directing his contemplations elsewhere. Since that is his duty, contemplate he must. To emphasize the poet's destiny, Gide modifies the myth. No abandoned Echo appears, no death closes the tale. The poet is eternal. But the individual *persona* has also escaped by an effort of will from self-destruction.

Yet, while self-destruction is the danger it is not inevitable. Philoctetes, whose confused murmurings set the self above all external pressures, whether human or superhuman, reconciles himself with his physical and psychical isolation and is duly rewarded. But he has little vitality. His function is to express an attitude of mind, not a human being. Candaules, on the contrary,

[1] *Œd.*, pp. 253–4.
[2] Tome I, livre II, troisième partie, IV: 'L'erreur de Narcisse'. See also J. O'Brien, *Portrait of André Gide*, chs. III, IV.

a man totally preoccupied with himself and constantly seeking his reflection in others, demonstrates the risks run by the Narcissus character caught up in the world of passionate men.

There is yet another example of the contemplative man provided by Icarus in *Thésée*; but here the dangerous element of experience is less that of self-absorption than the loss of contact with the world of men and action. Icarus' endless and insoluble metaphysical inquiries pursued eternally by his anguished spirit after death furnish an extreme illustration of the over-intellectual, unbalanced human personality. He admirably demonstrates the functioning of intelligence isolated from reality as described by Henri Morier:

L'intelligence, cette brillante manifestation de la vie intérieure, n'est en soi ni une propriété de l'âme, ni un organe cérébral, mais bien l'union des deux. Elle est le produit de la force animique utilisant les relais du cortex. C'est l'âme qui élance ses ondes à travers les circuits organisés de la pensée, galvanise les neurones et prend connaissance de leur message, compulse les dossiers de la mémoire, propose les échanges, associe les images et les concepts par voie d'analogie et de différence. Elle y trouve des machines à calculer: .... Cependant, ces mécanismes logiques ne peuvent fonctionner par eux-mêmes sans folie. Livrés à eux-mêmes, et si brillants soient-ils, les syllogismes de la dialectique aboutissent à des solutions creuses. Ses communications avec le monde réel coupées, l'intelligence fonctionne à vide, avec la liberté et la gratuité du rêve: elle oublie des données essentielles au problème qu'elle considère, et fournit des résultats incomplets, parfois absurdes.[1]

Unhappy Icarus!

Since Candaules, a Narcissus who does not draw back, contrives his own ruin in attempting to confirm his own existence through others, and since Icarus wanders in an agonized metaphysical labyrinth, it is hardly surprising that both Oedipus and Theseus flatter themselves on their lack of introspection: 'la logique n'est pas mon fort; je procède par intuition', says Oedipus; 'si je m'interroge,' says Theseus, 'ce que je ne fais jamais volontiers. . . .'[2] Perhaps indeed they do protest too much. Nevertheless, by the emphasis they place on the life of effort and of action, they

---

[1] *La Psychologie des styles*, p. 36.   [2] *Thésée*, p. 14.

separate themselves markedly from the early figures of Narcissus, Philoctetes, the Damocles of *Le Prométhée*, and King Candaules. The separation is so great that we might briefly consider how much Gide himself might be vulnerable to the Narcissus attitude.

From his writings alone, we might guess at a considerable attraction, which he recognised in himself, expressed in his youth, and later deliberately controlled, giving priority to opposing qualities. Gide's *Journal* reveals a great deal of his introspective youth. On the 3rd of January 1892, at the age of twenty-two, for instance, he examines himself anxiously: 'Je m'inquiète de ne savoir qui je serai', he writes; 'je ne sais même pas celui que je veux être; mais je sais bien qu'il faut choisir. . . . La vie d'un homme est son image. A l'heure de mourir, nous nous refléterons dans le passé, et, penchés sur le miroir de nos actes, nos âmes reconnaîtront *ce que nous sommes*. Toute notre vie s'emploie à tracer de nous-mêmes un ineffaçable portrait.' The image of 'penchés sur le miroir de nos actes' recalls Narcissus; but the ideas of choice and the revelatory nature of a lifetime lead forward towards decision. Gide's own judgement of his ' "journaux" de jeunesse', reread in 1920, is unnecessarily harsh: 'Je ne les relis pas sans exaspération — et n'était *l'humiliation* salutaire que je trouve à leur lecture, je déchirerais tout. Chaque progrès dans l'art d'écrire ne s'achète que par l'abandon d'une complaisance. En ce temps je les avais toutes, et me penchais sur la page blanche comme on fait devant un miroir.'[1] It is Narcissus he condemns in his youthful excesses in writing. Still later, in 1929, he explains his early self-centredness as the result of his being the only child of devoted parents.[2] Such entries suggest that Gide recognized the tendency to introspection as a danger which must be overcome by an effort of will, both in choosing and in acting. An important entry of August 1893 (not long before he left for Africa) heralds the future. Admittedly it expresses a momentary state of exasperation with his immediately past self-absorption, but it takes a form that is to become central to Gide's subsequent thought: 'J'en arrive, par réaction,' he writes, 'à souhaiter de ne plus m'occuper du tout de moi-même; à ne pas m'inquiéter, lorsque je veux faire

[1] *Journal*, p. 684, 28 octobre 1920.   [2] Ibid., p. 923, 26 avril 1929.

quelque chose, de savoir si je fais bien ou mal; mais tout simplement de la faire, et tant pis! Je ne désire plus du tout des choses
bizarres et compliquées; les choses compliquées, je ne les comprends même plus; je voudrais être normal et fort, simplement
pour n'y plus songer.'[1] Here is a moment of rebellion that forecasts Prometheus, and that will condemn the unfortunate Candaules to death. The personal entries in the *Journal* thus confirm
the impression formed from the imaginative works that Gide,
like his own Narcissus, warned by his own André Walter,
deliberately turns away from the over-sensitive image in the river
to welcome the 'normal and strong' heroes such as Gyges,
Oedipus, Theseus, to name only the figures from mythology.
When we remember Gide's sickly childhood, his over-protected
adolescence, and the serious illness of his Algerian sojourn, the
attraction of the normal and strong hero is the more understandable. *Les Nourritures terrestres* is a work of convalescence, as he
writes;[2] *Le Prométhée* may be the work of a writer extricating
himself from narcissism.

In a sense, however, Narcissus never dies. Delay defines
narcissism as being both 'physique ou psychique, selon qu'il
désigne un regard de l'œil ou de la conscience',[3] and sees both in
the writer of *Les Cahiers d'André Walter*; but when Delay goes
on to declare that 'le journal intime est au narcissisme psychologique un accessoire aussi nécessaire que le miroir au narcissisme
physique',[4] we recognize the writer of the *Journal* (continued
until the 12th of June 1949), and the memoirs, *Ainsi soit-il*,
written until the 13th of February 1951, six days before his death.
More questionably, we may see Gide's whole body of work as
self-revelatory. His friend, Jacques Rivière, thought the work up
to 1911 to be so: 'L'œuvre est tout entière de confession; loin
de le masquer, elle trahit sans cesse son auteur, et même quand
elle semble ne point le vouloir.'[5] There seems no reason to confine
such a statement to the early works alone. However that may be,
the imaginative works increasingly centre on the 'normal and

---

[1] *Journal*, p. 39.   [2] Préface de l'édition de 1927, O.C. ii. 227.
[3] Delay, *La Jeunesse d'A.G.*, p. 541.   [4] Ibid., p. 543.
[5] J. Rivière, *Études*, Paris, N.R.F. 1911, p. 178.

strong' character at the expense of the introspective one. The ruthlessness with which Icarus is treated—he is almost a caricature of André Walter—may very well have originated in the voluntary repression of narcissistic tendencies.

The 'civic man' also recurs in Gide's world although he is relatively simple in conception. He believes, in general, in the future progress of mankind, or, in a narrower sense, in the pre-eminence of the State. The first appearance of the protector and the inspirer of mankind is, of course, Prometheus. If it seems premature to call him 'civic', given the primitive condition of men to whom he gives fire and the arts that spring from it, he goes on to arouse within them both consciousness and con-science, two essential agents of civilization. And he caps his account of his benefactions to men by saying that: 'Échauffant leurs esprits, en eux je fis éclore la dévorante croyance au pro-grès.'[1] In a way, then, he is the predecessor of Theseus, builder of cities, whose 'grande force', as he says, 'était de croire au progrès'.[2] And in a way, too, particularly in the Aeschylean version of the myth, he is the martyr to his devoted service of mankind. Gide's hero has been interpreted in this fashion: '[Prometheus] epitomizes the writer's fondest thoughts: revolt against the established order, energy directed to progress and, most important, self-assertion through altruistic self-sacrifice. Prome-theus manifests Gide's own aspiration to martyrdom predicated up-on a compulsive feeling of guilt.... If Prometheus ... eats his eagle, this is not to be interpreted as a repudiation of his martyrdom.'[3]

But the Gidian Prometheus considers the belief in progress to be 'dévorante', his allegorical tale of Tityrus confirms his attitude, and he turns his back on devotion to men and civilization to look after himself. As Gide uses the myth, the benefactions to mankind are a matter of the past; the immediate concern is with the liberation of the hero. Prometheus is therefore the earliest agent of civilization as he is the first rebel against the authority he has helped to establish.

[1] *PME*, O.C. iii. 134.   [2] *Thésée*, p. 108.
[3] G. I. Brachfeld, 'The Myth Maker', *L'Esprit créateur*, no. 1, Spring 1961, pp. 33–35.

The ideas he embodies must await Theseus for their final statement. Meanwhile, Gide turns to the more limited concept of
the importance of the State. His two treatments of Ulysses, in
Philoctète and in 'Ajax', offer mechanical claims for the State above
the individual man. The earlier Ulysses defines human duty as
'la voix des dieux, l'ordre de la cité, l'offrande de nous à la Grèce'.[1]
The grouped classifications suggest how unfruitful such an attitude would be to Gide; if the voice of the gods must be confused with the duties to city and country, there are too many
incompatible loyalties. The Ulysses of 'Ajax' is even more intransigent, since he believes that all personal loyalties and all rights of
human justice should be subordinated to the State. Gide as the
defender of individual rights thus finds himself in an untenable
position. How can the need for individual development be reconciled with the general welfare of the State?

Henceforth Gide directs his attention to humanity in general
rather than to the concept of the State; his Oedipus dreams of a
better world, 'la terre couverte d'une humanité désasservie, qui
considérera notre civilisation d'aujourd'hui du même œil que
nous considérons l'état des hommes au début de leur lent progrès';[2] his Persephone adds pity to hope when she descends to the
suffering world of the shades. Only when we reach his Theseus
do we find a hero capable of recognizing the value of the individual man, the possibility of general human progress, the
needs of the City and the Citizen as compatible. He is the only
hero to reconcile the privileges of men with the prosperity of
mankind. He does so partly by his expedient division of men into
an *élite* and a *peuple*, as we have seen; partly by drawing on all his
own personal powers. To put his ideals into practice he uses both
'force et astuce',[3] behaviour which suggests to one critic the
emergence of the Machiavellian prince.[4] But Machiavelli, after
all, had the good of his own country at heart, as has the hero who
serves Athens with all his powers of action, intelligence, and
idealism.

[1] *Phil.* O.C. iii. 25.   [2] *Œd.*, p. 283.   [3] *Thésée*, p. 100.
[4] J. R. Loy, 'Prometheus, Theseus, The Uncommon Man and an Eagle', *Yale
French Studies*, vii, 1951, p. 41.

When we consider Gide's treatment of the man of emotional capacity, however, we must count Theseus out. Devotion to his City he possesses, passionate devotion to other human beings never. As a young man, as he says, he could not, nor would not, resist women but he abandons them as readily as he frees himself from Ariadne. Among all his early amorous conquests Hippolytus' Amazon mother came closest to touching his heart: 'De toutes, Antiope fut le plus près de m'avoir', he says reflectively.[1] But the young Amazon queen, as muscular as the athletes of Athens, as untamed and as furious as a wild cat, is more boy than woman and her conquest a special kind of physical triumph. As the husband of Phaedra he is dutiful but unobservant, spending all his energies and care on his people, dangerously neglecting, as Pirithous points out, a young and beautiful wife. When the tragic tempest subsides, leaving Theseus as a bereaved and inconsolable father, he barely notices Phaedra's suicide. She is dismissed in a postscript: 'Que Phèdre, sitôt ensuite, consciente de son forfait, se soit fait justice, c'est bien', he remarks, and closes the subject.[2]

Oedipus as lover and husband is even more perfunctory. The myth forces him to mention his love for Jocasta which he very properly describes as 'quasi filial et conjugal à la fois', but once Jocasta, too, dies by her own hand he never refers to her again. When we remember how the unfortunate Nyssia was passed from hand to hand like a precious but inanimate object, it is not surprising that the later play reduces Jocasta's role to that of an ill-fated burden. Persephone's betrothal to Triptolemus is simply decorative ritual to explain the cyclical process. The only relationship that contains any feelings at all, as we have noted before, is the friendship bordering on love, suggested in the slight figure of Neoptolemus, developed more fully in Gyges, and producing the anguished experience of Saul.

To confine human emotion to sexual love of whatever form would be, however, too narrow. The theme of filial love recurs from time to time: between mother and daughter in the fragmentary 'Proserpine'; father and daughter, more effectively, in Œdipe; father and son in Thésée. Nevertheless, this does not carry

[1] *Thésée*, p. 17.   [2] Ibid., p. 115.

sufficient weight and conviction to offset the impression given by Gide that positive emotion, directed towards another human being, is absent. Except Saul, no character's happiness depends on the existence of another, no one sets concern for another before concern for self. A psychologist deduces, from the evidence provided by Gide's private and public relations as well as his writings, that Gide's personal experience is incomplete: 'Trop de signes nous avertissent que ce chantre du risque et de l'aventure a refusé le grand risque, a refusé la grande aventure, la seule qui puisse justifier les autres: l'amour qui n'écoute plus rien que lui-même.'[1]

If the positive emotion of outgoing human love is absent from Gide's work, so, too, is the negative emotion of moral suffering, of regret and remorse. Again excepting Saul, no hero suffers from the sense of guilt, the destructive awareness of remorse. These elements of Saul's tormented experience throw into relief the absence of such feelings in others. There is the minor character of Damocles who, having profited by the unexpected and unex-plained gift of money from heaven in *Le Prométhée*, explains his imminent death as due to duty and the remorse arising from trying to free himself from that duty: 'Le devoir, Messieurs,' he says, 'c'est une chose horrible; moi, j'ai pris le parti d'en mourir. . . . Le devoir est horrible, Messieurs . . ., mais combien plus horrible le remords d'avoir voulu se décharger d'un devoir. . . .'[2] However, Damocles is more allegorical than human, as his threatened name suggests; his chief function is to warn Prometheus of the dire effects of duty and remorse. Prometheus learns quickly. If they can kill, avoid them. The eagle must die.

Candaules suffers more from regret for his own foolish rashness than from any stronger feeling. If he knows natural jealousy of Nyssia and Gyges, he masters it easily enough. He, too, must die. But, in fact, Candaules only lives for and in his extravagant offer of wife to friend. Once the decision has been taken his part is virtually at an end. It is the shadow of a king that the rising

[1] P. Archambault, *Humanité d'André Gide*, essai de biographie et de critique psychologiques [Paris], Bloud et Gay, 1946, p. 328.
[2] *PME*, O.C. iii. 145.

fortunes of Gyges must extinguish, not a man. The inevitable consequences of a foolish action kill him, not remorse caused by an inhuman disregard for his wife.

After *Le Roi Candaule* no hero undergoes a similar experience. Naturally enough, as the introspective nature disappears from Gide's works, so does the self-blaming. Besides, what is the origin of the sense of fault and hence of guilt? Surely it arises with the acceptance of either a supernatural morality against which one transgresses or in the recognition of interdependent human needs and rights. Gide's later heroes acknowledge neither. His Oedipus blinds himself by his own will, not through penitence or a desire to propitiate the offended gods: 'C'est volontiers que je m'im-mole', he says. 'J'étais parvenu à ce point que je ne pouvais plus dépasser qu'en prenant élan contre moi-même.'[1] So, too, Theseus takes the responsibility for the death of Hippolytus. Poseidon may execute it but the will to destroy is Theseus' own: 'C'est sur mon fils innocent que j'appelai la vengeance de Dieu. . . . Par volonté subite, irraisonnable, passionnée, je me trouvais avoir tué mon fils.'[2] He declares his inconsolability but he does not acknowledge culpability. He has lost his heir and regrets the loss. But the thought that he has wilfully cut short a young and independent life does not cross his mind. Neither the superhuman nor the human codes of behaviour cause a sense of guilt. Nor do they in Oedipus. When he discovers his incestuous situation he is no more concerned for the other victims of it than he is for the outrage to divine prohibitions: 'j'épousai ma mère, hélas! hélas!' he laments, 'et avec elle tout mon passé. Ah! je comprends à présent pourquoi ma valeur dormait. En vain m'appelait l'avenir. Jocaste me tirait en arrière... Jocaste, qui follement prétendis supprimer ce qui devait être, toi que j'aimais comme un mari et, sans le savoir, comme un fils... Il est temps. Quitte-moi! Je romps l'attache.'[3] But Jocasta as victim of tragic destiny? His children? The Sophoclean Oedipus feels responsible for the shame-ful heritage he is leaving his children and so for their shattered future. The Gidian Oedipus thinks only of himself: 'Et vous,

[1] *Œd.*, p. 301.   [2] *Thésée*, pp. 114–15.
[3] *Œd.*, p. 294.

enfants . . .', he says in taking leave of them, 'c'est sans vous qu'il me faut entrer dans mon soir pour accomplir ma destinée.'[1]

Such invulnerability is the logical enough outcome of a philosophy centred on the self. But it indicates a weakness in Gide's vision of life. It is possible to live without belief in divine providence; it is not possible to live entirely alone. Gide's adoption of the first attitude separates him, as we shall see, from the Greeks; his acceptance of the second separates him from most of us and explains the emotional immunity of most of his heroes. 'Rien de plus vain que les regrets', he notes in his *Journal*,[2] and observes their absence in his daughter as in himself[3] with some satisfaction. Naturally enough his heroes are spared such human weaknesses.

Oedipus, as he appears in *Thésée*, is the only representative of the 'spiritual man'. The earlier Tiresias is too prosy and too sanctimonious to be so considered in his own right. He is the spokesman of an orthodoxy against which Oedipus must, for his own development, consistently struggle, and he is presented in such a way that all sympathy is alienated from his point of view. As we have seen, the later figure of Oedipus, although representing the attitude of individual mysticism, not that of dogmatic orthodoxy, comes perilously close to producing the same effect. As Theseus' peer he is able to express an alternative summing-up of human experience, but Gide is content to allow him to speak only, making no other attempt to establish him as a man, to humanize him, as it were. It is sufficient that he throws into relief the more vigorous and more admired philosophical stance of the hero.

Nevertheless, Oedipus too is allocated the expression of ideas of central importance, although they are not fully developed. It is almost in passing that Oedipus at Colonus interprets his earlier situation as he was forced to understand it and in so doing he touches on the myth's main attraction for Gide. As he describes the experience of tragic discovery, it consists in the sudden realization of the real nature of his immediate happiness: 'je pris soudain conscience de ceci', he explains to Theseus: 'que j'avais

---

[1] *Œd.*, pp. 294-5.   [2] *Journal 1939-1949*, p. 60, 14 octobre 1940.
[3] Ibid., p. 314, 1947, Feuillets d'automne.

assis mon humaine souveraineté sur un crime, de sorte que tout ce qui s'ensuivait en fût conséquemment souillé.'[1] Expressed in these terms, his discovery is understandably terrible. If contentment be based on a crime, it is only too obvious that it should become irretrievably contaminated. Gide, by the extreme statement he is now making, is in a way masking his original interpretation of *Oedipus the King*; for, as he writes in an unpublished notebook, Oedipus' happiness was founded on a lie and so could not endure. True happiness can be attained but it cannot be based on a false situation. This is what Gide, by analogy with his own experience, suddenly understands in the Oedipus story:

L'histoire d'Œdipe s'éclaira brusquement pour moi et . . . j'eus la subite révélation de sa signification profonde, tel jour précis et telle heure que je pourrais désigner, une révélation imprévue m'ayant appris sur quel mensonge j'avais édifié jusqu'alors mon bonheur, l'éblouissant mirage de ce bonheur chancela tout à coup se déchira, s'ouvrit et me laissa sombrer comme Œdipe au plus profond du désespoir. Si, depuis, j'ai pu atteindre de nouveau le bonheur . . . c'est comme par delà la mort, et avec un tel détachement que la mort ne puisse m'enlever grand chose, qu'elle ne m'enlevera que la vie. Cette fois ce bonheur est donc véritable. C'est celui d'Œdipe à Colone; je ne m'occupe aujourd'hui que d'Œdipe roi.[2]

But while the revelation of the inner meaning of the Oedipus myth may have come to him suddenly, it is but an extension of his lifelong desire for the sincere, or the explicit attitude in art and in life. Gide's 'sincerity' has been much debated,[3] but it is nevertheless a tenet of his own philosophy. From his early entry in the *Journal* of the 31st of December 1891, where he considers literary sincerity: 'La chose la plus difficile, quand on a commencé d'écrire, c'est d'être sincère. Il faudra remuer cette idée et définir ce qu'est la sincérité artistique'; or, a few days later when he finds himself in the general dilemma of desiring to be both moral and sincere,[4] he is constantly aware of the disparity between the

---

[1] *Thésée*, p. 120.

[2] Fonds Gide, Bibliothèque littéraire J. Doucet, γ 906, p. 8.

[3] See, for instance, H. Peyre, *Literature and Sincerity*, New Haven and London, Yale U.P. 1963, ch. 9, 'André Gide: Martyr and Hero of Sincerity'.

[4] *Journal*, p. 29, 11 janvier 1892.

crude experience and the artistic (literary in his terms) distillation of it in a work of art. Nothing seems, however, more inevitable or more natural. Any attempt to organize experience into a meaningful pattern demands the exercise of the controlling mind which, in order to communicate the experience, must intervene to order it intelligibly. This truism of the artistic method brings out one of the reasons for the appeal of mythological subject-matter to later writers since the myths we know come to us through literature, having been chosen by writers for their moving and meaningful character which is further thrown into relief by the literary presentation.[1]

However, Gide's so often discussed opinions of 'sincérité' are less relevant to his interpretation of the Oedipus myth than his characteristic mistrust of what is hidden from the world; he writes in his autobiography: 'j'avais une particulière horreur pour ce que l'on fait en cachette; s'il m'est arrivé par la suite et trop souvent, hélas! de devoir dissimuler, je n'ai jamais accepté cette feinte que comme une protection provisoire comportant le constant espoir et même la résolution d'amener bientôt tout au grand jour. Et n'est-ce pas pourquoi j'écris aujourd'hui ces mémoires?'[2] With such an attitude, recognized and expressed some years before the creation of his own Œdipe, Gide is prompt to seize upon its mythological 'correlative'. Oedipus the King is the dramatization of the discovery of truth: Gide's personal need to disclose the truth as he understands it, which governs such imaginative works as L'Immoraliste (1902), La Symphonie pastorale (1919), Les Faux-Monnayeurs (1926), not to mention the didactic Corydon (1924) or the autobiographical Si le grain ne meurt (1926), is similarly urgent. Le Roi Candaule obliquely approaches the same theme, since the hero discloses the source of his own happiness only to find that it dissipates in the process. The final persona of Theseus, freed from any sense of constraint by the death of his prudish son, recounts his life with apparently total frankness, including his weaknesses, or worse (for instance, the murder of the worthy Scyron among the bandits, the abuse of Minos' hospitality, the death of Egeus); and the result of this frank recognition of fault as well as of creditable achievement is peace of mind.

The myth of Oedipus is capable of expressing other Gidian themes. When Oedipus at Colonus explains his self-mutilating action to Theseus, he describes it as 'je ne sais quel secret besoin de pousser à bout ma fortune, de rengréger sur ma douleur et d'accomplir une héroïque destinée'.[1] At the end of his life he can thus analyse motives common to all the earlier heroes although they are less conscious of them and so less articulate.[2] From Adam to Theseus, they all thrust on in the self-realizing actions that lead them to their heroic destiny, whatever form that may take. 'Or, laisser insatisfait un désir,' says Theseus with echoes of William Blake, 'c'est malsain'.[3] But no Gidian hero voluntarily suffers from such a disease. Theseus again is the spokesman: apropos of his abduction of Phaedra from Minos' palace, he says: 'J'abusais évidemment. Mais il n'était pas, il n'est jamais en moi de me laisser arrêter par des scrupules. Sur toutes les voix de la reconnaissance et de la décence, celle de mon désir l'emportait. Tout coup vaille. Il faut ce qu'il faut.'[4]

The object of desire may vary: it may be the self-sufficing isolation of Philoctetes or the destructive intimacy sought by Candaules; the independence of Prometheus or the humanitarian devotion of Persephone; the self-chosen exile of Oedipus or the patriotic foundation of Theseus' life. The pursuit of satisfaction may lead to contentment or to death. But the motive and the self-realizing process are common to all the experiences. For the heroic destiny is the discovery and the development of the authentic self. As Gide writes in 1930: 'Le seul drame qui vraiment m'intéresse et que je voudrais toujours à nouveau relater, c'est le débat de tout être avec ce qui l'empêche d'être authentique, avec ce qui s'oppose à son intégrité, à son intégration. L'obstacle est le plus souvent en lui-même. Et tout le reste n'est qu'accident.'[5] Or,

---

[1] *Thésée*, p. 121.
[2] See Brée, *André Gide*, ch. v.
[3] *Thésée*, p. 88. See Blake, *Le Mariage du ciel et de l'enfer*, traduction par André Gide, Paris, Corti, 1942, p. 23: 'Le Désir non suivi d'action engendre la pestilence.'
[4] *Thésée*, p. 94. [5] *Journal*, p. 995, 3 juillet 1930.

as Oedipus teaches his sons, the monsters to be defeated may be within us.

There are, however, some external obstacles to be overcome or to be circumvented. External authority, for instance, whether exercised by divine providence or by the family, is such a threat. Rebellion against one or both manifestations of authority, as has long been recognized, is the characteristic behaviour in many Gidian heroes. The early heroes pit themselves against divine authority, Adam against paradisiacal order, Prometheus against Zeus; neither of them has to worry about family ties, of course, while Philoctetes is similarly free. But with the last two heroes, the conflict with supernatural authority is paralleled by the clash between sons and fathers. Oedipus' complicated family history provides a double example of what has been called 'la lutte des générations', an experience which is present in most legends.[1] For Oedipus not only kills his true father, though unwittingly, but he is conscious of enormous relief and freedom when he discovers his independence of Polybius, his father by adoption. His cutting of family ties is occasion for jubilation, never for regret, and the condition of bastard (as elsewhere in Gide's work) is pure benefit: 'Jailli de l'inconnu', he says triumphantly to Creon; 'plus de passé, plus de modèle, rien sur quoi m'appuyer; . . . Personne à qui ressembler, que moi-même.'[2]

Theseus is more decorous in public when his father dies as a result of the misleading black sails which he omitted to change but he is no less contented with his new-found power. He institutes ceremonial lamentations to be alternated with celebrations of his accession as proper public rites, but he cannot personally lament his father's death, even though Egeus was 'quelqu'un de très bien', as he judges him. For Egeus stood in his way and may even have threatened his future: 'obstruant ainsi ma carrière', Theseus observes, 'alors que c'est chacun son tour'.[3] Thus, the black sails did not fly at the mast through simple forgetfulness but through the elemental need for self-assertion. Each in his turn. Gide interprets the accidental and disastrous negligence of the myth as due

---

[1] M. Delcourt, *Œdipe*, p. 80.
[2] *Œd.*, p. 272. [3] *Thésée*, p. 14.

to the basic drive which directs the rising fortunes of the son and heir.

In the struggle between the generations there is no fortuitous accident but rather the action of the 'fatalité intérieure' which governs human lives. Myths to Gide, as we have seen, are embodiments of psychological truths, but they embody the truths he has learnt on his own pulse, all concerned in one way or another with the liberation and development of the individual man. His interpretations may seem to pervert the generally understood meaning of a myth—would a Gidian Orpheus, as hero, not have turned deliberately towards Eurydice in order to consign her eternally to Hades?—but they do follow an intelligible, if not always logical, pattern of his own ideas. They trace the heroic search for self-understanding and self-expression even if that search requires a personal and eccentric reading of traditional subject-matter. Theseus' sin of omission serves Gide doubly as early as 1919. The myth illustrates his theory of inner fate which replaces the supernatural *Fatum* of antiquity. On the one hand, given Theseus' ambitious and dominating character what else could he do but bring about his royal father's suicide? In the same way he was compelled to rid himself of Ariadne. Both were stumbling-blocks in his path: 'Et l'on n'a rien compris au caractère de Thésée', Gide writes, '. . . si l'on admet que l'audacieux héros . . . ait laissé par simple inadvertance la voile noire au vaisseau qui le ramène en Grèce, cette "fatale" voile noire qui, trompant son père affligé, l'invite à se précipiter dans la mer, grâce à quoi Thésée entre en possession de son royaume. Un oubli? Allons donc! Il oublie de changer la voile comme il oublie Ariane à Naxos.'[1] But it is also generally true that the son must supplant his father—a doctrine which may be dangerous. 'Et je comprends que les pères n'enseignent pas cela aux enfants . . .', Gide adds. Thus, seen in a certain light, the life of Theseus illustrates the universal struggle between the generations in which he triumphs over both his father and his own son, and eliminates both threats to his position. As Sartre writes: 'Il n'y a pas de bon père.'[2]

[1] 'Myth. grecque', O.C. ix. 150.
[2] J.-P. Sartre, *Les Mots*, Paris, Gallimard, 1964, p. 11.

Yet, while Gide is aware of this central core of meaning (although he does not suggest Theseus' subconscious intention in the death of Hippolytus, explaining his curse as a sudden explosion of passion) he expands his presentation of rebellion against the father to include all family ties and the *mores* of a group as obstacles to self-development. As his Prometheus and Philoctetes free themselves from socially accepted concepts of progress or patriotism by abandoning them, so his Oedipus, caught up by his immediate circumstances, breaks out of the trap by violence against himself and by total renunciation of his situation: 'Je ne suis plus un roi', he declares; 'plus rien qu'un voyageur sans nom, qui renonce à ses biens, à sa gloire, à soi-même.'[1] He is the last and most important of the heroes to undergo uprooting and departure, that formative ordeal which only the strong-spirited will find rewarding: 'Instruction, dépaysement, déracinement', as Gide writes in 1897; '— il faudrait pouvoir en user selon les forces de chacun . . .'.[2] By his own choice Theseus undertakes the Cretan adventure but it only teaches him how deeply his roots are down in his own country: wiser and forewarned, he returns to rule where he had once obeyed.

There are thus many common elements in the situations as in the heroic conduct which Gide found congenial in mythology: the necessity for uprooting with the capacity to endure and profit by it; the rejection of all authoritarian pressures and the acceptance of independence as condition and aim of life; the ideal of self-development as directing principle. But what general impressions can be formed from the group of particular heroes chosen from among the riches of Greek mythology? The dominant impression is certainly that of Gide's admiration for the physically strong man governed by strong will, a will which enables him to transcend or ignore all conventional restraints on his pursuit of individuality. He realizes himself in action, not in reflection; he is moved by intuition rather than by reason, although reason can be brought into play to support the intuitive impulse. In the successful hero, the combined forces enable him to control

[1] *Œd.*, p. 303.
[2] 'A propos des "Déracinés"', O.C. ii. 442.

any tendency to excessive introspection. His action once initiated, it must be pursued to the end, regardless of its destructive effect on others or even himself. His first thought is always for himself but none the less he possesses a desire to devote himself to something beyond self. When personal relations fail him, when vague feelings of pity for others are dissipated (for the world belongs to the strong, after all) he is capable of devoting himself to the general good of mankind.

He inhabits a world that is reassuring, without mysteries or invincible monsters: for reason explains the one, courage and effort defeat the other. It is a world without shadows, for the hero lives through his experience in the open day, without physical or mental suffering, for death itself seems accidental and incidental. It seems a world as it might be conceived by a very young man, a very healthy man, or a Stoic. But is it the world of the Greeks?

9

GREECE OR GIDE?

THE question would not be worth asking, were it not for the protective, possessive attitude Gide adopted for the Greek cultural spirit to which France seemed to him to be the natural heir. His lifelong interest in things Greek and his use of the Greek myth which showed the way to so many succeeding writers, as has often been noted,[1] might suggest a particular compatibility between antiquity and the modern writer, a particular sympathy capable of bridging the long gap in time. Yet a Greek critic emphatically denies that Gide possessed any such special sympathy. 'Dans sa première période', he writes of Gide, '. . . la Grèce ancienne passe et repasse; on dirait presque des souvenirs de collège, enregistrés par le génie. . . . Plus tard il y est revenu, en puisant librement dans la littérature hellénique des sujets qu'il renouvelait sans trop se soucier de leur origine ou de leur sens profond. Je ne crois pas qu'il puisse être question de la tradition de la Grèce ancienne dans l'œuvre d'André Gide.'[2]

There are thus further questions to be asked. If Gide set himself up both explicitly as essayist and implicitly by his use of myth as the defender of Greece, why did he misunderstand the true sense of Greek literature? If the misunderstanding was deliberate (and not a simple failure in comprehension which is more than unlikely in such a sensitive reader) what was its origin? And, finally, why did he choose the Greek heroes as his frequent subject-matter?

In an attempt to answer the first query Schlegel's examination of the satisfactions to be found in Greek tragedy may be illuminating: 'No: it is not the aspect of suffering which constitutes the

---

[1] See McLaren, *The Theatre of André Gide*, p. 90; Trousson, *Prométhée*, ch. VIII. iii, etc.

[2] C. Dimaras, 'Gide et la Grèce', *Revue d'Athènes*, avril 1951, p. 42.

charm of a tragedy', he writes. 'The satisfaction which we derive from the representation of the powerful situations and overwhelming passions in a good tragedy, must be ascribed either to the feeling of the dignity of human nature, excited by the great models exhibited to us, or to the trace of a higher order of things, impressed on the apparently irregular progress of events, and secretly revealed in them; or to both of these causes together.'[1]

Nevertheless, suffering, whether of body or soul, is an integral part of the Greek tragic experience. As Professor E. R. Dodds traces the extension of meaning of the Greek term *ate* from its early application to the irruption of the irrational in human behaviour to its later and wider sense of 'ruin', supernaturally determined, which may include both the 'sinner's state of mind' and 'the objective disasters resulting from it',[2] the two manifestations of suffering are combined. Suffering was also accepted, according to Simone Weil's quotation of Aeschylus, as part of the Eleusinian Mysteries, as part, in fact, of human life: 'Eschyle dit, citant évidemment une parole sacrée des Mystères. . . . Par la souffrance l'enseignement (accordé par Dieu à l'homme).'[3] But we have lost the same comprehensive vision today, as Albert Camus observed in 1948. In a comparison between the Greek tragic imagination as manifest in what he calls 'la tragédie du sang' and today, Camus singles out precisely the treatment of physical suffering in the two ages as one of his points of contrast: 'Quelle imagination aurions-nous donc pour cet équilibre supérieur', he asks, 'où la nature balançait l'histoire, la beauté le bien, et qui apportait la musique des nombres jusque dans la tragédie du sang! Nous tournons le dos à la nature, nous avons honte de la beauté. Nos misérables tragédies traînent une odeur de bureau et le sang dont elles ruissellent a couleur d'encre grasse.'[4]

Certainly the Gidian hero is spared physical suffering. If blood

---

[1] A. W. Schlegel, *A Course of Lectures on Dramatic Art and Literature*, translated by J. Black, London, Baldwin, Cradock and Joy, 1815, i. 76–77.

[2] E. R. Dodds, *The Greeks and the Irrational*, Berkeley and Los Angeles, University of California Press, 1951, p. 38.

[3] Simone Weil, *La Connaissance surnaturelle*, Paris, Gallimard, 1950, p. 316.

[4] A. Camus, 'L'exil d'Hélène', *Permanence de la Grèce*, Les Cahiers du Sud, 1948, pp. 382–3.

runs, from Prometheus' side, down Oedipus' cheeks, it dries at once. It is transparent, arising not from damaged tissue but from the mind. And it leaves no trace. Gide's intention, whether satiric or didactic, in his two first important Greek figures, Prometheus and Philoctetes, masks the fact that he has chosen two heroes who are called on to endure enormous physical suffering. But Prometheus, chained to the Caucasus, tortured daily by the eagle, becomes involved in Gide's version in a curiously complex relationship with his tormenting eagle, a masochistic form of love-play: '[L'aigle] occupait de ses morsures le prisonnier qui l'occupait de ses caresses, qui maigrissait et s'épuisait d'amour, tout le jour caressant ses plumes, sommeillant la nuit sous son aile et le repaissant à loisir. — L'aigle ne le quittait plus, ni la nuit ni le jour.'[1] The overtones of allegory inevitably obscure the legendary suffering. And the Gidian Prometheus' carefree invitation to dine on his eagle takes place in a world quite other from that of the Aeschylean Titan, buffeted by tempest and inconquerable in spirit.

The choice of Philoctetes is just as remarkable, since as he appears in Sophocles' tragedy all his sufferings are due to his incurable and repulsive wound. Isolation, a rugged existence of survival, and a tormenting sense of injustice, all make up Philoctetes' situation; but they are consequent on the corrupt flesh that functions within the tragic action and produces his individual destiny. The spectator is never allowed to forget the wound: it caused the abandonment of Philoctetes in the past; it draws lamentation from him now; its agony forces him to hand his miraculous bow to Neoptolemus, and so deliver his last power into the hands of the enemy; and it must be cured before he can accomplish his heroic future. Lessing's famous analysis of *Philoctetes* stresses the physical suffering he must endure: 'the lamentations are those of a man, but the acts are those of a hero. Both compose the manly hero who is neither effeminate nor hardened, but at one time appears as the former, at another as the latter . . .'.[2]

But how does Gide present such extremity of pain? His

---

[1] *PME*, O.C. iii. 125–6.
[2] G. E. Lessing, *Laocoon*, translated by R. Phillimore, London, Macmillan, 1874, p. 45.

Philoctetes certainly speaks of it but in a way that symbolizes the poet, not the sufferer from a putrefying wound: 'depuis que je ne m'en sers plus pour manifester ma souffrance, ma plainte est devenue très belle; à ce point que j'en suis consolé', he tells the invaders of his solitude.[1] It would be unfair, of course, to reproach Gide for failing to produce an effect he never intended. *Philoctète* is a Symbolist treatise and stays within its conventions. Nevertheless, the physical sufferings of Philoctetes distinguish him from other men, and in Gide's version, as in the dramatic figure of Oedipus, they remain declarations, not experience painfully endured. If we allowed ourselves to test either work by the criteria of reality, we would agree with Lessing when he states that 'everything stoical is unsuited to the stage, and our sympathy is always proportioned to the suffering which the object of interest expresses'.[2]

The treatment of death in Gide's mythological subject-matter is equally neutral. Indeed, he may eliminate it altogether, as in *Le Narcisse*, he may pass over it rapidly, as in the death of Phaedra or Hippolytus, or he may treat it as almost incidental, as in Candaules' suppression from the rising curve of Gyges' fortunes. Nevertheless, in a way Gide approaches the Greek conception of death. For him, as for the classical Greek, human life ends in death, without consequence and without influence. In Gide's world (always of the myth) death comes with sudden and unexpected violence and totally eliminates the figure: his *personae* withdraw from life, as it were, and are barely remembered by their fellows. Damocles sees his own death as the end of his sufferings, while Prometheus learns his profitable lesson from it and sweeps his companions off to lunch: 'laissons les morts ensevelir les morts', he says briskly, 'et allons vite déjeuner.'[3] Gyges' murdered wife hardly crosses his mind again and Candaules is forgotten in the new rights of king and husband. Oedipus never mentions Jocasta again, nor Theseus Phaedra; even Hippolytus' death does not disturb the contented tenor of Theseus' old age. Every death suggests the total disappearance of the living creature. Theseus' achievement

---

[1] *Phil.*, O.C. iii. 32.   [2] *Laocoon*, p. 11.
[3] *PME*, O.C. iii. 157.

will survive his death, but he is the only one to think beyond his own experience: the tomb effaces the others.

If the Greeks did not conceive of total obliteration for the dead (for they passed into the world of shades) they entered a state so removed from life and so powerless to affect it that they became negligible entities: 'In the Homeric age', as Otto writes,

the primal thought that the dead were impotent and dreamy shadows became central to the entire belief in the dead. All that remains of the deceased is actually no more than a delicate breath in human form without either will or power to act. An infinite chasm seperates him from the world. . . . The persistence of the dead is no longer an imitation of life; the essentials of life they have lost once and for all. And yet there they stand, solemnly and turned inward upon themselves, an eternal image. With this the Greek idea of death was fixed.[1]

Since will and the power to act are essentials of life, as Gide understands it, their loss in death totally eliminates the human spirit. Gide's dead do not persist even in the human memory of others which is one form of immortality. His view of death then approaches the Greek view although it is not, of course, identical with it.

For life, according to Otto, was naturally the greatest good. The gods of the Greeks responded fully to the demands of the living but they abandoned the dying who must meet the dreamless sleep of death with what heroism and dignity they could find in their own nature. When we think of Theseus' last words, we see the likeness between the two conceptions with their emphasis on the independence of man at the approach of death: Theseus, after a long and crowded life, awaits his death serenely and alone: 'J'ai vécu', he concludes.

But Theseus is the only hero to have completed his natural life (if we except Oedipus in his momentary appearance at Colonus), to have found serenity in a realistic setting (we must exclude *Philoctète*), and to have proved capable of incorporating rebellion, occasions for remorse, hypocrisy for the general good

---

[1] Walter F. Otto, *The Homeric Gods*, translated by Moses Hadas, London, Thames and Hudson [1954], pp. 143–4.

within a long and fruitful life. In a sense he is the apotheosis of
the Gidian hero. But he is uncharacteristically contented; the
experience of younger heroes of Gide's own earlier days is
naturally incomplete, unless ended in untimely death. Again, the
perspective given by Theseus' longevity (and his author's) justifies
a detachment and hence an ironical tone which is less surprising
here than it is in the earlier works.

We need perhaps to exercise some historical imagination today
to realize just how incongruous and indeed shocking the tone of
Le Prométhée must have seemed on its first appearance in 1899.
For the process of 'désacralisation du mythe héroïque' initiated by
Gide's Prometheus, 'ce petit écrit caustique et satirique',[1] has since
become the new orthodoxy. The disparity between solemn
mythological subject-matter and its expression has now become
so familiar that it is the serious treatment of, say, O'Neill's *Mourn-
ing becomes Electra* (1932) that is more novel than the 'désolennisa-
tion' of Cocteau, Giraudoux, Anouilh, or T. S. Eliot. As a critic
says of the tone of recent French plays based on the Greek myth:
's'il y a un trait commun à toutes ces pièces, c'est bien leur
irrévérence.'[2]

But irreverence is the dominating attitude of *Le Prométhée*: it
was impossible to treat the venerable theme with 'une plus
apparente désinvolture, un plus évident souci de désolenniser la
légende du grand Révolté'.[1] But it is not only the youthful work
which exploits the deflating tone: *Œdipe*, too, is controlled by the
same attitude. When we recall that Gide considered these two
tragedies the most solemn in antiquity,[3] the attitude he adopts
towards them seems the more remarkable and the more deliberate.
It may well manifest a Gidian revolt against authority, a writer's
revenge on the deified figures of European literature, analogous
to the chosen subject-matter of rebellion against authority. The
Gidian Prometheus must have seemed sacrilegious on his first
appearance, although the sacrilege renewed the myth's vitality,
potentiality, and range.[1]

---

[1] Trousson, *Prométhée*, ii. 435.
[2] J. de Romilly, 'Les mythes antiques dans la littérature contemporaine',
loc. cit., p. 171.   [3] *Journal*, p. 342, Feuillets.

In themselves, the myths of Prometheus and Oedipus possess the greatest authority, partly because of the nobility of their themes, partly through the respect in which they have always been held, partly, as we saw above, because of the distinction of the writers who had chosen to re-create them;[1] and, chiefly, because of the unfailing elevation of thought and poetic expression. Their original tone, the tragic tone, controls the dramatic experience. The criticism one writer makes of the tone employed by Anouilh in his *Antigone* may be equally applicable to *Œdipe*, at least; *Le Prométhée's* satiric intention sets it rather apart: 'Ce n'est pas un vain respect de la forme', he writes, 'qui m'incite à dire qu'il y a un ton tragique dont il n'est pas prudent de s'écarter. Je n'en fais pas une question d'ambiance, de solennité, mais de situation relative. Il y a une certaine distance qu'il faut établir entre les personnages d'une tragédie et nous, une distance optima, unique: plus loin du héros nous ne le plaindrions pas assez, mais plus près de lui, nous le jugerions trop. C'est le ton qui nous indique notre place.'[2]

The Gidian tone functions in two ways. It seems at once to bring us too close to the characters, and to separate us from them. Certainly, the familiarity with which Gide handles his Prometheus and his Oedipus is intended to diminish the larger-than-life heroes: the setting, in one case, the stuffy mediocrities who surround Oedipus, in the other, bring both heroes within the realm of common day. Despite Prometheus' unusually deep voice, both express themselves in everyday colloquial speech, as modern men among their contemporaries. So deliberate is Gide's attempt to render the superhuman and the great simply human and familiar that his practice contradicts his theory. In 'L'évolution du théâtre' (of 1904) he defends the choice of subjects remote in time, since the passage of time has eliminated all episodic irrelevancies, as he defends the distance established between characters and audience; both are means of producing the pure work of art which is something quite other than, and apart from, reality: 'le dépaysement que l'artiste cherche à produire en éloignant de nous ses personnages, indique précisément ce désir: nous donner son œuvre d'art

---

[1] See ch. III.
[2] H. Gignoux, *Jean Anouilh*, Paris, Éditions du Temps Présent, 1946, pp. 114–15.

pour une œuvre d'art, son drame pour un drame, simplement — et non courir après une illusion de réalité qui, lors même qu'elle serait obtenue, ne servirait qu'à faire avec la réalité pléonasme'.[1]

Yet, in *Œdipe* particularly, details of setting, situation, and character all lessen the distance between hero and spectator; while the overall tone reduces Titan and Theban alike to the stature of ordinary men.

Again, it is the manipulation of tone that controls the emotional pattern of both works, as we noted above in the case of *Œdipe*, where Creon's fatuous interjections deflate the rising feeling of the tragic situation. In this way, the Gidian tone intervenes between experience and audience, destroying the growing sympathy as it develops and establishing a barrier between the dramatic events and their spectator.

This tone is so personal, sometimes so outrageous, that we inevitably question its origin. Rebellion against the orthodox literary gods may certainly be related to Gide's rejection of authoritarianism. But, in general, could the tone be understood as the result of an effort of will, a deliberate effort to master a side of his nature that he thought over-sensitive, even sentimental? At twenty, he set himself to 'dry out' his heart: 'on y moisit, dans mon cœur', he observes,[2] and consequently disciplines his reading. Twenty-five years later, in reading the work of Maurice de Guérin, he grudgingly acknowledges a fundamental similarity in attitude: 'Je n'ai jamais beaucoup aimé, ni même bien lu Maurice de Guérin, agacé d'entendre que je lui ressemblais. Mais il est vrai que je *sens* cette page [du *Journal*], jusque dans le moindre détail de son rythme et de sa force, comme si je l'avais écrite moi-même — et que j'aurais voulu l'écrire.'

Gêné aussi par la calligraphie du *Centaure* et de la *Bacchante* (qui me sont à peu près insupportables), par le *geignement* latent de sa pensee . . . .[3] At once attracted and repelled by such a sensibility Gide may well have exaggerated his own self-discipline.

[1] 'L'évolution du théâtre', O.C. iv. 205.
[2] *Journal*, p. 21, 10 juin 1891.
[3] Ibid., p. 538, 8 février 1916.

Irony would naturally result from a voluntary reaction against the vulnerability of his own nature.[1]

But the explanation may be found elsewhere. The origin of this provocative tone could lie at a deeper level, below the action of consciousness and will-power. Certain entries in the *Journal* are so revealing that we may briefly disregard his famous advice: 'C'est du point de vue de l'art qu'il sied de juger ce que j'écris. . .',[2] to consider whether the detached attitude, and the ironical tone which expresses it, is not more probably an essential trait of character than an acquired characteristic. Gide's reaction to violent events, even when they are potentially dangerous to him, is curiously illuminating: he is never involved himself and assumes the role of audience of an interesting but remote spectacle. When there was an attempt made on the Spanish king's life, for instance, Gide happened to be very close by; yet his account shows his detachment: 'De cette place j'entendis fort bien la bombe. . . . De nouveau je pus constater en moi la difficulté de *prendre au sérieux* l'événement. . . . Il ne me semblait pas que ce fût de la vie véritable. Le tableau fini, les acteurs allaient revenir saluer.'[3] More closely involved, physically, in a railway accident which resulted in four or five deaths and a score of injured victims, he remained equally psychologically detached, and recorded: 'Pour moi, constaté à neuf la grande difficulté où je suis de prendre au tragique, au sérieux même, l'accident fortuit. Je reste amusé, comme au spectacle, exalté plutôt et prêt à dépenser une ressource d'activité subite.'[4] Since the accidents of real life seem theatrically unreal to him his casual fashion of presenting them in his work is not surprising. In *Le Prométhée*, for example, when Cocles accidentally loses an eye, an event with subsequent meaning for Damocles, it is recounted with terrifying speed: 'Un oiseau . . . obscurit un

---

[1] S. Ullman, *The Image in the Modern French Novel*, p. 6, examines Gide's images as being produced despite an 'uncompromising inner censorship', and notes 'an unresolved conflict between his natural bent and the restraint imposed by the austere side of his personality'. This view is similar to the present interpretation although it seems probable that irony offers an acceptable means of resolving inner conflict.

[2] *Journal*, p. 658, 13 octobre 1918.

[3] Ibid., pp. 162–3, mai 1905.   [4] Ibid., p. 544, 2 mars 1916.

instant le ciel du boulevard — fond comme un tourbillon vers le café, brise la devanture, et s'abat, crevant l'œil de Coclès d'un coup d'aile, et . . . s'abat sur le flanc droit de Prométhée.'[1] The *sotie*, of course, profits by such fantastic speed; but this incident is merely one of the more extreme examples of Gide's characteristically casual presentation of painful events. They happen fortuitously and without emotional overtones.

This emotional reticence may be due to Gide's refusal to commit himself completely to any single idea, emotion, or personal experience. Psychological biography is not the intention of this study. Nevertheless, any attempt to explain a persistent literary trait must record Gide's own analyses of his character. For he recognizes his ambivalent attitude to his own experience where a deep dichotomy continually prevails. As early as 1892, he examined his own complexity and preferred it to the simplicity of others: 'Je vois toujours presque à la fois les deux faces de chaque idée et l'émotion toujours chez moi se polarise. Mais, si je comprends les deux pôles, je perçois fort nettement aussi, entre eux deux, les limites où s'arrête la compréhension d'un esprit qui se résout à être simplement personnel, à ne voir jamais qu'un seul côté des vérités, qui opte une fois pour toutes pour l'un ou pour l'autre des deux pôles.'[2] The continual changes in his work no doubt result from this basic attitude but, more relevantly, it explains the emotional void in his works and the consequent deficiency of emotional impact on his reader or spectator. To submit to emotional experience, to suffer from it, demands, ultimately, surrender to it. And of this total surrender of the being Gide was incapable. He had his own protective device which he described to Valéry in 1896: 'Pour moi j'ai toujours dans mon armoire quelque petite idole devant qui je me console de la perte des autres.'[3]

Such a philosophy of substitution is no doubt prudent and guarantees an easy life. But it entails a diminishment of the being. And it divides Gide from his Greek tragic models. For Antigone and Andromache, Oedipus and Orestes, Prometheus and

---

[1] *PME*, O.C. iii. 118. [2] *Journal*, p. 31, 12 mai 1892.
[3] *Correspondance*, p. 274 [29 août 1896].

Philoctetes did not protect themselves from suffering by alternatives. Whatever the particular circumstances of the hero, he is totally involved in his experience, without second thoughts, without evasion. But, except Saul, no Gidian hero so surrenders himself to his experience, while the double vision that produces irony protects his creator. In a discussion of the *Correspondance* between Gide and Valéry, Gide's characteristic reservations have been observed: 'Gide est moins libre devant Valéry . . . pour être aussi moins libre devant lui-même',[1] and by consequence: 'On ne peut donc attendre de lui, à aucun moment, une expression définitive, et c'est parce qu'il le sait qu'il ne cesse, dans ses lettres, de se préserver et de réserver.'[2]

However, simple indifference too can be protective and this is a condition that Gide himself acknowledges as he ages. In 1929 he writes, 'je ne tiens authentiquement plus à grand'chose, plus à rien, depuis que j'ai perdu ce à quoi je tenais le plus. (Mais ceci depuis douze ans seulement.)'[3] (He is alluding, presumably, to his despair when, after his departure for England in 1918, his wife destroyed all his early letters to her and, in so doing, seemed to destroy his past.) But this recognition of indifference comes relatively late in his life; it seems more likely that it derives from his life-long self-protection and, ultimately, from his refusal to commit himself wholly to his experience.

If the suffering that Schlegel considered integral in the Greek tragic experience is absent in Gide's versions of myth so, too, is the involvement of his reader or audience. The 'combat des idées' may engage the mind but the emotions are left untouched. This was Gide's avowed intention for *Œdipe*, of course, but it demonstrates how remote from the spirit of Greek tragedy all his re-creations are since all of them stimulate the mind and anaesthetize the feelings. Greek tragedy, despite the special conditions of its presentation, addresses itself directly to the heart as to the mind of its audience: in a sense, it is a 'chant de deuil sur les malheurs de l'humanité'.[4] The Gidian detachment builds a wall of

---

[1] G. Picon, *L'Usage de la lecture*, T. II [Paris], Mercure de France, 1961, p. 117.
[2] Ibid., p. 118.　　　　　　　[3] *Journal*, p. 940, 8 octobre 1929.
[4] É. Faguet, *Notes sur le théâtre contemporain, 1888*, Paris, Lecène et Oudin, 1889,

glass between the spectator and the imaginative experience. He
may approve, he may admire, but he is never moved.

Nor does he feel awe. When Schlegel distinguishes the sense
of a supernatural ordering as one of the elements of the tragic
experience he throws into relief the other essential divergency of
Gide's concept from the Greek. For Gide acknowledges no superhuman force: 'Je crois plus facilement aux dieux grecs qu'au
Bon Dieu', he writes. 'Mais ce polythéisme, je suis bien forcé
de le reconnaître tout poétique. Il équivaut à un athéisme foncier.'[1]
As atheist, therefore, he is radically opposed to the Greek spirit
which apprehended the manifestation of the supreme *Fatum* in
human lives. Whatever the roles the heroes are called on to play,
one force directs them all. They may become its victims, like
Oedipus or the Trojan women; propitiatory sacrifices, like Iphi-
genia or Antigone; instruments of vengeance, like Orestes; its
agent of punishment or of crime, depending on the point of view,
like Clytemnestra: but the unknowable force is always in action,
a power that transforms the violence and confusion of human
action into a meaningful pattern.

Gide denies this mysterious power. As he understands the
myth, there is no need to glorify simple chance and elevate man's
failure in understanding to the force of divinity:

l'erreur, c'est de ne consentir à ne reconnaître dans le mythe que
l'expression imagée des lois physiques, et de ne voir dans tout le reste
que le jeu de la *Fatalité*. Avec ce mot affreux l'on fait au hasard la part
trop belle; il sévit partout où l'on renonce à expliquer. Or je dis que
plus on réduit dans la fable la part du Fatum, et plus l'enseignement
est grand.... Que nous enseigne le Fatum, chaque fois que nous le laissons reparaître? A nous soumettre à ce dont nous ne pouvons point
décider.[2]

To call the *Fatum* chance is to diminish it immediately, and to

p. 219. A revival of *Oedipus Rex* leads Faguet to distinguish three ways of
appreciating Greek tragedy: as work of art, as philosophic comment, as melo-
drama: 'Il y a un intérêt de contemplation, un intérêt de méditation et de pitié, un
intérêt de curiosité', he writes (p. 225).

[1] *Les Nouvelles Nourritures* (1935), with *Les Nourritures terrestres*, Paris, Gallimard
[1942], p. 248.

[2] 'Myth. grecque', O.C. ix. 149.

interpret it as the substitute for human decision, operating in a void, as it were, when free choice proves too difficult to make, is to negate it altogether. The positive force governing the mythological experience, as Gide understands it, is the evolution of individual psychological fate, the self-engendered, self-directing destiny of human nature.

This interpretation controls his own handling of the myth. Deities are eliminated or so reduced in stature, Zeus as 'Miglionnaire', Poseidon as agent, that they might as well be absent. The Erinnyes, particularly, are unknown; they have no place in Gide's world of man. If there is no code of supernatural morality, there can be no transgressions against it. The Gidian hero is thus spared the sense of guilt and fear of punishment, just as he has eliminated the terror of the incomprehensible from his life. He would be utterly alien in the world of the Greek tragic poets, that world dominated by the inherited 'archaic guilt-culture' whence arose, as Professor Dodds says, 'some of the profoundest tragic poetry that man has produced'.[1] The Gidian Oedipus does not breathe the same air as the Sophoclean king, for: 'It was above all Sophocles, the last great exponent of the archaic world-view, who expressed the full tragic significance of the old religious themes in their unsoftened, unmoralised forms—the overwhelming sense of human helplessness in face of the divine mystery, and of the *ate* that waits on all human achievement—and who made these thoughts part of the cultural inheritance of Western Man.'[1] The Gidian hero does not know guilt or fear, protected as he is by rationalization. He does not necessarily escape from natural feelings of remorse, but since he readily sheds his past he avoids the remorse it might warrant.

Gide's theory and treatment are thus consistent. Where others may stress the myth's metaphysical meaning, as Simone Weil does when she writes: 'Le fondement de la mythologie, c'est que l'univers est une métaphore de vérités divines',[2] Gide emphasizes its psychological truth and that truth alone: 'La fable grecque,' he writes, 'à partir de Troie, perd sa signification symbolique,

---

[1] *The Greeks and the Irrational*, p. 49.
[2] *La Connaissance surnaturelle*, p. 145.

mais se charge de valeur psychologique et poétique, pour le profit des dramaturges. Il n'y a plus lieu de chercher le sens secret de ces histoires; elles n'ont rien de mythique; leur pathos admirable doit suffire au poète ingénieux.'[1] Seen in this light, the Greek heritage is inexhaustibly rich, valuable in itself, potentially valuable to other poets. But it is not the light of Greek antiquity. The mythical element dissipates, and the narrative on a human level only is left. All that does not conform to the psychological explanation is ignored: 'La fable grecque est essentiellement raisonnable', Gide writes,[2] but he puts aside all its irrational aspects.

He is, in fact, logical in his beliefs as a non-believer. Greek myth is useful to him as the Christian terminology is useful. When he passes through a spiritual crisis in 1916, he writes of hell and 'le Malin' in all sincerity and solemnity, but he adds: 'Je me sers consciemment ici, comme précédemment, d'un vocabulaire et d'images qui impliquent une mythologie à laquelle il n'importe pas absolument que je croie. Il me suffit qu'elle soit la plus éloquente à m'expliquer un drame intime.'[3] Both Christian and Greek mythology help him to explore and explain his own intimate crises as, by his use of the synonymous terms of 'le côté Prométhée' (or 'le côté Christ'), they clarify his philosophic thought. They are means of communication, and with the whole of Greek mythology available to him, the writer need only make his personal choice. The myths 'represent', as the young Gide demanded, the eternal human experience in its infinite variety.

Nevertheless, choice reveals the man as much as style and his problems and purposes may be many. Gide's use of the myth is so persistent that it raises some general problems of cause and effect that have been much discussed recently in relation to the remarkable resurgence of mythological subject-matter in the past forty years. Gide's own definition of the myth's meaning, while widely acceptable today, was not formulated until his middle age and does not illuminate his earlier versions of myth.

It has been suggested that the familiar matter of myth offers the writer an easy solution to his problem of choosing a subject.

[1] *Journal 1939–1949*, pp. 283–4, 17 février 1945.
[2] 'Myth. grecque', O.C. ix. 148.   [3] *Journal*, p. 541, 16 février 1916.

This may be an advantage, as one critic thinks: earlier presentations have accentuated the moving and meaningful character of
the myth and the writer is free to meditate upon it, elaborate it,
and make his own commentary.[1] Another, on the contrary,
considers that reliance on the literary mythical subject is a sign of
weakness in the author who chooses it: he includes Gide, with
his *Œdipe* and his *Perséphone*, among those writers who manifest
such weakness: '[ils] trahissent peut-être', he writes, 'dans leur
reprise de sujets cent fois traités, la faiblesse secrète de tant d'auteurs
modernes: le manque de fougue imaginative, la crainte de puiser à
même la vie, souvent vulgaire, et brutale, et la préférence pour la
matière déjà épurée, sublimée et filtrée par maint prédecesseur.'[2]
When we recall *L'Immoraliste*, *La Porte étroite*, *La Symphonie
pastorale*, *Les Faux-Monnayeurs*, we may rule out the idea of
Gide's fear of subjects drawn from life, not literature. It is note-
worthy, all the same, that Gide draws on the myth particularly
at the beginning and towards the end of his creative career, while
his interest in hellenism in his maturity is confined to unfinished
fragments and to critical examination and exposition. His later
recourse to it suggests a weakening of imaginative invention: 'les
figures mythologiques offrent de nouveau à sa pensée la succession
d'images riches de signification qu'il lui est difficile d'extraire de la
vie.'[3] The extreme difficulty with which Gide wrote his *Œdipe*,
recorded in the *Journal*, might suggest failing inspiration but,
again, the astonishing outburst of creative energy which produced
Thésée might deny it. And there may have been other and deeper-
seated reasons for the slower creation of *Œdipe*.

Gide's most frequent use of the myth is evident in the first
ten years of his literary life, a fact that has been explained in many
ways. One writer sees it as an exploratory period in which Gide
was seeking his proper path:[4] she thinks, too, that the mythical
figures were 'legendary disguises' for his 'arresting and original

[1] J. de Romilly, 'Les mythes antiques dans la littérature contemporaine',
loc. cit., pp. 170–1.
[2] H. Peyre, *L'Influence des littératures antiques sur la littérature française moderne*,
pp. 80–81. See also E. Ludovicy, 'Le mythe grec dans le théâtre français contemporain', *Revue des langues vivantes*, xxii, 1956, p. 415.
[3] Brée, *André Gide*, p. 330.   [4] Ibid., p. 186.

drama';[1] while another develops the thought of disguise yet
further to understand Gide's adoption of the myth as a 'ruse'
which enabled him 'to give his "dangerous thoughts" some kind
of circulation in the heavy pre-1914 world in which he found
himself. . . . He wrote his books under the protection of the
myth.'[2] Again, one simple reason may lie in the existing literary
tradition. Certainly, the choice of Narcissus was dictated by
fashion and even, in a spirit of audacity, so may have been
Prometheus. And Gide, a dedicated writer from his adolescence,
may simply have followed his predecessors: this is another critic's
opinion when he writes: 'Fidèle à la grande tradition littéraire
française classique, il ne crée pas son sujet. Il l'emprunte à la
mythologie. A proprement parler, il n'invente rien. Et pourtant,
il invente tout. Car si les faits sont ceux de la légende traditionnelle,
l'interprétation qu'il nous en donne est toute personnelle.'[3] Seen
in this way Gide would not only have been faithful to the French
classical tradition but also to the classical tradition itself. For the
Greek poets drew on the myth to re-create it in their own imaginative modes: 'Les personnages d'Æschyle semblent des Titans,
ceux de Sophocle des Héros, ceux d'Euripide des hommes. . . .'[4]
Yet, while the individual imagination of the Greek writers played
over the given myth, transforming it in their own tragic or comic
vision, the tragic writers particularly, as a modern author observes, transmitted the myth as still infinitely potential: 'Parce
qu'elle a mis sur le théâtre non des individus, mais des figures,
non des caractères mais des destins, la tragédie grecque a laissé
à ses héros, qu'aucun cerne ne limite, des possibilitées illimitées
de développement. Debout sur une frontière d'ênigmes où la
personnalité humaine se débat pour s'affirmer dans les anneaux
monstrueux d'un cosmos encore nocturnes, ils sont offerts à toutes
les questions et prêts pour toutes les réponses. . . . '[5]

---

[1] Brée, Gide, p. 99.
[2] L. Bogan, Selected Criticism, London, Peter Owen, 1958, pp. 321–2. (A
review of Imaginary Interviews, 1944.)
[3] B. Guyon, 'Le testament d'André Gide', La Vie intellectuelle, juin, 1951, p. 59.
[4] L. Ménard, Du polythéisme hellénique, p. 85.
[5] Thierry Maulnier, 'Les mythes grecs chez les auteurs d'aujourd' hui, Le
Théâtre dans le monde, T. VI, no. 4, 1957, p. 290.

And the examination of human destiny and its relationship with its surrounding world is what lies at the centre of Gide's major presentations of myth, although his method may vary. In differing forms, the theme runs through the works until it reaches man's domination over both situation and circumstances in *Thesée*.

In the less important works, such as *Le Narcisse* or *Philoctète*, Gide handles the mythological figures as abstractions. They serve him as symbols of function, as in Narcissus the Poet, or as allegorical representations of conflicting points of view, as in *Philoctète*. And the Dioscuri, in their alliance with Helen as Beauty and Clytemnestra as Passion, are employed in the same way. The mythological figures here provide a rapid communication of ideas, in today's prevailing manner: that is, as a form of abstract language which is used by the intelligence and appeals only to the intelligence. It is, however, anti-humanist, anti-classical, and anti-poetic.[1] And it does not satisfy Gide for long, nor does it help him in expressing his major problems. The ideas, even for the writer who was later to claim the predominance of conflicting ideas in his *Œdipe*, remain too remote from their imaginative environment. Narcissus' contemplation by the symbolic river is too static, his situation too unnatural, while Philoctetes is subjected to a metaphysical metamorphosis that has little to do with life and nothing to do with how best to live.

Nevertheless even here there is the first appearance of a man coming literally to grips with his surroundings in Adam, even if his act entails destruction; and there is the tentative affection of Neoptolemus, which offers another way for man to adjust to his situation.

The next use to which Gide puts the myth is the exploration of man's situation, where this is more significant than the character involved. This seems the case in *Le Prométhée*. The question that Gide poses is how best to conduct a life in certain circumstances rather than what kind of man has to decide. 'Où vont-ils?'

---

[1] J. Thomas, 'Les mythes antiques dans le théâtre français contemporain', *Lettres d'humanité*, T. III, 1944, Paris, 'Les Belles Lettres', Association Guillaume Budé, p. 156.

Prometheus asks about the Parisian and preoccupied crowds. His final solution is to extricate himself from the pressures exercised by his surroundings upon him, just as Damocles is overcome by them and Cocles, the complacent, comes to profitable terms with them. *Le Prométhée* is concerned with the alternative means of living with society, either by evasion or by capitulation, but not with the nature of the figures involved. In a sense, it offers a more vital presentation of abstract ideas, but they are handled with such wit, provocativeness, and complexity that the exploration of situation has a life of its own. But it still does not produce a human being in his particular set of circumstances.

This aim is more fully realized in *Le Roi Candaule* and in *Saül*. For here, apart from the natural dramatic advantage in presenting a convincing human being, the situation to be explored is brought about by the character's own actions. Both Candaules and Saul influence their immediate environment. Events move beyond their control but they result from their individual although fatally ill-understood natures. At this stage, Gide's concern is primarily with the crisis of character and the consequences of unpredictable and uncontrollable human motives. The man contrives the situation that will destroy him. It is precisely because Ajax is incapable of self-direction, however disastrous it may prove, that Gide abandons his projected drama.

In Gide's treatment of Oedipus, that 'organic myth' as it has been called,[1] and *Perséphone*, the problem of man and his situation is presented from yet another angle. For if there were ever myths where the situation could be supposed to control and overpower the central figure, they might be recognized in Oedipus, trapped in the inescapable destiny shaped for him before his birth, caught in *La Machine infernale*, as Cocteau describes the same process, or in Persephone, driven from earth to the underworld and back again in her eternal cyclical destiny. Yet in both Gidian presentations the title figure achieves mastery over the situation by the exercise of will. At the point where Oedipus understands the

[1] R. Las Vergnas, 'Le renouveau des mythes dans la littérature française contemporaine', *Marche romane*, Cahiers de l'Association des romanistes de l'Université de Liège, T. IX, no. 1, 1959, p. 12.

trap of destiny, he voluntarily acts against himself in self-mutilating violence, in a voluntary act of self-immolation, as he says.
By such an act he regains the power of decision and, in the tragic
light, becomes master of his own destiny again. Persephone's
way of dominating her destined situation is similarly achieved
through an act of her own will. Compassion takes her voluntarily
down to the underworld and love for her mystical bridegroom,
Triptolemus, brings her back to the sunny spring surface of the
earth. If the given situation in which the central character finds
himself is thus inescapable yet the exercise of individual will,
whether directed against himself in what may seem a negative
way or in capitulating to conditions, which may seem equally
negative, can also be understood as a positive force to use against
potentially overpowering conditions.

Theseus alone is capable of both creating and dominating the
situations of his increasingly complex life. As he passes from youth
to age, he undertakes the varying exploits of heroic history, as we
have seen, and having physically conquered the bandits in his first
youth, surpasses Hercules, as he says, in overcoming the monstrous
Minotaur by physical strength and psychological endurance, and
goes on to fulfil the destiny predicted for him by Daedalus. But
the foundation of a City as destiny is in a sense a neutral prophecy.
It is neither the negative entanglement in circumstances in which
Oedipus finds himself nor is it a gift from the gods. It is a privilege
that must be actively and laboriously achieved. Theseus prides
himself on his devotion to the immediate task, whatever form it
may take: he learns from his father that 'l'on n'obtient rien de
grand ni de valable, ni de durable, sans effort'.[1] He is, if we except
Prometheus' early benefits to man which antedate his immediate
story, the only hero who is capable of sustained effort, of 'dévouement à la tâche'. This is the attribute that distinguishes him from
the other heroes, that enables him to fulfil his heroic destiny in
more than the exercise of physical strength and courage, that
directs him and endows him with the power to influence his
environment according to his own aspirations, and to satisfy
himself in the creation of an enduring memorial to his own life.

[1] *Thésée*, p. 11.

Perhaps he over-rationalizes a characteristic deficiency when he brushes aside his failure in his emotional relationships, but his history offers its own reason. In the end, he can offset his personal loneliness by his sense of the enduring story of mankind.

In *Thésée*, Gide, for the first and last time in his works based on myth at least, achieves the 'mythical slant' of the artist's eye that Thomas Mann writes of as desirable both in the artist and in the individual man. It engenders the capacity to see historical life as a 'sacred repetition' of human experience of immemorial age. In *Thésée* it is partly brought about by the autobiographical form of the old man's account of his life but it is chiefly due to the personal and comprehensive vision held by Theseus: he alone is able to recognize (and it is the youthful Gide's own ideal duty imposed on men)

the extent to which his life is but formula and repetition and his path marked out for him by those who trod it before him. His character is a mythical role which the actor just emerged from the depths to the light plays in the illusion that it is his own and unique, that he, as it were, has invented it all himself, with a dignity and security of which his supposed unique individuality in time and space is not the source, but rather which he creates out of his deeper consciousness in order that something which was once founded and legitimized shall again be represented and once more for good or ill, whether nobly or basely, in any case after its own kind conduct itself according to pattern.[1]

It is this final and fully realized treatment of man's 'representative' mission in the *persona* of Theseus that brings serenity to the fictional character and justifies in the deepest sense the ironical light that plays over the whole narration. For Gide's tone in this last work seems of a different quality, because of a different origin, from that of such earlier works as *Le Prométhée*, or even that of *Œdipe*. It originates, as we have noted earlier, in the sense of perspective rather than in the exploitation of incongruity that underlies the treatment of Prometheus in Paris or the juxtaposition of Creon and Oedipus' tragic fate. It is, it seems, the irony to be found, as Thomas Mann writes, in 'the gaze which the

[1] T. Mann, 'Freud and the Future' (1936), *Essays of Three Decades*, translated by H. T. Lowe-Porter, London, Secker and Warburg (n.d.), pp. 422–3.

mythically oriented artist bends upon the phenomena about him—
an ironic and superior gaze ... for the mythical knowledge resides
in the gazer and not in that at which he gazes'.[1]

Again, it is remarkable that in *Thésée* Gide returns to his long-
felt admiration for Goethe to echo Faust's final speech (*Part Two*)
in Theseus' last words. When Theseus says: 'J'ai fait ma ville. ...
Il m'est doux de penser qu'après moi, grâce à moi, les hommes se
reconnaîtront plus heureux, meilleurs et plus libres. Pour le bien
de l'humanité future, j'ai fait mon œuvre. J'ai vécu',[2] there is a
strong reminiscence of the dying Faust's last words:

> I work that millions may possess this space,
> If not secure, a free and active race.
> Here man and beast, in green and fertile fields,
> Will know the joys that new-won region yields,
> Will settle on the firm slopes of a hill
> Raised by a bold and zealous people's skill.
>
> Such busy, teeming throngs I long to see,
> Standing on freedom's soil, a people free.
> Then to the moment could I say:
> Linger you now, you are so fair!
> Now records of my earthly clay
> No flights of aeons can impair—
> Foreknowledge comes, and fills me with such bliss,
> I take my joy, my highest moment this.[3]

But Faust's task and his belief in eternally glorious achievement
are delusion: the clashing spades do not turn bog into fertile land;
they prepare his grave. He dies in this delusion. Theseus, however,
created by a master of irony, speaks entirely without ambiguity:
his last words are an affirmation of faith.

Thésée, the last of Gide's myth-based works, is, it seems, the
only one to create the feeling of myth in itself, in a way that has
little, though not, of course, nothing to do with the given myth
of Theseus. 'Les mythes n'ont pas de vie par eux-mêmes', Camus
writes of the Promethean myth. 'Ils attendent que nous les

---

[1] T. Mann, loc. cit   [2] *Thésée*, p. 123.
[3] *Faust, Part Two*, Act V, pp. 269–70.

incarnions.'[1] *Thésée* is Gide's creation which carries a meaning over and above the heroic aspects of youth or even the achievement of age which are present in the given matter. It possesses a unity that is lacking in the earlier examinations of partial experience, where the characters are never fully enough explored to communicate any sense of an action complete in itself. The unity of *Thésée* comes partly from its subject of a lifetime, partly from its tone, but chiefly from its concept of man's unified and continuous history. In one sense, this is produced by the selection of incidents within the story of the hero; the span of the episodes, their nature as representative phases of a life, the very economy and generality of their presentation stress the typical aspect of Theseus, one of the *élite* among men certainly, but one whose long life epitomizes many lives. And that life, however remarkable and successful, is one link in the lengthening chain of human lives. Theseus' recognition of his debt to his father, even if necessities of succession may seem to drive him to ruthless inaction, establishes his relationship to the past; his relationship to the future, in the absence of his son to inherit his power, is guaranteed by his legacy to his citizens.

The plot is thus concerned to establish the concept of the continuous process of human life, both in individual histories and in the racial history of men. Theseus' reminiscence of Ecclesiastes: 'Il est un temps de vaincre . . ., puis un temps de cultiver . . .',[2] works poetically to convey the same feeling of a process active in man and race alike. And it is this feeling of a general truth concerning both life and history, engendered by *Thésée*, that creates its own myth. This is Gide's great achievement among his works based on mythology, if not among his total works.

Its subject, its orientation, and its declarations establish the primacy of man. Man is the only concern of men, Theseus says angrily to Pirithous. And Man is the child of this earth alone, he believes. In this way, Gide's last work, codifying as it were what has gone before, brings him close to the spirit of Greek antiquity.

[1] A. Camus, 'Prométhée aux enfers' (1946), *L'Été*, Paris, Gallimard, 1954, p. 88.
[2] *Thésée*, p. 107.

By the importance he attaches to human life on earth, to the individual development of innate capacities, the enjoyment of the pleasures and privileges of living, with the duty to increase them for others, if it is possible, Gide holds something of the Greek view of man as centre and measure of his world.

When he accepts human weaknesses as the inevitable accompaniment to living, Gide also recalls the Greek attitude. We are to believe that every aspect of human character and behaviour is natural and so admissible: the constant theme of Gide's last years is, as Theseus says to Oedipus, that 'l'homme, quelqu'il soit et si taré que tu le juges, doit faire jeu des cartes qu'il a'.[1] In this way, Gide's attitude is closer to Euripides than to his great predecessor's. As Aristotle notes, 'Sophocles . . . said that he drew men as they ought to be, and Euripides as they were'.[2]

None the less, if Gide accepts human frailty and does not expect any miraculous transformation of human nature, he does not fail to demand the best from men. In so doing he replies in his own way and age to one of the great issues of classical Greek controversy which questioned 'the springs of human conduct—why do men behave as they do, and how can they be induced to behave better?'[3] Gide furnishes his own twentieth-century answer. Man's duty is to develop his capacity to its human limits: he cannot hope to transcend those limits as the Sophoclean Oedipus does in his death. All remains, as Gide would have said of philosophy as he says of art, 'à 'l'échelle de l'homme'.[4] But man has duties to himself as to others that must be assumed and, in the end, he must take the responsibility for his own life. It is not an easy task, since it requires as much moral strength as physical endurance. It is a concept that some may find over-arduous, that many must find unsatisfactory: and, indeed, Gide's early mythological heroes did not always appreciate the consequences of their assertion of independence and the impulsive actions that manifested it. Yet finally there is *Thésée* and thus a hero capable of self-understand-

---

[1] *Thésée*, p. 122. See also *Journal 1939–1949*, p. 67 n., 12 janvier 1941; p. 248, 26 juin 1943.

[2] Aristotle, *De Poetica*, translated by I. Bywater, *Works*, vol. xi, Oxford, Clarendon Press, 1924, 1460^b 33, 34.

[3] E. R. Dodds, *The Greeks and the Irrational*, p. 183.   [4] *Divers*, p. 43.

ing, self-direction, and self-transcendence in his concern for future men.

The life of Theseus provides Gide with his last medium for the testing of personal experience which has governed his myth-based works throughout. In his turn he has added to the myth itself by his own imaginative re-creation. The given legend has allowed him to evaluate the long experience of his life and to express it memorably. Such an evaluation of the experienced and the known by means of the myth succeeds, as has recently been suggested, in enhancing the 'resonance that the content [of the myth] awakens in us'.[1]

Gide's artistic achievement in individual works based on the myth may seem uneven. It cannot fail to do so when we consider the range of presentation from the confrontation of abstractions, as in *Philoctète*, to the superior equanimity, if not Goethean 'banalité', of *Thésée*. Nevertheless his total achievement is of inestimable value. His use of the myth as an intimate means towards self-understanding showed the way to many recent writers, playwrights, and philosophers alike, and proved, if such proof were necessary, its perennial validity. And when Gide placed man alone in the centre of his universe, he raised for us all today, if he did not always solve, the grave problems of human responsibility.

[1] Kerényi, *Prometheus*, p. xxiv.

INDEX

PRINTED IN GREAT BRITAIN
AT THE UNIVERSITY PRESS, OXFORD
BY VIVIAN RIDLER
PRINTER TO THE UNIVERSITY